DIVORCE
AND REMARRIAGE

Recent Titles in
Contributions in Women's Studies

Pariahs Stand Up! The Founding of the Liberal Feminist Movement in France, 1858-1889
Patrick Kay Bidelman

Separated and Divorced Women
Lynne Carol Halem

Female Soldiers—Combatants or Noncombatants? Historical and Contemporary Perspectives
Nancy Loring Goldman, editor

A Woman's Issue: The Politics of Family Law Reform in England
Dorothy M. Stetson

"Traitors to the Masculine Cause": The Men's Campaign for Women's Rights
Sylvia Strauss

Women in the Resistance and in the Holocaust: The Voices of Eyewitnesses
Vera Laska, editor

Saints and Shrews: Women and Aging in American Popular Film
Karen M. Stoddard

Women of the English Renaissance and Reformation
Retha M. Warnicke

Face to Face: Fathers, Mothers, Masters, Monsters—Essays for a Nonsexist Future
Meg McGavran Murray, editor

God's Handiwork: Images of Women in Early Germanic Literature
Richard J. Schrader

As Minority Becomes Majority: Federal Reaction to the Phenomenon of Women in the Work Force, 1920-1963
Judith Sealander

Women in Colonial Spanish American Literature: Literary Images
Julie Greer Johnson

DIVORCE AND REMARRIAGE

PROBLEMS, ADAPTATIONS, AND ADJUSTMENTS

Stan L. Albrecht,
Howard M. Bahr, and
Kristen L. Goodman

Contributions in Women's Studies Number 42

Greenwood Press
Westport, Connecticut • London, England

Albrecht, Stan L.
    Divorce and remarriage.

    (Contributions in women's studies, ISSN 0147-104X ;
no. 42)
    Bibliography: p.
    Includes index.
    1. Divorce—West (U.S.) 2. Remarriage—West (U.S.)
I. Bahr, Howard M. II. Goodman, Kristen L. III. Title.
IV. Series.
HQ834.A685   1983   306.8'9'0979   82-24250
ISBN 0-313-23616-X (lib. bdg.)

Library of Congress Catalog Card Number: 82-24250
ISBN: 0-313-23616-X
ISSN: 0147-104X

First published in 1983

Greenwood Press
A division of Congressional Information Service, Inc.
88 Post Road West
Westport, Connecticut 06881

Printed in the United States of America

10 9 8 7 6 5 4 3 2 1

Contents

	List of Figures and Tables	*vii*
	Preface	*xi*
1	Introduction	3
2	Marriage, Divorce, and Remarriage in Social and Historical Context	29
3	The Divorced and the Non-Divorced	75
4	The Decision to Divorce	93
5	Reactions to Divorce and Adjustments After	119
6	Remarriage	141
7	Concluding Thoughts on Replication, Regional Specification, and Future Research	157
	APPENDIX A—Research Methodology	169
	APPENDIX B—Demographic Description of the Sample	185
	Bibliography	*199*
	Index	*207*

List of Figures & Tables

Figures

1 Marriage Rates per 1,000 Population for Nevada, Idaho, Utah,
  and the U.S., 1870-1980   35
2 Divorce Rates per 1,000 Population for Nevada, Idaho, Utah, and
  the U.S., 1870-1980   44

Tables

1 Approximate Distribution among Topical Categories of 154 Journal
  Articles on Divorce, 1980-1981   10
2 Research Site, Number of Divorced/Separated Respondents, and
  Type of Sampling Universe for Empirical Research on Personal
  Experience of the Divorce Process   12
3 Major Monographs on the Process and Aftermath of Divorce,
  1930-1980   19
4 Marriage Rates per 1,000 Population for the U.S. and the Mountain
  States, 1870-1980   31
5 Divorce Rates per 1,000 Population for the U.S. and the Mountain
  States, 1870-1980   32
6 Percent Distribution of First Marriages and Remarriages for Brides
  and Grooms, U.S. and Selected Mountain States, 1960-1977   34
7 Marriage Statistics for Nevada, Idaho, Utah, and the U.S., 1870-1980 36
8 Marriage Rates per 1,000 Unmarried Women Aged 15 and Over,
  Nevada, Idaho, Utah, and U.S., 1890-1970   40
9 Median Duration of Marriage Before Divorce for Nevada, Idaho,
  Utah, and the U.S., 1880-1979   41

10   Divorce Statistics for Nevada, Idaho, Utah, and the U.S.,
     1870-1980   42
11   Refined Divorce Rates per 1,000 Married Women, Nevada,
     Idaho, Utah, and the U.S., 1890-1979   46
12   Age-Specific Divorce Rates by Age of Husband and Wife
     at Time of Decree, Idaho, Utah, and the U.S., 1970   47
13   Remarriage Rates per 1,000 Previously Married Population
     14 Years and Older, Idaho, Utah, and the U.S., 1970   48
14   Legal Minimum Age at Marriage for the Mountain States,
     August 1958 and March 1981   52
15   Economic Indicators for Nevada, Idaho, Utah, and the U.S., 1979   56
16   Mean Number of Children per Divorce with Children
     Reported for Nevada, Idaho, Utah, and the U.S., 1870-1977   57
17   Mean Number of Children per Divorce and Child Involvement
     Rate per 1,000 Population Under 18 Years, Idaho, Utah,
     and the U.S., 1950-1979   58
18   Correlates of Divorce   64
19   Correlates of Remarriage   67
20   Age at First Marriage and Current Marital Status   78
21   Relationship Between Parents' and Spouse's Parents'
     Marital Status and Current Marital Status of Respondent   80
22   Marriage Setting and Current Marital Status   81
23   Religious Identity and Current Marital Status   82
24   Religious Activity and Marital Status   83
25   Educational Level and Current Marital Status   85
26   Race and Marital Status   86
27   Perceived Marital Happiness Compared with Happiness of Others   88
28   Marital Happiness Compared with Expectations prior to Marriage   89
29   Relationship between Stability and Happiness
     in Marital Relationships   95
30   Factors Found to Differentiate between High and Low
     Cohesive Marriages   97
31   Satisfaction with Former Marriage Compared with
     Perceived Satisfaction of Other Couples   98
32   Satisfaction with Former Marriage Compared with
     Expectations prior to Entering the Marriage   99
33   Major Reasons Why Marriage Failed   100
34   Perceived Barriers to Obtaining Divorce   103
35   Factors Influencing Decision to Divorce   106
36   Percent of Family and Close Friends Who Approved of Divorce   109
37   Percent of Close Friends Who Are Divorced   110
38   Percentage of Respondents Whose Own or Former Spouse's
     Parents Were Divorced   110

39 Divorce Experience of Own and Spouse's Brothers and Sisters   111
40 Has Own Divorce Encouraged Anyone Else to Divorce   113
41 Who Initiates Divorce Action   113
42 Characterization of Experience in Seeking and Obtaining Divorce   122
43 Characterization of Worst and Best Periods in Obtaining Divorce   124
44 Living Arrangements after Filing for Divorce   127
45 Property Settlements   128
46 Feelings About Property Settlements   129
47 Impact of Divorce on Participation in Organizations and Clubs   130
48 Contact with Own and Spouse's Relatives before Divorce   131
49 Change in Contact with Own and Spouse's Relatives
    following Divorce   132
50 Contact with Former Spouse   133
51 Income Compared with Closest Friends and Associates   135
52 Satisfaction with Present and Former Marriage
    Compared with Perceived Happiness of Other Couples   147
53 Satisfaction with Present and Former Marriage
    Compared with Expectations prior to Entering the Marriage   147
54 Major Problems Identified in Current Marriage   150
55 Pearson Correlations between Three Measures of Satisfaction
    with Remarriage and Selected Independent Variables   152
56 Response Rates for Phase I   172
57 Response Rates for Phase II   174
58 Marital Status of Respondents, by Sex, for Each Mountain State   188
59 Comparison of Percent Married Persons, Intermountain
    Divorce Study 1976 and U.S. Census 1970   190
60 Comparison of Ever-Married/Divorced Persons, U.S. Census 1970
    and Intermountain Divorce Study 1976   191
61 Religious Preference of Respondents, by State   192
62 Years of Schooling Completed by Respondents, by State   193
63 Occupation of Employed Respondents, by Sex   194
64 Income in the Mountain Region   197

Preface

The dramatically increasing rates of divorce in this country have, in recent years, attracted growing attention from professionals and laypersons alike. In 1980 there were an estimated 1,182,000 divorces, a record high. This represents an increase of 67 percent over the 1970 total and is three times the total number of divorces recorded in 1960.

The important effect of increasing divorce rates on the form and structure of the current American family can be seen from statistics on the number of children living in single parent families. Paul Glick has projected that the proportion of children under 18 living with two parents may be expected to decline to 56 percent by 1990. The situation for black children is even more extreme. In 1978 only 44 percent of black children under 18 were living with two parents (including those in remarriages as well as those in first marriages). Unless current trends change, by 1990 only about one-third of all black children will be living with both natural parents in their first marriage.

Paul Glick and Arthur Norton also point out that if we assume that the future divorce experiences of today's young adults will mirror the experience of older adults in recent years, then we can project that approximately 40 percent of women now in their late twenties will terminate their marriage in divorce. Of the three-quarters of these who will later remarry, about 44 percent will redivorce. The majority of divorces will occur during the first ten years of marriage and the probability of divorce during this period increases dramatically if the marriage has occurred between teenagers.

It is clear that the upsurge in the divorce rate in the United States during the last decade has been stimulated by a growing acceptance that divorce is a reasonable and, at times, even desirable alternative to an unhappy marriage. Norton and Glick note that the increase coincides with a number of other important societal trends including: (1) a liberalization and reform of divorce laws in a great number of states, including a widespread trend toward the establishment of no-fault divorce; (2) changes in the traditional roles and status of women which are resulting in more women being employed outside the home and women seeking greater personal freedom and fulfillment; (3) a period of challenging many basic social institutions and values that have, in the past, been supportive of more traditional family forms; (4) a decline in fertility rates which results in more women having fewer or no children which, in turn, affects the level of participation of women in the labor force and contributes to their greater economic independence; and (5) an increase in premarital conception—particularly among younger girls—which has been found to be conducive to higher rates of divorce.

There is much current disagreement regarding what the increasing frequency of divorce means for the family as a social institution. Many critics view the recent divorce statistics as indicative of the final demise of the nuclear family. From this perspective, the family is no longer a viable institution, in that it has lost many of the important functions that it once fulfilled in the past and now fails to fulfill those with which, supposedly, it has been left. Some critics who accept this view feel that the family ought to be replaced with other arrangements that "impose fewer unnecessary restrictions on humanity."

Just as there are vocal critics of the family as an institution, so also are there equally committed defenders who view and interpret the statistics quite differently. For example, Michael Novak argues that the one unforgettable law that has been learned through a thousand years of oppression, disaster, and injustice is that "if things go well with the family, life is worth living; when the family falters, life falls apart."

Jessie Bernard reminds us, however, that divorce per se has ceased to be a salient issue since all jurisdictions make provision and permit a variety of grounds for divorce. Divorces have occurred and will continue to occur among all segments of the population. We must take this as a given. What remains, then, are the important questions about why it occurs, where it does occur, and what its impacts are for the family as an institution, for the larger society, and for individual family members.

This book has been written to examine the divorce experience from the perspective of the individual who actually experiences it. Therefore, while we will occasionally make some observations about the impacts of divorce on the larger society or on the structure of the family, our primary concern is at the individual level—how the individual makes the decision to terminate an unsuccessful marriage, the constraints that are imposed on this decision, how these constraints are overcome, the adjustment process following the divorce, and so on. In addition, we will give some attention to the question of remarriage since a majority of those who divorce eventually marry again. In other words, our story does not end at the divorce court but examines what happens to individuals following divorce, and concludes with a description of the nature of the adjustment that they make in subsequent marriages if, indeed, they do remarry.

The book is based on a rather detailed study of a sample of divorced persons living in the eight intermountain states (Arizona, Colorado, Idaho, Montana, Nevada, New Mexico, Utah, and Wyoming). One of the primary intents of the study was to develop a research sample that would be both large enough for detailed analysis and generally representative of the larger population of divorced persons living within a definable geographic locale. The research process is described in detail in Appendix A. The first two chapters of the book place the study in context by examining the literature on divorce and by discussing in some detail significant patterns and trends in divorce and remarriage in this country and in the region where the study was conducted. The next three chapters then review the experience of our divorced respondents. Chapter six looks at the process of remarriage for those respondents who had married again following a divorce. Chapter seven concludes discussing important future trends of divorce and remarriage.

We are grateful for the assistance of colleagues who aided in the initial research effort or who read and commented on various drafts of the manuscript. They include Bruce Chadwick and Philip Kunz of Brigham Young University and Adrienne Mayor, the copyeditor. We also appreciate the assistance of the editorial staff at Greenwood Press, including Lynn Sedlak who served as production editor. Finally, we acknowledge the important role of Lori Vernon who so ably typed the various drafts of the manuscript during its preparation.

Chapter 1

Introduction

"Shocking," wrote Sonya Herman in 1977, referring to the tendency among the general public and social science professionals alike to ignore or deny the problem of divorce.[1] "Insufficiently recognized, little studied," echoed Wallerstein and Kelly three years later, ". . .the number of investigations, given the magnitude of the problem, is perilously low."[2] Nobody knows just how much study and service the magnitude of the problem *should* generate, but these statements no longer describe the arena of divorce research. Indeed, a review of the recently published literature on the subject points to a "knowledge explosion" now underway.

The writers quoted made the statements before the remarkable surge of scientific interest in divorce was obvious. Today the trend is apparent and striking. True, it is part of a larger trend of increased research and writing about marriage and the family. The annual inventories of marriage and family literature published by the University of Minnesota describe the pattern as a "mushrooming interest in research and theorizing about marital and family relationships" and their computerized counts of articles on marriage and family matters reveal three times as many publications in 1979-1980 as in 1973-1974.[3] But the growth of the divorce literature far outstrips that of the family generally. Simple counts of items listed in the Minnesota inventories reveal 6.5 times as many pieces on divorce and separation in 1979-1980 as in 1973-1974: for the 1979-1980 period there were 274 articles on divorce and separation (including "custody"), compared to 42 in 1973-1974.[4] In 1973-1974, articles on divorce and separation amounted to 1.7 percent of the published family literature; in 1980, they accounted for 5.4 percent.

The rate of increase in published work on divorce and separation has even outpaced the increases in the national divorce rates, but this comparison probably does not mean much, because the amount of scientific work on divorce was so miniscule even a decade ago. We can say, however, that the era of scientific disinterest in the problem of divorce seems to have ended.

This book is a fragment of the contemporary "explosion" in empirical research about divorce and separation. The primary objective of this first chapter is to place the Intermountain Divorce Study in context and to show how it differs from and in some ways extends previous work. At the same time, the descriptions of representative as well as exemplary work on divorce by other researchers will highlight the perceptions of the present study.

Research Context

Initially, let us define the context for this book as including both the objective national situation—the incidence of divorce and how divorce rates seem to have changed—and the interpretations of that situation by scholars and other interested observers. More specifically, the context consists of (1) national trends and the way they are interpreted; (2) the contemporary research context, the body of recent work which reveals some accepted styles of research and typical ways of defining the social and scientific problems posed by divorce; and (3) landmark studies, which have served to define and illuminate the entire field. These major studies, some of them several decades old, must be taken into account because they changed the way people looked at divorce, contributed new insights or literally offered "discoveries," and sensitized researchers to issues, problems, and approaches, thereby shaping future work.

National trends and interpretations. The national trends are readily stated. Between the early 1960s and the late 1970s, the divorce rate, however measured, increased substantially, more than doubling in the 15-year period 1963-1978. Since 1978, the divorce rates have plateaued at an annual rate of between 5.2 and 5.4 per 1,000 population (the 1981 divorce rate was 5.3 per 1,000 population, compared with 5.2 in 1980).

This more-than-doubling of the divorce rate during a 15-year period has been interpreted by many as denoting drastic and possible fatal changes in the American family. The divorce statistics mean, in fact, that there are more people involved in divorce than there used to be. They say nothing about the quality of American marriage or the relative happiness or commitment to family values of persons who divorce compared with those who do not. Here is one critic's cogent summary of the multiple errors people fall into when they try to generalize from divorce statistics to statements about the vitality of the family:

The divorce statistics, variously calculated, tell us only one thing: they tell us how many marriages were legally dissolved in a given period of time. They do not tell us, or give us justification for claiming that the statistics represent the number of failures in marriage; nor do the statistics indicate the degree of marital health within a society, sub-culture, or age sub-set. To appeal to divorce statistics in order to make a case for the supposed decay of marriage or the breakdown of the family without careful consideration of the historical context is to use statistics in an illegitimate and unwarranted manner. To use the statistics in such a manner is spurious and gives rise to conclusions which then form the ''authority basis'' for public speeches, political statements, sermons, and propaganda heralding the decay and/or demise of the institutions of marriage and the family.[5]

There are many ways to discount the apparently high divorce rates. For instance, imagine that in the United States, now and historically, one marriage in every five has been a truly unhappy union. Historically, to dissolve that union via divorce has been more costly from economic, religious, or social standpoints than have other ways of coping with a bad marriage. But in an era when the legal impediments to divorce have been greatly reduced, and when divorce is common enough in most communities that the stigmatization to be endured seems manageable, couples might choose divorce more often as the way to deal with a miserable marriage. Other options still exist, but may seem less attractive than the ''new start'' a divorce offers:

Divorce is, after all, only one solution to the problem of an unsatisfactory marriage. Still others are continuing to live in ''empty shell'' marriages. . . , permanent separation, separation and reconciliation, and interventions that modify the marriage for the better.[6]

There are still more alternatives, including desertion, pseudo-divorce,[7] and suicide (see Simon and Lumry's provocative ''Suicide of the Spouse as a Divorce Substitute'').[8]

In our scenario, the coping alternative chosen by the one desperately mismatched couple in every five depends on their estimation of the costs of the different alternatives. The increase in divorce rates over the past 15 years might be defined as a function of a growing popular awareness that divorce is a less punishing way to deal with dead marriages than are the more traditional approaches. Indeed, some analysts have suggested that part of the increase in divorce during the past decade is a result of legal changes and greater public tolerance for divorce allowing mismatched couples to divorce sooner than they otherwise would have done, thus temporarily pushing up divorce rates:

The elimination of many barriers previously inhibiting divorce has been relatively recent and rapid. Consequently, it seems reasonable to speculate that at least part of the recent increase in the divorce rate may represent an acceleration in the timing of divorces that, under previous conditions, would have been spread over a longer number of years. If this is the case, one might expect the rate of divorce either to eventually decline or at least to level off.[9]

There are various ways to interpret the increase in divorce rates without making of it a national crisis, but the research literature (not to mention the journalistic treatments of trends in divorce) does convey a sense of urgency, crisis, and possible family collapse. For example, a review article begins with reference to the "precipitous increase" in divorce;[10] an excellent book on impacts of divorce upon children refers to these children and their parents as a population "expanding explosively," driven apart by "a truly extraordinary rise in the incidence of divorce."[11]

Articles in the staid journal *Demography* are more subtle. There are references to "remarkable changes" in the rates of marital dissolution, comments that "a *very large* [emphasis added] proportion of marriages are now ending in separation and/or divorce," and descriptions of the upward trend in number of divorces as "dramatic" and "precipitous."[12] Studies of children and divorce are more apt to use terms like "alarming," "spiraling," and "phenomenal"[13] and the editorial introduction to the new *Journal of Divorce* adopts a metaphor of natural destructive force when it refers to the "avalanche" of divorce.[14] That the scientific community has also assumed there is a crisis is apparent in the first sentence of a useful theoretical piece on the divorce process which points to "the mushrooming concern of counselors in regard to divorce."[15]

Perhaps we should be more cautious with our metaphors. These changes in divorce rates, while sizable, may not properly elicit—at least on a societal scale—response comparable to those required by the pressing, life-threatening natural emergencies in which they are metaphorically clothed. We must face a deluge or an avalanche at once, or risk being swept away; precipices are dangerous to life and limb, unless viewed from a distance. But demographic trends may properly yield more deliberate action, lest a "crisis"-provoked reaction make things worse or inhibit more constructive approaches. Indeed, there are some who, viewing these same trends, cheerfully interpret the dramatic "spiraling" as either positive or at least mixed in consequence, and not disastrous either for individuals or the larger society.

Among the analysts who define divorce as simply another family stage is Constance Ahrons, who reminds us that divorce does not *dissolve* the family, but merely redefines it.[16] The new entity that divorce produces, she argues, is not non-family or a-family at all, but rather is a different kind of family, one she labels the "binuclear system." The divorced family may *appear* shattered, but that is only appearance, created by a general lack of experience with the post-divorce family. Divorce and remarriage create a series of transitions and stresses, but these changes may be viewed as stages in a continuing family system rather than collapses of the system. Defining the divorced family as a continuing family system emphasizes that parents can continue to provide a coparental relationship. The binuclear family concept "provides a family style which does not force the child to sever the bond with either parent, but which allows both parents to continue their parental roles post-divorce."[17]

Another fairly positive approach to the divorce "crisis" is one that identifies the strains leading to divorce in many American families as structural, not personal strains. In this perspective, the culture is seen as defining personal fulfillment as the reason for marriage and family life, but the constraints imposed by external organizations—economic, political, religious, educational, professional—all, in fact, demand higher priority than emotional-nurturant needs of families. The family fails as a unit, and sometimes dissolves in divorce, because it cannot provide for the emotional well-being of all of its members. Instead, "work which provides routine necessities takes priority; emotional well-being must be continually compromised." The family structure, the argument goes, is not conducive to meeting each member's emotional needs as they arise, and therefore "the woman is structurally positioned to fail."[18]

Although the problem is essentially one of structure, not personality, the couples whose lives are bedeviled by the cross-pressures and built-in failure mechanisms define their problems as personal rather than structural. Divorce is defined as a way out of the trap:

Locating the source of problems within the couple reinforces the myth that marriage to the "right" person will result in a happy family life. Thousands of people explain their marital difficulties by appealing to this rationale—that they made a "poor choice" and should "try again" in another marriage.[19]

In either of the above approaches—whether divorce is a "normal" family stage in modernized societies or a regrettable but inevitable consequence of conflict between culturally induced expectations and anti-family organizational constraints—the "family crisis" or "family collapse" interpretations of contemporary divorce trends seem inappropriate, and may limit understanding and impede positive programs rather than facilitating them.

Much of the writing about American divorce is about trends in numbers and rates, or correlates of these trends. Ordinarily the changes (in recent times usually upswings) are described and possible causes or consequences are listed or weighed against each other. Also, much scholarly effort has been devoted to comparing divorced people and their children with non-divorcing, "intact" families. The *process* of divorce—the sequences in seeking and obtaining a divorce and perceptions of changes in one's social world during and after the divorce—has received less attention.

In most of the chapters of this book, we will try to tell about divorce as it was experienced from the standpoint of the individual, or, more accurately, from a sample of individuals. We are much less concerned with the consequences of divorce upon the wider society and its institutions. In other words, we are not concerned with the "goodness" or "badness" of divorce from the viewpoint of the community or the nation. Instead, we summarize divorced persons' perceptions of what happened to them as they terminated a marriage and entered a new marital status, and what they thought about what happened to them.

Let us illustrate the concerns we explicitly avoid, and those we will stress, with an example. Divorced people are still the objects of prejudice and discrimination. From the standpoint of the larger society, the stigmatization of divorced persons may have some positive functions; from the perspective of the divorced persons the stigma may be costly, painful, or apparently pointless. Whether, on balance, it is "right" or "wrong" for the divorced to be stigmatized, and whether and to what extent society benefits, is beyond our purview. Whether divorced persons have *felt* stigmatized, however, and how they have reacted, are matters of great concern to us.

Contemporary Research Context

As part of the heightened volume of divorce research, there are now scientific journals wholly devoted to the topic. In Fall 1977, the *Journal of Divorce* began publication, adding a specialized outlet to the many journals[20] that already defined divorce and its sequelae as appropriate subject matter. As noted above, in the editorial statement of its first issue, the journal was justified as a response to "the divorce avalanche."[21]

To place our study of divorced people in the intermountain region in context within the large volume of research accomplished since that editorial appeared, we shall identify our study in reference to the kinds of divorce research being published in the journals.

We will not attempt a definitive review of the divorce literature. That has been aptly done for the scientific literature in two recent articles, Kitson and Raschke's "Divorce Research: What We Know; What We Need to Know," and Price-Bonham and Balswick's decade review on divorce, desertion, and remarriage.[22] Nor are we much interested here in substantive findings; instead, we want to summarize topics of inquiry that have dominated research on divorce and separation, and the research procedures that have been used in exploring these topics. In other words, we want to describe what has been studied and the way the studies have been done.

Range of topics. The popularity of certain topics of research is subject to change because as a scientific field matures, dead ends are abandoned and more fruitful avenues of work are explored and extended. Moreover, there are fads in scientific research as in other areas of life, and some changes in topical interest may be attributed to changes in fashion whether or not they represent scientific advancement. As applied to our review of the topics presently receiving attention from divorce researchers, this means that our summary of topics is by nature a "snapshot," a cross-sectional approximation of the kinds of work being done in the specified period, and may not be at all congruent with the distribution of research effort observed only a short time before or after.

Our estimate of how divorce research is presently divided among topics is based on a rough content analysis of articles listed in the *Social Science Citation Index*. For all of 1980 and January through August of 1981, the *Social Science Citation Index* was searched for articles with titles containing the words "divorce," "divorced," "divorcees," "divorces," or "divorcing." Citations were typed on cards and sorted. Articles containing the key words but apparently not relevant to the social scientific study of contemporary divorce (for example, a hypothetical "Divorce in the works of Hawthorne and Melville") were dropped, as were letters to journal editors and book reviews. The 154 citations remaining for the 20-month period were categorized by title, with the category system growing out of the sorting process in the manner of "grounded theory."[23] That is, titles dealing with related topics were grouped together, and then a label was sought which best included the range of pieces in that category. Admittedly, the final typology of contemporary research-production on divorce is *ad hoc* and tentative. There are undoubtedly many articles that should have been included in the total list that were not, and the coding into categories is very rough, based as it is entirely on what the title conveyed about the article. Nevertheless, the rough break-down by topic of research serves to illustrate where "the action" is in divorce research today.

The distribution shown in Table 1 highlights a contemporary dominance of two types of study; namely, analysis of effects of divorce upon children, and general descriptions or theoretical treatments of some aspect of divorce (essentially the latter was a residual category for pieces that did not fit under the other five more specific headings). These two categories accounted for about half of the published articles for the period. The demography of divorce, broadly defined, accounts for another one-seventh of the articles. Three other topics—divorce and the law, divorce counseling and therapy, and studies of the divorce process—each account for about one-eighth of the published articles. The Intermountain Divorce Project belongs in this final category.

We do not claim any greater generality for our rough classification of the topics of divorce research than is inherent in the procedure described. That is, pieces published prior to 1980 might show a different distribution by topic, as might those published late in 1981 or in 1982. Furthermore, it is technically incorrect to speak of pieces published in a given year as "current" work, inasmuch as there may be lags of a year or more between submission of a manuscript and its publication.

Methods in empirical research on divorce process. We tried to get a feel for the locales and types of samples being studied by divorce researchers by systematically examining the articles on divorce in two major journals which deal with marital instability, the *Journal of Divorce* and the *Journal of Marriage and the Family*. In all, we examined 36 issues (16 from the *Journal of Divorce*, 20 from the *Journal of Marriage and the Family*) for the period 1977-1981.

The first four volumes of the *Journal of Divorce*, covering the period 1977-1981, contained 111 articles. By our reckoning, 32 of these were empirical studies of the divorce process from the standpoint of the divorcing person. Between 1977 and 1981 the *Journal of Marriage and the Family* issued 5 volumes. The 20 separate issues for this period contained 33 articles treating divorce in some way. Of these, 8 focused on the individual experience of marital dissolution, which is the focus of the present book. Combining the 32 pieces from the *Journal of Divorce* with these 8 yields a total of 40 articles on process of divorce.

These articles were compared with regard to the place where the research was done, the way respondents were chosen, and the sample size. The results of this comparison, summarized in Table 2, permit us to answer such questions as, Where is the research on the process of divorce being done? Who are the respondents? What types of divorced populations comprise the universes from which samples of divorced persons are selected for study?

Tentative answers to these questions for the 1977-1981 period, *as represented in the two journals analyzed*, are given in Table 2. Remember that the unit of

Table 1

Approximate Distribution among Topical Categories of 154 Journal Articles on Divorce, 1980-1981

Categories of Divorce Research	Number of Articles	Percent	Illustrative Titles
Impacts on children	41	27%	The teacher's role in facilitating a child's adjustment to divorce
Descriptive and theoretical	36	23	Older mothers' perceptions of their child's divorce
			Managerial behavior and stress in families headed by divorced women-- a proposed framework
Demographic trends, including critiques of statistics and procedures	21	14	A comparative analysis of divorce rates in Canada and the United States, 1921-1967
			Those unsatisfactory statistics on divorce
Legal issues	20	13	Minimizing taxes in separation and divorce
Clinical/therapeutic approaches	19	12	Divorce counseling or marriage therapy--a therapeutic option
Divorce process (personal experience)	17	11	Empirical investigation of emotional reactions to divorce
TOTAL	154	100%	

Source: All articles listed in <u>Social Science Citation Index</u>, 1980 and January through August 1981, whose titles contained the words divorce, divorced, divorcees, divorces or divorcing.

analysis in this tally of research is the published article, not the research project. That is, some projects, and some authors, are represented several times among the 40 articles listed in Table 2. If a single project, say the work by Chiriboga and his associates,[24] produced several articles published in these two journals during the period in question, that project was allotted several times the numerical impact of a project that published only one article. In fact, the project producing only a single article may have been far more important, but for purposes of our rough survey, we have adhered to the "one publication-one vote" rule.

On that basis, it is apparent that contemporary knowledge of the divorce process, at least what is published in journals like the two represented, is highly localized: only a handful of research sites accounted for most of the work. Among the 34 pieces that identified a research site, eight were California metropolitan areas. Midwestern metropolitan areas were also well represented, with Detroit, Dayton, and Chicago accounting for eight articles and three unnamed midwestern metropolitan areas accounting for two more; if Kalamazoo County, Michigan, is included, then metropolitan areas in the Midwest account for one-third (11 of 34) of the published reports. Notably underrepresented in this body of research are the South (one "large southeastern city" was a research site), and the East Coast (two articles treated samples from Buffalo, New York, and two others dealt with unnamed eastern or East Coast cities). Also underrepresented, with the exception of California, are the western states, with one study of divorced persons in an Oregon county, two from Boulder, Colorado, and two (representing the project described in the present book) drawing upon the eight intermountain states. National studies are almost non-existent: the only two were reports of a study of divorced ministers.

These 40 articles reveal a preponderance of court records as the primary sampling source, with special interest organizations (almost entirely Parents Without Partners) the second-most-frequent source of populations of divorced and separated people for study. The next most common sampling sources are social services agencies and organizations, such as marriage and divorce counseling agencies, and day-care centers. The reliance upon court records is greater than it appears, for several of the "social service" agencies were associated with a court, for example, a marriage and divorce counseling service operated in conjunction with a county court.

An underrepresentation of men in studies of the divorce process is also evident in Table 2. Only 6 of the 39 articles reporting the sex distribution of respondents had at least equal representation of men and women. In the other 33 pieces (85 percent of the articles) fewer than half of the respondents were men, and the populations studied in 11 of the articles (28 percent) included no men at all.

Landmark studies and other books. In our view, the most important body of previous work on the process of divorce as personally experienced is represented in the eight monographs described in Table 3. Some people may fault choosing these and neglecting others more important by their criteria. But these eight, we we feel, represent adequately the core of well-researched books summarizing

Table 2
Research Site, Number of Divorced/Separated Respondents, and Type of Sampling Universe for Empirical Research on Personal Experience of the Divorce Process

Citation	Research Site	Divorced/Separated Respondents Total	Men	Court Records	Pub./Priv. Soc. Serv. Agencies	Spec'l Int. Organizat'n	Other Sources
1977							
Bloom, et al.	Boulder CO	503	a				X
Brown, Perry & Harburg	Detroit MI	253	0		X		
Chiriboga & Cutler	Dayton OH	73	18			X	
Raschke	2 midwestern cities	277	91			X	
1978							
Brown & Manela	Detroit MI	253	0		X		
Chiriboga, Roberts, & Stein	San Francisco & Alameda Cnty's CA	309	126	X			
Deckert & Langelier	Quebec	222^c	54	X	X	X	X
Gray	a	126	50			X	
Jacobson (a)	Los Angeles CA	30	0	X	X		
Jacobson (b)	Los Angeles CA	30	0	X	X		
Jacobson (c)	Los Angeles CA	30	0	X	X		
Kurdek and Siesky	Dayton OH	73	18			X	
McKenry, White, & Price-Bonham	large southeastern city	20	10	X			
1979							
Albrecht	8 western states	500	207				X
Chiriboga, et al.	San Francisco & Alameda Cnty's CA	310	185	X			
Colletta (a)	Buffalo NY	48	0		X		
Colletta (b)	Buffalo NY	48	0		X		
Goetting	Kalamazoo Cnty MI	180	90	X			
Granvold, Pedler, & Schellie	a	53	0		X	X	
Hutchison & Hutchison	United States	157	157				X
Spanier & Casto	Centre Cnty PA	50	22	X			
White	Nebraska	136	63				X
1980							
Ahrons	San Diego CA	41	19	X			
Albrecht & Kunz	8 western states	500	207				X
Alexander	East Coast urban area	63	26			X	
Brown, et al.	Detroit MI	192	75		X		
Chiriboga & Thurnher	San Francisco & Alameda Cnty's CA	298	121	X			
Goldsmith	Cook Cnty IL	129	52	X			

		Divorced/Separated Respondents		Sampling Universe			
Citation	Research Site	Total	Men	Court Records	Pub./Priv. Soc. Serv. Agencies	Spec'l Int. Organizat'n	Other Sources
1980 (Continued)							
Hayes, Stinnett & DeFrain	Oklahoma	138	51	X			
Hutchison, Nichols & Hutchison	U.S.	160	160				X
Kurdek & Siesky (a)	Dayton OH	74	14			X	
Kurdek & Siesky (b)	Dayton OH	71	14			X	
Pino	"urban, large eastern private practice"	50	25		X		
Stern	a	49	0			X	
Woodward, Zabel, & Decosta	midwestern city	59	25	a			
Zeiss, Zeiss, & Johnson	Lane Cnty OR	133	59	X			
1981							
Berman & Turk	a	106	25	X		X	
Bloom & Caldwell	2 southern CA Cnty's plus Boulder CO	288	104	X			X
McLanahan, Wedemeyer, & Adelburg	a	45	0				X
Nelson	a	15	0	X			

a. not reported
b. Based on surveys of Volumes 1-4 of Journal of Divorce and Volumes 39-43 of Journal of Marriage and the Family.
c. Total sample was 229, but sex distribution was provided only for 222.

Full citations for the 40 articles listed in the table are as follows:

Journal of Divorce
Ahrons, Constance R., "Joint Custody Arrangements in the Post-divorce Family," 3 (Spring, 1980): 189-205.
Albrecht, Stan L., and Phillip R. Kunz, "The Decision to Divorce: A Social Exchange Perspective," 3 (Summer, 1980): 319-337.
Alexander, Sharon J., "Influential Factors on Divorced Parents in Determining Visitation Arrangements," 3 (Spring, 1980): 223-239.
Bloom, Bernard L., William F. Hodges, Robert A. Caldwell, Laura Systra and Antonia R. Cedrone, "Marital Separation: A Community Survey," 1 (Fall, 1977): 7-19.
Brown, Prudence, Barbara J. Felton, Victor Whiteman, Roger Manela, "Attachment and Distress Following Marital Separation," 3 (Summer, 1980): 303-317.

Table 2 (continued)

Journal of Divorce (continued)

Brown, Prudence and Roger Manela, "Changing Family Roles: Women and Divorce," 1 (Summer, 1978): 315-328.

Chiriboga, David A., Anne Coho, Judith A. Stein and John Roberts, "Divorce, Stress, and Social Supports: A Study in Helpseeking Behavior," 3 (Winter, 1979): 121-135.

Chiriboga, David A. and Loraine Cutler, "Stress Responses Among Divorcing Men and Women,"1(Winter, 1977): 95-106.

Chiriboga, David A., John Roberts and Judith A. Stein, "Psychological Well-Being During Marital Separation," 2 (Fall, 1978): 21-36.

Chiriboga, David A., Majda Thurnher, "Marital Lifestyles and Adjustment to Separation," 3 (Summer, 1980): 379-390.

Colletta, Nancy Donohue, "The Impact of Divorce: Father Absense or Poverty?" 3 (Fall, 1979): 27-35.

Deckert, Pamela and Régis Langelier, "The Late-Divorce Phenomenon: The Causes and Impact of Ending 20-Year-Old or Longer Marriages," 1 (Summer, 1978): 381-390.

Goetting, Ann, "The Normative Integration of the Former Spouse Relationship," 2 (Summer, 1979): 395-414.

Goldsmith, Jean, "Relationships Between Former Spouses: Descriptive Findings," 4 (Winter, 1980): 1-20.

Granvold, Donald K., Leigh M. Pedler, and Susan G. Schellie, "A Study of Sex Role Expectancy and Female Postdivorce Adjustment," 2 (Summer, 1979): 383-393.

Gray, Gloria M., "The Nature of the Psychological Impact of Divorce upon the Individual," 1 (Summer, 1978): 289-301.

Hayes, Maggie P., Nick Stinnett and John Defrain, "Learning about Marriage from the Divorced," 4 (Fall, 1980): 23-29.

Hutchison, Katherine R., William C. Nichols and Ira W. Hutchison, "Therapy for Divorcing Clergy: Implications from Research," 4 (Fall, 1980): 83-94.

Jacobson, Doris S., "The Impact of Marital Separation/Divorce on Children: I. Parent-Child Separation and Child Adjustment," 1 (Summer, 1978): 341-360.

Jacobson, Doris S., "The Impact of Marital Separation/Divorce on Children: II. Interparent Hostility and Child Adjustment," 2 (Fall, 1978): 3-19.

Jacobson, Doris S., "The Impact of Marital Separation/Divorce on Children. III. Parent-Child Communication and Child Adjustment, and Regression Analysis of Findings from Overall Study," 2 (Winter, 1978): 175-194.

Kurdek, Lawrence A., and Albert E. Siesky, Jr., "An Interview Study of Parents' Perceptions of Their Children's Reactions and Adjustments to Divorce," 3 (Fall, 1979): 5-17.

Kurdek, Lawrence A., and Albert E. Siesky, Jr., "Sex Role Self-Concepts of Single Divorced Parents and their Children," 3 (Spring, 1980): 249-261.

Kurdek, Lawrence A., and Albert E. Siesky, Jr., "Effects of Divorce on Children: The Relationship Between Parent and Child Perspectives," 4 (Winter, 1980): 85-99.

McKenry, Patrick C., Priscilla N. White, and Sharon Price-Bonham, "The Fractured Conjugal Family: A Comparison of Married and Divorced Dyads," 1 (Summer, 1978): 329-339.

Nelson, Geoffrey, "Moderators of Women's and Children's Adjustment Following Parental Divorce," 4 (Spring, 1981): 71-83.

Pino, Christopher J., "Research and Clinical Application of Marital Autopsy in Divorce Counseling," 4 (Fall, 1980): 31-48.

Raschke, Helen J., "The Role of Social Participation in Postseparation and Postdivorce Adjustment," 1 (Winter, 1977): 129-140.

Spanier, Graham B. and Robert F. Casto, "Adjustment to Separation and Divorce: An Analysis of 50 Case Studies," 2 (Spring, 1979): 241-253.

Stern, Edgar E., "Single Mothers' Perceptions of the Father Role and of the Effects of Father Absence on Boys," 4 (Winter, 1980): 77-84.

Woodward, John C., Jackie Zabel and Cheryl Decosta, "Loneliness and Divorce," 4 (Fall, 1980): 73-82.

Zeiss, Antonette M., Robert A. Zeiss and Stephen M. Johnson, "Sex Differences in Initiation of and Adjustment to Divorce," 4 (Winter, 1980): 21-33.

Table 2 (continued)

Journal of Marriage and the Family
    Albrecht, Stan L., "Correlates of Marital Happiness Among the Remarried,"
      41 (November, 1979): 857-867.
    Berman, William H., and Dennis C. Turk, "Adaptation to Divorce: Problems
      and Coping Strategies," 43 (February, 1981): 179-189.
    Bloom, Bernard L., and Robert A. Caldwell, "Sex Differences in Adjustment
      During the Process of Marital Separation," 43 (August, 1981): 693-701.
    Brown, Prudence, Lorraine Perry and Ernest Harburg, "Sex Role Attitudes
      and Psychological Outcomes for Black and White Women Experiencing
      Marital Dissolution," 39 (August, 1977):549-561.
    Colletta, Nancy Donohue, "Support Systems After Divorce: Incidence and Impact,"
      41 (November, 1979): 837-846.
    Hutchison, Ira W., and Katherine R. Hutchison, "The Impact of Divorce upon
      Clergy Career Mobility," 41 (November, 1979): 847-855.
    McLanahan, Sara S., Nancy V. Wedemeyer, and Tina Adelburg, "Network Structure,
      Social Support, and Psychological Well-Being in the Single-Parent Family,"
      43 (August, 1981): 601-612.
    White, Lynn K., "Sex Differentials in the Effect of Remarriage on Global
      Happiness," 41 (November, 1979): 869-876.

the characteristics and experiences of divorcing people. With one exception, we specifically excluded works whose primary focus was on another aspect of divorce, even though they contained material on the process of divorce. Noteworthy among these is Jessie Bernard's *Remarriage*,[25] which considers the process of marital break-up from time to time, but which generally maintains a focus on remarried people: their characteristics and courtships, the solidarity, competition and conflict in their remarriages, and their overall marital success. Another important study whose information on the characteristics of the divorced is tangential to the main message of the book is Harvey Locke's *Predicting Adjustment in Marriage*,[26] in which a sample of 525 divorced people from one Indiana county are used as criterion cases of poor marital adjustment in contrast to 404 "happily married" respondents.

In recognizing the monographs represented in Table 3 as the models and stimuli for our own work, there is no intention to ignore or downplay the sizable literature on divorce available in the professional journals and in books which do not strictly fit the monograph format applied here. There are at least three other classes of books which deserve mention, namely scientific anthologies, demographic and statistical studies, and clinical or journalistic efforts designed to sensitize and educate people about divorce.

The scientific anthologies usually combine essays and summaries of research findings, with recognized authorities describing the current state of their specialties. Thus, Paul Bohannan's *Divorce and After*[27] includes an introduction by Jessie Bernard, two articles on the process of divorce, three on its aftermath, three on "divorce around the world," and two on needed legal and social reforms. Represented among its contributors are a family sociologist, four anthropologists, the director of an Institute of Sex Research, two law professors, and a psychoanalyst.

Another respected anthology, slightly more technical, is Levinger and Moles's *Divorce and Separation: Context, Causes, and Consequences*.[28] This book is a revision and expansion of a 1976 special issue of the *Journal of Social Issues*. Its contributors include clinical psychologists, professors of education, sociologists, human development specialists, psychiatrists, psychologists, social psychologists, and demographers. Many of the pieces are theoretical essays or assessments of qualitative and impressionistic data, but there are also articles on the divorce process based on sample surveys, notably an innovative view of break-ups among couples who live together without marriage ("Breakups Before Marriage: The End of 103 Affairs"), and an analysis of marital break-up among the 2,126 women interviewed in the National Longitudinal Survey of Labor Market Experience ("Work Life and Marital Dissolution"). Counterbalancing these statistical depictions are the more numerous qualitative assessments of interviews with small samples (e.g., Robert Weiss's "The Emotional Impact of Marital Separation") based on insights and experiences gained in group discussions with "the separated" conducted at the Harvard Laboratory of Community

Psychiatry; Spanier and Casto's "Adjustment to Separation and Divorce: A Qualitative Analysis," based on interviews with 50 persons who had filed for divorce in the 1974-1976 period in Centre County, Pennsylvania; and Kohen, Brown, and Feldberg's "Divorced Mothers: The Costs and Benefits of Female Family Control," based on interviews with 30 Boston-area mothers who had a child under 16 living with them and had been divorced 1 to 5 years.

Some useful anthologies have a focus wider than divorce per se, yet include research findings relevant to the situation of divorced persons. Thus, Jeanne Gullahorn's *Psychology and Women: In Transition* includes some tangential pieces such as "The American Family: A Twenty-Year View," but also the first-rate work of Mavis Hetherington *et al.*, on "Stress and Coping in Divorce: A Focus on Women."[29] The Hetherington project, a two-year study of the impact of divorce on family functioning and child development, used many different data collection techniques to make illuminating contrasts between families having experienced divorce and intact families having similar characteristics.

Another large and respected category of writing about American divorce has taken the nation as its laboratory and has drawn upon vital statistics and governmental records to identify variations in marital stability over time and to attempt to interpret the possible causes and consequences of the changes. Indeed, many of the most respected books on divorce and remarriage published in the past decade are not summaries of individual experiences, but analyses of demographic or economic data relevant to apparent trends in the incidence, causes, and consequences of divorce. For example, Ross and Sawhill's oft-cited *Time of Transition*[30] draws mainly upon census data, labor statistics, and other federal sources to show that an increasing number of household heads are women, and considers possible implications of this trend. Similarly, Andrew Cherlin's widely praised *Marriage, Divorce, Remarriage*[31] deftly sketches the continuities and changes in marriage, divorce, and remarriage as they appear in national demographic data, and then attempts to explain the trends and predict their consequences. Another influential work of similar approach is Carter and Glick's near-classic *Marriage and Divorce*.[32]

In addition to the studies of trends and correlates of divorce, there is a broad popular literature ostensibly aimed at helping those who anticipate divorce or already are divorced to cope with their new personal realities. Some of these books draw upon research to illustrate their points, but mostly they are books of advice and anecdotes by people who have themselves been divorced or who, as practitioners, have counseled and treated the divorced. Thus, Cull and Hardy bring the perspectives of clinical psychology and transactional analysis to their *Deciding on Divorce: Personal and Family Considerations*;[33] in *The Courage to Divorce*[34] psychotherapists Gettleman and Markowitz try to show that in contemporary society "divorce can be and often is a wholly liberating and positive experience." In *The American Way of Divorce*[35] author Sheila Kessler makes a book-length appeal for "equal time":

Traditional marriage is not being dethroned but rather asked to share its crown with other covenants. The Single. The Commune. The Family. The Divorced. The Partners. Each sacred in its own right.

And Mel Kranzler's acclaimed *Creative Divorce*[36] tantalizes the reader with the positive outcomes of his own experience:

As a professional counselor and a divorced man, I saw divorce as an emotional process with its own internal time schedule that a divorce decree can hasten or delay, but not eradicate. It is a crisis that must be lived through. More than that, however, more than just a time for picking up the pieces, divorce is a new opportunity to *improve* on the past and create a fuller life—*if* you can come to terms with the past, recognize self-defeating behavior, and be willing to change it.[37]

Kranzler's book is designed to help people see "the promise in the pain," to understand "the healing process of mourning," and to "avoid the nine emotional traps of the past" as they learn to cope with new realities and "new ways of relating to people."

Other helpful popular books on divorce include Esther Oshiver Fisher's *Divorce: The New Freedom*,[38] an attempt to describe the process of divorce counseling from making the decision to divorce through post-divorce adjustment. The high interest recently shown in the idea of divorce mediation has spawned several volumes, such as *Divorce Mediation: A Rational Alternative to the Adversarial System*,[39] and *Divorce Mediation: A Practical Guide for Therapists and Counselors*.[40]

Having mentioned some of the important books not listed in Table 3, let us now turn to the eight "landmark" monographs. The table gives details on when, where, and how each project was done, along with illustrative comments on the techniques used and particular emphases or biases in the objectives or interpretations of findings. The geographical scope of these landmark studies is fairly limited. Apart from the two British studies, these major contributions to existing knowledge about divorce represent portions of the divorced population of four American metropolitan areas (Philadelphia, Detroit, Boston, and San Francisco), plus non-representative volunteers from various unspecified parts of the country.

Two of the monographs—Goode's *After Divorce* and Thornes and Collard's *Who Divorces?*—have a predominantly quantitative emphasis, but descriptive, qualitative work is the dominant approach among the landmark studies. Illustration, not statistical representation, has been the primary objective, and participant observation, depth interviews, and the collection of case histories have been the methods of choice.

Intermountain Divorce Study

Now that we have outlined the methods applied in the major monographs, and reviewed the emphases and techniques of the contemporary journal literature, we are in a position to show how the present study fits into the body of research

Table 3
Major Monographs on the Process and Aftermath of Divorce, 1930–1980

Waller (1930)[a]	Goode (1956)[c]
Data Collection When: 1927-1929 Where: Largely Philadelphia vicinity Method: Case histories, some obtained by interview, others from written life histories; includes some autobiographical material. **Respondents** Characteristics: 33 cases, mostly middle and upper-middle class; Waller states them to be "rather well distributed" in social characteristics, although literary and intellectual types are over represented How Selected: Not explained fully; some were members of Waller's social network; others were referred to him by friends.	**Data Collection** When: 1948 Where: Detroit, Michigan Method: Interview **Respondents** Characteristics: 425 women divorcees, all mothers aged 20-38 at time of divorce and divorced 2-26 months at interview. Included both Blacks and Whites. How Selected: Wives in all divorces listed in county courthouse records for four time periods. **Comments** "We have approximated a random sample . . . We seem to have achieved a representative sample of the urban, divorced mothers in the ages 20-38 years at the time of the divorce, resident in the metropolitan area of Detroit." (p. 31) ". . . confining one interview to the ex-wife is unfortunate, but it is not the lack of the ex-husband that is damaging, but the lack of genuine observation." (p. 27)

Comments

". . . Waller is concerned with the means of adjustment rather than with the social conditions relating to divorce and remarriage. He writes about utilizing the experience of divorce effectively, and he discusses minimizing the personal and social costs of divorce . . . Waller divides social scientists into two groups—"those who want what they say to be true and as demonstrable as possible, whether it is significant or not, and those who do not so much care whether what they say is exactly true as whether it is significant if it is true, or if it has some truth in it." Waller identifies himself as belonging to the latter group. The technique used in The Old Love and the New is the case study method. Waller believes that the method "is based upon the notion that what happens in one case will happen in another, and that understanding can be had from a study of the ideal typical, which may represent nothing which ever happened but something which always tends to happen."

Table 3 (continued)

Hunt (1966)[d]	Weiss (1975)[e]

Data Collection

When:	1962-1965	When:	1971-1974
Where:	"various parts of the United States"	Where:	Cambridge, Mass. in Middlesex County, Boston Vicinity, Mass.
Method:	Multiple-method, including personal interviews, participant observation, expert-informant interviews, and a questionnaire survey.	Method:	Multiple-method, including collection of illustrative material; case studies intensive interview studies of small samples.

Respondents

Characteristics: 200 separated and divorced persons, both men and women (interviews); 169 "middle-class and upper-middle-class adults of all ages, religions and educational attainments, scattered all around the country."

How Selected: Volunteers either members of Parents Without Partners or acquaintances of professionals (marriage counselors, travel agents, sociologists) who serve the formerly married.

Characteristics: Number undefined, over 50 persons both men and women; respondents were members of Parents Without Partners; participants in seminars for the separated sponsored by Laboratory of Community Psychiatry, Harvard University Medical School.

How Selected: Self-selected, although there were quotas designed to assure both men and women in seminar groups.

Comments

"This is a description of the world of the separated and divorced in America, an eye-witness report on the mores, problems, and experiences of people who inhabit a half-secret subculture outside the realm of conventional marriage and family life. . . . I have limited myself almost entirely to the middle class. . . . Like the anthropologist, I have sought to report and interpret, rather than to exhort or give advice. . . . The sample is . . . a reasonably good one; nevertheless, since the proportions do not match those of an ideally representative sample, and since the respondents were all volunteers, I have used my statistical findings sparingly and with caution." (pp. ix, 296)

Comments

"Although this book has, I believe, a strong empirical foundation, I cannot draw on the kind of survey necessary for quantitative statements: for estimates for example, of the proportion of separated individuals who have had specific experiences. Nor can I say with confidence which of various fairly common experiences occur most frequently, although I may be able to say that some experiences appear to occur often and others to be rare. Much in this book is theoretical in nature. . . . Almost all these theoretical formulations seem to me to be supported by my own observations and by those of others." (pp. xii-xiii)

Hart (1976)[f]

Data Collection

When: 1968-1970
Where: "Riverton" a Midlands University city, England
Method: Participant Observation, Depth-Interviews.

Respondents

Characteristics: 58*, including 35 women and 23 men; 52% divorced, 22% legally separated, 26% informally separated. All were members of a club for divorced and separated.

How Selected: "Club Regulars" were observed and interviewed. Casual attenders excluded.

Comments

"Because my study is grounded in the experiences of a small number of people and because these experiences appeared to have been at worst traumatic and at best difficult, the main focus has been on problematic features of marital breakdown and its aftermath. I have been content to draw a one-sided picture, an extreme typification of the negative aspects of divorce and separation in Britain." (p. 215)

"The people on whom this study is based may not be typical of the divorced and separated at large in British society. For a number of reasons . . . their problems of adjusting to the status passage were extremely harsh. It was this which in part led them to the Rivertown Association for the Divorced and Separated . . ." (p. xi)

*author states she collected detailed case material on 63 persons, but published Tables include only 58.

Hunt and Hunt (1977)[g]

Data Collection

When: 1975-1976
Where: U.S. generally (specific locations not given
Method: Questionnaire, depth interviews, observation

Respondents

Characteristics: The national survey: 984 separated and divorced people, one-third of them male; the depth interviews: characteristics not given, except that they are separated or divorced persons.

How Selected: The national survey: questionnaire was published in monthly magazine of Parents Without Partners, plus selective distribution of questionnaires by marriage and divorce counselors, and other marriage and family specialists. The depth interviews: mode of selection not given.

Comments

"It is a non-random volunteer sample, but in most of its demographic characteristics it is quite similar to the national population of separated and divorced people. . . where our data could be compared with those obtained by sociologists and psychologists currently doing research in this field, the results were usually reassuringly close. . . ." (p. 272)

"The book is the end product of an intensive research program. . . . It is not a compilation of statistics, and not a "how to" guide, but a book of human experiences. Data are given where the numbers are particularly surprising, enlightening, or fascinating, but in the main our significant findings are presented through case material and descriptions of behavior; these are far more accessible to most people than are tables, charts, and graphs, and the voices of divorced people are far more persuasive than our own." (pp. xiii-xiv)

21

Table 3 (continued)

| Thornes and Collard (1979)[h] | Wallerstein and Kelly (1980)[i] |

Data Collection

When: 1972-1973
Where: West Midlands, England
Method: Interviews

Respondents

Characteristics: 520 divorced persons, 336 women and 184 men, who had petitioned for divorce and had decree granted between September, 1970 and March, 1972. Comparison data were also collected from a "continuing married sample of 520 persons (199 men and 371 women) married at least two years, still in their first marriage.

How Selected: Sampling frame constructed from names of petitioners published in local newspaper; 95 percent lived within 20-mile radius of the divorce court. All "petitioners" were those who legally requested the divorce, and not "respondents" whose names and addresses were not always available. "Continuing marrieds" names were drawn from electoral registers of the same area where the divorced respondents lived.

Comments

"This present study . . . compares those who divorce with those who are continuing with their primary marriages, and it is possible that factors which are part of the underlying mechanisms of marital unhappiness may not be powerful discriminators between the survey divorced and continuing married, if the latter includes unhappily married informants." (p. 12)

Data Collection

When: 1971-1977
Where: Suburban San Francisco
Method: Multiple clinical interviews with divorcing parents and their children, with data forms filled out by clinicians following the interview sessions. Parents were interviewed weekly (children slightly less often) during a six-week baseline period, then again one year later and five years later. All respondents were interviewed separately. Data were also collected by interviews from the children's school teachers. During final follow-up some interviews were by telephone.

Respondents

Characteristics: Sixty divorcing couples, largely white, middle-class, and their 131 children. Respondents, participating at each stage included 47 fathers, 59 mothers, and 131 children at baseline period; 41 fathers, 53 mothers, and 108 children at first follow-up; and 41 fathers, 54 mothers, and 101 children at five-year follow-up. Families selected were judged to have "normal" children who had no histories of psychological or intellectual dysfunctions. Fifteen percent of the fathers and 20 percent of the mothers were clinically assessed as "severely troubled." Two-thirds of the fathers and one-third of the mothers had college degrees.

How Selected: The 60 families initially volunteered for a free six-week child-centered divorce-counseling service. Parents were separated and filing for divorce at the time. Most were referred to the program by social workers, attorneys, ministers, or friends. A few were referred by the superior court.

" . . . an attempt was made to construct a model for divorce. . . . which incorporated the notions on the one hand of personal vulnerability and on the other, of environing disadvantage, which could be singly or jointly present. . . . The extent to which those who divorce may be considered as more vulnerable or more disadvantaged than those who continue with their marriages could not be explored in great depth in this survey. . . ."

Comments

"Our research objective in seeing parents and children separately, and in getting independent information from the schools, was to obtain a complex and rich set of data about each family collectively and as individuals within that family. . . . These multiple sets of data enabled us to triangulate often irreconcilable appearing data into a meaningful psychological portrait of the family and its members in the midst of divorce." (pp. 319-320)

a. Willard Waller, The Old Love and the New (Philadelphia: Liveright, 1930), republished with introduction by Bernard Farber, Carbondale: Southern Illinois University Press, 1967.

b. Bernard Farber, "Introduction" to Willard Waller, The Old Love and the New, pp. xviii, xxxiv.

c. William Goode, After Divorce (Glencoe, Ill.: Free Press, 1956).

d. Morton M. Hunt, The World of the Formerly Married (New York: McGraw-Hill, 1966).

e. Robert S. Weiss, Marital Separation (New York: Basic Books, Inc., 1975).

f. Nicky Hart, When Marriage Ends: A Study in Status Passage (London: Tavistock Publications, 1976).

g. Morton Hunt and Bernice Hunt, The Divorce Experience (New York: McGraw-Hill, 1977).

h. Barbara Thornes and Jean Collard, Who Divorces? (London: Routledge and Kegan Paul, 1979).

i. Wallerstein and Kelly, Surviving the Breakup.

on divorce, and to highlight its strengths and weaknesses. The Intermountain Divorce Study is based on a two-stage data collection process which, in the end, netted a sample of 500 divorced individuals who were roughly representative of the divorced population of eight western states. The first stage instrument, a modest 31-item schedule, collected enough demographic detail to permit the identification of divorced people and to provide essential contrasts in demographic and social characteristics between the divorced and the non-divorced. The second phase of the data collection was a mail survey of the divorced people identified in stage one. The nine-page questionnaire included 68 items on the nature of the kinship, friendship and organizational networks experienced before, during, and after the divorce. There were also some key indicators of how the divorce process itself was experienced, and a brief section on characteristics of a remarriage, if any.

Our report includes no cautionary tales, no personal accounts of the psychological balance sheet at the way-stations of divorce. Indeed, the approach is almost wholly sociological: not "How did you feel?" but "To what did you belong?"; not "What psychic supports did you discover?" but "How often did you attend church?"

The objective has been to chart the effects of divorce upon the networks of personal affiliation—to measure the remembered variations in "belonging" to friends, family, church, and clubs—as one changed from the normal status of "married" to the deviant one of "divorced."

The Intermountain Divorce Study differs from much of the previous research on divorce in several other ways:

1. It represents a more heterogeneous population with respect to stage of divorce. Much previous work focused on people in the process of divorce or recently divorced. We obtained questionnaires from the ever-divorced.

2. It represents a wider geographic base. Respondents in most earlier studies were drawn from court records, agency client rosters, or were participants in organizations serving a given city or county. The geographic base for the Intermountain Divorce Study is an eight-state region.

3. Not only is the geographic base wider than in most divorce research, but it is different. As far as we can tell, this is the first major study of divorce in the intermountain West. It will be recalled that the locales for much of the prior research on divorce are the metropolitan areas of the Midwest and of California.

4. Our method of data collection has been rarely used in divorce research. Where systematic surveys have been done, the interview rather than the structured questionnaire has been the preferred method.

5. Use of mail survey techniques made it possible to obtain data from a much larger sample than is usually available. Of the 40 articles listed in Table 2, only one reported a sample larger than the 500 Intermountain Divorce Study respondents, and among the landmark monographs, only three—the books by Goode, Hunt and Hunt, and Thornes and Collard—had samples in the same general size range or larger.

6. Our method of sampling is almost without precedent in the divorce literature. We sampled the general population from telephone directories, and screened that sample via

a first-wave mailing to identify divorced persons. Those who indicated they had ever been divorced were invited to participate in the second stage mail survey which focused on the divorce process.

7. Finally, the Intermountain Divorce Study has a better representation of divorced people of both sexes than is typically the case.

Besides those differences, we recognize the biases inherent in using telephone books as an initial sampling frame, the problems of selective recall in retrospective data, and the limitations of a two-wave questionnaire design which permitted easy non-response or refusal. On the other hand, the advantages in scale (number of respondents, size and population of area represented), scope or range of experience (obtaining data from the ever-divorced rather than the recently divorced or the currently divorcing), and representativeness (all divorced persons residing in an area were defined as potential respondents, rather than merely those who had obtained their divorce in a given jurisdiction) are also considerable. We recognize and lament the lack of qualitative detail in the data. At the same time, we affirm that the trade-off for representativeness, scale, and scope may be worth it, at least in one monograph.

We cannot say that we know our respondents as Weiss, or Wallerstein and Kelly, or Waller knew theirs. Indeed, we are envious of the depth, warmth, and apparent exchange of help that characterized some of the research represented in the major monographs. But if our respondents were not friends, confidants, or clients, in the sense that is expressed so well by Wallerstein and Kelly,[41] they were courteous but confidential collaborators. They took time to share aspects of their experience in the hope that someone would fit it into meaningful patterns and thereby, perhaps, discover some commonalities or insights unavailable, probably invisible, to the divorcing individual. In the chapters that follow we have tried to do that.

Notes

1. Sonya J. Herman, "Women, Divorce, and Suicide," *Journal of Divorce* 1 (Winter 1977):108.

2. Judith S. Wallerstein and Joan B. Kelly, *Surviving the Breakup: How Children and Parents Cope with Divorce* (New York: Basic Books, 1980), p. 5.

3. David H. Olson, ed., *Inventory of Marriage and Family Literature, Vol. VII, 1980* (Beverly Hills: Sage Publications, 1981), p. vii. See also, for example, David H. L. Olson and Nancy S. Dahl, *Inventory of Marriage and Family Literature, Vol. III, 1973 and 1974* (St. Paul: University of Minnesota, Family Social Science, 1975).

4. The inventories also reveal increased interest in research on the children of divorce; a special category on "custody" was first added to the "divorce and separation" section in the 1977-1978 volume.

5. John F. Crosby, "A Critique of Divorce Statistics and Their Interpretation," *Family Relations* 29 (January 1980):51; see also Lincoln Day, "Those Unsatisfactory Statistics on Divorce," *Australian Quarterly* (December 1979):26-31.

6. Gay C. Kitson and Helen J. Raschke, "Divorce Research: What We Know; What We Need to Know," *Journal of Divorce* 4 (Spring 1981):3.

7. David G. Rice, "Pseudo-Divorce: A Factor in Marital Stability and Growth," *Psychotherapy: Theory, Research and Practice* 13 (Spring 1976):51-53.

8. Werner Simon and Gayle K. Lumry, "Suicide of the Spouse as a Divorce Substitute," *Diseases of the Nervous System* 31 (September 1970):608-12.

9. Arthur J. Norton and Paul C. Glick, "Marital Instability in America: Past, Present, and Future," in George Levinger and Oliver C. Moles, eds., *Divorce and Separation: Context, Causes, and Consequences* (New York: Basic Books, Inc., 1979) p. 13.

10. Kitson and Raschke, "Divorce Research: What We Know; What We Need to Know," p. 1.

11. Wallerstein and Kelly, *Surviving the Breakup,* p. 5.

12. Arland Thornton, "Marital Dissolution, Remarriage, and Childbearing,"*Demography* 15 (August 1978):361; Robert T. Michael, "The Rise in Divorce Rates, 1960-1974: Age-Specific Components," *Demography* 15 (May 1978):177.

13. Ulrich C. Schoettle and Dennis P. Cantwell, "Children of Divorce," *Journal of the American Academy of Child Psychiatry* 19 (1980):453; Judith S. Wallerstein and Joan B. Kelly, "Children and Divorce: A Review," *Social Work* 24 (November 1979): 468; Janice M. Hammond, "Children of Divorce: A Study of Self-Concept, Academic Achievement, and Attitudes," *Elementary School Journal* 80 (no. 2, 1979):55.

14. Esther Oshiver Fisher, "The Journal of Divorce," *Journal of Divorce* 1 (Fall 1977):5.

15. Connie J. Salts, "Divorce Process: Integration of Theory," *Journal of Divorce* 2 (Spring 1979):233.

16. Constance R. Ahrons, "Divorce: A Crisis of Family Transition and Change," *Family Relations* 29 (October 1980):533-40.

17. Ibid., p. 539.

18. Roslyn Feldberg and Janet Kohen, "Family Life in an Anti-Family Setting: A Critique of Marriage and Divorce," *Family Coordinator* 25 (April 1976):155-56.

19. Ibid., p. 158.

20. *The Journal of Marriage and the Family, Journal of Marital and Family Therapy, Family Relations, Social Work, Journal of Family Law, Family Law Quarterly, American Journal of Orthopsychiatry, Social Casework, Journal of Clinical Psychology* are a few of the journals addressing divorce topics.

21. Its role was envisioned in the introductory editorial as ". . . a literary clearinghouse of ideas and skills, exchange of information, dialogue, cooperative study, and joint professional development. . . . The *Journal of Divorce* is the first professional journal to be devoted entirely to research, counseling, and therapy for use by this wide variety of helping professionals involved with divorce."

22. Kitson and Raschke, "Divorce Research: What We Know: What We Need to Know"; Sharon Price-Bonham and Jack O. Balswick, "The Noninstitutions: Divorce, Desertion, and Remarriage," *Journal of Marriage and the Family* 42 (November 1980): 959-72.

23. Barney G. Glaser and Anselm Strauss, *The Discovery of Grounded Theory*, (Chicago: Aldine, 1967).

24. The four articles are listed in the citations at the bottom of Table 2.

25. Jessie Bernard, *Remarriage: A Study of Marriage* (New York: Russell & Russell, 1956, 1971).

26. Harvey J. Locke, *Predicting Adjustment in Marriage: A Comparison of a Divorced and a Happily Married Group* (New York: Henry Holt, 1951).

27. Paul Bohannan, ed., *Divorce and After* (Garden City, N.Y.: Doubleday & Co., 1970).

28. George Levinger and Oliver C. Moles, eds., *Divorce and Separation: Context, Causes, and Consequences* (New York: Basic Books, 1979).

29. Jeanne E. Gullahorn, ed., *Psychology and Women: In Transition* (New York: John Wiley & Sons, 1979); E. Mavis Hetherington, Martha Cox and Roger Cox, ''Stress and Coping in Divorce: A Focus on Women,'' pp. 95-128 in Gullahorn, 1979.

30. Heather L. Ross and Isabel V. Sawhill, *Time of Transition: The Growth of Families Headed by Women* (Washington, D.C.: The Urban Institute, 1975).

31. Andrew J. Cherlin, *Marriage, Divorce, Remarriage* (Cambridge, Mass.: Harvard University Press, 1981).

32. Hugh Carter and Paul C. Glick, *Marriage and Divorce: A Social and Economic Study* (Cambridge, Mass.: Harvard University Press, 1976).

33. John G. Cull and Richard E. Hardy, *Deciding on Divorce* (Springfield, Ill.: Charles C. Thomas, 1974).

34. Susan Gettleman and Janet Markowitz, *The Courage to Divorce* (New York: Simon and Schuster, 1974).

35. Sheila Kessler, *The American Way of Divorce: Prescriptions for Change* (Chicago: Nelson-Hall, 1975).

36. Mel Krantzler, *Creative Divorce: A New Opportunity for Personal Growth* (New York: M. Evans and Co., 1974).

37. Ibid., p. 28.

38. Esther Oshiver Fisher, *Divorce: The New Freedom* (New York: Harper & Row, 1974).

39. Howard H. Irving, *Divorce Mediation: A Rational Alternative to the Adversarial System* (Toronto: Personal Library Publishers, 1980).

40. John M. Haynes, *Divorce Mediation: A Practical Guide for Therapists and Counselors* (New York: Springer, 1981).

41. Wallerstein and Kelly, *Surviving the Breakup*, pp. 7-8.

Chapter 2

Marriage, Divorce, and Remarriage in Social and Historical Context

Introduction

The purpose of this chapter is to describe, from a historic and comparative point of view, trends in marriage and divorce in the mountain states (Arizona, Colorado, Idaho, Montana, Nevada, New Mexico, Utah, and Wyoming). As mentioned in chapter one, these eight states are the region sampled in the Intermountain Divorce Study. To fit the patterns of divorce and remarriage in this region into the national context, we will make certain comparisons between states in this region and the United States as a whole. However, an analysis of the history and current status of divorce and remarriage in all eight of these states would be too lengthy for this chapter. Instead, we have chosen three—Nevada, Idaho, and Utah—for detailed treatment.

These three states were selected because of their distinctive histories of marriage and divorce. As everyone is aware, Nevada is unique in the United States in its high rates of marriage and divorce. Utah, with its strong religious heritage, is also an atypical state; although patterns of marriage and divorce tend to be quite consistent with the national pattern. Idaho falls somewhere between Utah and Nevada on many of the trends and is generally representative of the larger intermountain region. Much of the discussion of the historical, social, and demographic correlates of divorce and remarriage in this chapter will focus on these three states. The subsequent chapters, based on the empirical data collected, reflect perceptions of the ever-divorced in the entire eight-state region.

Regional Marriage, Divorce, and Remarriage in National Context

Demographers have long noted regional trends in marital statistics in the United States. Marriage and divorce rates are higher in the South than in the North and higher in western than in eastern states.[1] The mountain states have had higher than national divorce rates since 1870 and higher than national marriage rates since 1900.

Table 4 shows crude marriage rates per 1,000 population for the United States, the mountain states region, and each state in the region. Most states follow the national pattern of a gradual climb from 1870 through the 1940s (World War II boom), a short decline through the 1960s, and another slight increase in 1980 when there were 2,413,000 marriages in the United States.[2] Exceptions to the pattern include an extremely high marriage rate in Arizona, an atypically low rate for Colorado in 1940, and lower marriage rates in 1980 than in 1970 for Idaho and Nevada.

The general trend in marital dissolution for the last century has been toward an ever-increasing number of divorces, reaching an all-time national high of 1,182,000 divorces in 1980.[3] Divorce rates per 1,000 population for the United States and mountain states are shown in Table 5. Rates increased in each state and in the United States through the post-World War II boom into 1950, then experienced a slight decline during the 1960s, and another increase through 1980. Only Nevada continued a downward trend in divorce rates after 1960.

Remarriages are included in the crude marriage rates and have contributed to the overall pattern through the years. When analyzed separately, we learn that first marriages declined through the 1960s and into the 1970s, while remarriage rates began increasing in the 1960s and did not decline again until the last half of the 1970s.[4]

Historical data on remarriage rates for each state are not available. However, there are data on the proportion of marriages by previous marital status. Table 6 shows that the proportion of all marriages that are remarriages has increased over the last twenty years in the United States and in three of the mountain states.[5] In Montana, the proportion of remarriages decreased between 1960 and 1970, but had increased again by 1977. Table 6 also shows higher rates of remarriage after divorce than after widowhood. It is estimated that about three-fourths of the women and five-sixths of the men who divorce in the United States will eventually remarry.[6] Much smaller proportions of widowed men and women can expect to re-enter matrimony.

Marriage in Nevada, Idaho, and Utah

A more complete look at marriage and divorce statistics in specific states will illuminate the trends described above.

Crude marriage rates. Marriage rates for Nevada, Idaho, Utah, and the United States for the last century are detailed in Table 7 and plotted in Figure 1.[7] Before 1900, Nevada's crude marriage rate (number of marriages per 1,000 population) was lower than the national rate. After 1900, it ranged from 1.7 times as high as the U.S. rate in 1900 to 34.9 times as high in 1941 when Nevada's marriage rate was up to 443.3 marriages per 1,000 population and the U.S. rate was

Table 4
Marriage Rates per 1,000 Population for the U.S. and the Mountain States, 1870-1980

	1870	1880	1890	1900	1916	1930	1940	1950	1960	1970	1980[e]
United States	8.8[a]	9.0[a]	9.0[a]	9.3[a]	10.6	9.2	12.1	11.1	8.5	10.6	10.9
Mountain States	--	--	9.2	9.2	11.9[b]	13.9	26.7[a]	26.1	17.9[a]	22.6	21.2
Arizona	--	--	5.7	9.0	12.6	17.6	47.4	26.7	7.8	10.4	11.1
Colorado	8.3[b]	8.4[b]	11.3	10.1	10.3[b]	11.3	6.6	10.4[d]	9.1[a,d]	11.3	11.8
Idaho	4.4[b]	7.0[b]	7.5	8.5	10.2[b]	10.1	16.9	14.2	15.1	15.3	13.9
Montana	3.8[b]	8.5[b]	9.2	8.7	16.7	10.1	15.6[a]	12.2	8.7	10.0	10.6
Nevada	5.8[b]	5.3[c]	5.5[b]	15.4[b]	12.7	67.0	354.0	311.5[d]	208.1[d]	199.7	144.4
New Mexico	--	--	7.0	6.7	10.4[b]	20.5	22.9	33.3	11.6	12.2	12.6
Utah	--	--	11.0[c]	9.8[c]	12.1[b]	11.1	15.0	10.3[d]	8.0	11.0	11.7
Wyoming	10.1[b]	8.5[b]	6.9	9.1	11.1[b]	7.8	11.7	12.2	9.9	13.5	14.5

a. Estimated

b. Excluding non-reporting areas

c. Incomplete

d. Marriage licenses

e. Computed

Sources: National Center for Health Statistics, 100 Years of Marriage and Divorce Statistics, United States, 1867-1967. Table 7. Hyattsville, Md.: 1973.
National Center for Health Statistics, Vital Statistics of the United States, 1970. Volume III- Marriage and Divorce. Table 1-5. Hyattsville, Md.: 1973.

Table 5
Divorce Rates per 1,000 Population for the U.S. and the Mountain States, 1870-1980

	1870	1880	1890	1900	1916	1930	1940	1950	1960	1970	1980[d]
United States	0.3	0.4	0.5	0.7	1.1[b]	1.6	2.0	2.6	2.2	3.5	5.3
Mountain States	0.8[b]	0.8	1.2	1.3	2.0	2.9	4.1[a]	5.5[a]	4.2	5.9	7.5
Arizona	--	0.6	0.6	1.3	2.1	2.6	3.8	5.4	3.7	7.2	7.3
Colorado	1.2[b]	1.3[a]	2.1	1.5	1.2[b]	2.2	2.5[a]	3.3[a]	2.7	4.7	6.3
Idaho	0.9[b]	1.0[b]	0.5	1.3	2.3	2.2	3.2	4.6	3.9	5.1	7.0
Montana	0.8[b]	1.0[c]	1.6	1.5	3.0	2.5	3.0[a]	3.3	3.0[c]	4.4	6.3
Nevada	0.8	1.0[c]	1.2[c]	1.0[c]	8.2	28.7	47.1	55.7	29.6	18.7	17.1
New Mexico	--	0.1	0.4	0.7	1.2[b]	1.8	2.3[a]	3.9	3.0	4.3	8.0
Utah	0.9[c]	0.8	0.7	1.0	1.6	2.0	2.7[a]	3.1	2.4	3.7	5.4
Wyoming	1.4[c]	1.0	0.8	1.3	1.8[b]	2.9	4.0[a]	4.0[c]	4.0	5.4	8.4

a. Estimated

b. Excluding non-reporting areas

c. Incomplete

d. Computed

Sources: National Center for Health Statistics, 100 Years of Marriage and Divorce Statistics, United States, 1867-1967. Table 9.
National Center for Health Statistics, Vital Statistics of the United States. Volume III-Marriage and Divorce. Table 2-2.
National Center for Health Statistics, Monthly Vital Statistics Report, Births, Marriages, Divorces, and Deaths for 1980. Table 3. Hyattsville, Md: 1981.
U.S. Bureau of the Census, 1980 Census of Population and Housing, U.S. Summary, Final Population and Housing Counts. Washington, D.C.: U.S. Government Printing Office, 1982.

12.1. Since then both rates have decreased, but Nevada's crude marriage rate has decreased much more rapidly, reaching a point of 147.4 in 1979, only 13.9 times as high as the U.S. rate of 10.6 marriages per 1,000 population.

The historical fluctuations in state marriage rates have been greatly influenced by statutory changes. As a state has added requirements for physical examinations (or blood tests), waiting periods, or other restrictions on applications for marriage, some non-residents have been discouraged from seeking marriage in that state. In states not requiring waiting periods or blood tests, a higher proportion of marriage licenses are granted to non-residents than in states with more strict requirements. Nevada requires no blood test; there is no waiting for the license and no waiting period after the license is issued, making it the most lenient in regard to marriage laws. Utah requires a blood test but there is no waiting period either before or after issuance of the license. Idaho requires a blood test, but if both parties are over 18 years old, there is no waiting period for the license. There is a three-day waiting period prior to issuance if either party is under 18 but no mandatory wait after the license is issued.[8]

In Nevada, after a 1913 reduction in legal residency requirements, marriage rates increased sharply, influenced not only by persons who migrated to marry but also by those who came to divorce and found it convenient to remarry before they left. When the residency requirement was lowered again in 1931, marriage rates rose again. They peaked during World War II and have been on the decline since then. Nevertheless, Nevada's marriage rates continue to be far higher than those of other states.

While Nevada's crude marriage rates have consistently been very high, Idaho's crude marriage rates have oscillated both above and below national rates. Early in the century, Idaho's marriage rates were lower than the country's, but by 1930 the Idaho rate had risen to 10.1 marriages per 1,000 population, compared to a U.S. rate of 9.2. Crude marriage rates in Idaho continued higher than national rates, peaking in 1942 with an estimated 24.5 marriages per 1,000 population, not quite twice as high as the U.S. rate of 13.2. In 1943, rates dropped both nationally and regionally, such that Idaho marriage rates were lower than U.S. rates for 1944-1946. The U.S. marriage rate reached its highest point ever in 1946 (16.4). But after World War II, Idaho marriage rates again were higher than U.S. rates, peaking in 1966 with 24.6 marriages per 1,000 population, a figure more than two and a half times higher than the U.S. rate of 9.5 for 1966.

In 1967, the Idaho legislature established a three-day waiting period for persons under 18 years of age, and the marriage rates for the next few years were significantly lower than they had been during the early 1960s. Between 1970 and 1973, national marriage rates were higher than Idaho rates, then in 1974 both Idaho and the United States had 10.5 marriages per 1,000 population. Since 1977 U.S. rates have been increasing while Idaho rates have been decreasing. In 1980, Idahoans experienced approximately 13.9 marriages per 1,000 population, while the U.S. rate was 10.9 (see Table 7).

Table 6

Percent Distribution of First Marriages and Remarriages for Brides and Grooms, U.S. and Selected Mountain States, 1960-1977

	1960		1970		1977	
	Bride	Groom	Bride	Groom	Bride	Groom
United States [a]						
First marriages	80.5	81.4	78.4	78.1	71.7	70.0
Remarriages	19.5	18.6	21.6	21.9	28.2	30.0
Widowed	5.2	4.8	4.7	4.1	3.8	3.5
Divorced	14.3	13.8	16.9	17.8	24.4	26.5
Idaho						
First marriages	65.6	69.3	62.0	62.2	57.5	57.7
Remarriages	34.4	30.7	38.0	37.8	42.5	42.3
Widowed	6.4	3.4	6.9	4.0	4.4	3.2
Divorced	28.0	27.3	31.1	33.8	38.1	39.1
Montana						
First marriages	70.4	71.2	77.1	78.2	68.2	68.7
Remarriages	29.6	28.8	22.9	21.8	31.7	31.2
Widowed	7.7	4.8	5.1	3.5	4.0	3.0
Divorced	21.9	24.0	17.8	18.3	27.7	28.2
Utah						
First marriages	87.1	86.1	86.1	86.6	82.2	81.2
Remarriages	12.9	13.9	13.8	13.4	17.8	18.8
Widowed	4.0	3.0	2.5	2.6	2.2	2.0
Divorced	8.9	10.9	11.3	10.8	15.6	16.8
Wyoming						
First marriages	62.6	65.7	61.6	63.9	55.2	56.3
Remarriages	37.4	34.3	38.4	36.1	44.9	43.7
Widowed	7.3	4.6	6.3	4.2	4.1	3.4
Divorced	30.1	29.7	32.1	31.9	40.8	40.3

a. Marriage Reporting Area

Sources: National Center for Health Statistics, Vital Statistics of the United States, 1960, Vol III-Marriage and Divorce. Table 2-23. Hyattsville, Maryland: 1963.
National Center for Health Statistics, Vital Statistics of the U.S., 1970, Volume III-Marriage and Divorce. Table 1-23. Hyattsville, Md: 1974.
National Center for Health Statistics, Vital Statistics of the U.S., 1977, Volume III-Marriage and Divorce. Table 1-11. Hyattsville, Md: 1981.

From the beginning of the twentieth century until the beginning of World War II, Utah had higher marriage rates than the United States. From then until 1966, when both Utah's marriage rate and that of the nation were 9.5 per 1,000 population, Utah's marriage rates were lower than the U.S. rates. Since 1966 Utah's marriage rates have been somewhat higher than national rates, reaching ll.7 in 1980 compared to 10.9 for the country as a whole.

Refined marriage rates. The crude rates are computed per 1,000 population, and as Utah's population includes a relatively high proportion of children, the

Figure 1
Marriage Rates per 1,000 Population for Nevada, Idaho, Utah, and the U.S., 1870-1980

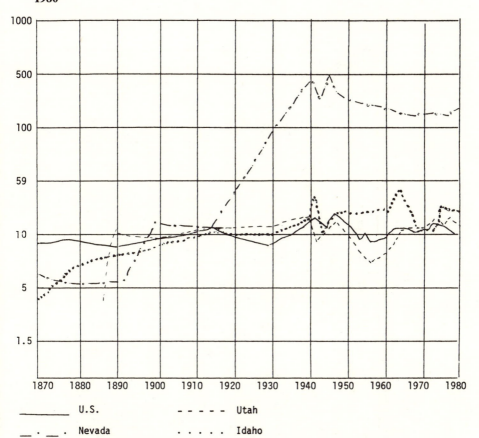

_____ U.S.   - - - - - Utah

__ . __ . Nevada   . . . . . Idaho

Sources: National Center for Health Statistics, Monthly Vital Statistics Report,
           Advance Report, Final Marriage Statistics, 1975. Hyattsville, Md: 1977.
           National Center for Health Statistics, Monthly Vital Statistics Report,
           Annual Summary for the U.S., 1976. Tables 1 and 3. Hyattsville, Md: 1977.
           National Center for Health Statistics, Monthly Vital Statistics Report,
           Advance Report, Final Marriage Statistics, 1977. Hyattsville, Md: 1977.
           National Center for Health Statistics, Vital Statistics of the United
           States 1960, Vol. III-Marriage and Divorce. Tables 1-D and 3-B.
           Hyattsville, Md: 1964.
           National Center for Health Statistics, Vital Statistics of the United States
           1965, Vol III-Marriage and Divorce. Table 1-8. Hyattsville, Md: 1968.
           National Center for Health Statistics, Vital Statistics of the United
           States 1974, Vol III-Marriage and Divorce. Tables 1-5, 2-2 and 2-6.
           Hyattsville, Md: 1977.
           National Center for Health Statistics, 100 Years of Marriage and Divorce
           Statistics: United States, 1867-1967. Tables 1, 7, and 9. Hyattsville,
           Md: 1973.
           National Center for Health Statistics, Monthly Vital Statistics
           Report, Births, Marriage, Divorces and Deaths for 1980. Hyattsville,
           Md: 1981.
           U.S. Bureau of the Census, 1980 Census of Population and Housing,
           U.S. Summary, Final Population and Housing Counts. Washington, D.C:
           1982.

Table 7
Marriage Statistics for Nevada, Idaho, Utah, and the U.S., 1870-1980

Year	Number of Marriages			Marriage Rate per 1,000 Population			
	Nevada	Idaho	Utah	Nevada	Idaho	Utah	United States[a]
1870				5.8[b]	4.4[b]		8.8
1880				5.3[d]	7.0[b]		9.0
1890			2,319	5.5[b]	7.5[d]	11.0	9.0
1900			2,715	15.4[b]	8.5	9.8	9.3
1916			5,036	12.7	10.2	11.7	10.6
1930	20,786		5,649	67.0	10.1	11.1	9.2
1939	39,030	6,313	8,254	193.8	12.1	15.0	12.1
1940	53,200	8,892	7,263	345.4[a]	16.9	13.1	12.7
1941	55,300	11,213[a]	6,081	443.3[a]	22.4[a]	9.5	13.2
1942	28,000	11,700[a]	6,705	403.6[a]	24.5[a]	10.8	11.8
1943	25,593	5,900[a]	6,262	185.4[a]	11.8[a]	10.0	11.7
1944	34,861	5,171	7,034	167.3	9.8	11.2	12.2
1945	59,186	4,377	9,781	234.0	8.6	15.4	16.4
1946	57,556	7,394	7,965	413.9	14.5	12.2	13.9
1947	52,360	8,029	7,327	386.3	15.4	10.9	12.4
1948	45,155	8,354	6,402	335.6	15.2	9.3	10.6
1949	49,872	7,565	7,110	287.6	13.3	10.2	11.1
1950	49,477	8,345	6,843	311.5	14.2	9.6	10.4
1951	51,703	7,849	6,752	299.1	13.4	9.2	9.9
1952	50,079	8,120	6,926	293.9	13.9	9.2	9.8
1953		8,486		27.13	14.3		

36

1954	50,553	8,915	6,295	253.0	14.9	8.3	9.2
1955	52,420	8,879	6,294	238.1	14.5	8.7	9.3
1956	54,915	9,132	6,657	228.7	14.8	8.1	9.5
1957	58,042	8,995	6,672	232.6	14.1	7.9	8.9
1958	55,832	9,522	6,600	215.4	14.8	7.7	8.3
1959	60,365	9,343	6,734	217.5	14.2	7.6	8.5
1960	59,373	10,325	7,202[c]	208.1	15.1	7.9	8.5
1961	63,967	11,151	7,401	196.6	16.3	7.9	8.5
1962	68,404	11,934	7,651	201.0	17.2	8.0	8.5
1963	73,233	12,679	8,263	198.5	18.4	8.4	8.8
1964	75,894	14,019	8,525	189.0	20.9	8.7	9.0
1965	81,024	15,864	8,736	191.6	22.9	8.8	9.3
1966	86,335	17,129	9,623	196.4	24.6	9.5	9.5
1967	86,426	14,108	10,220	194.4	20.1	10.2	9.7
1968	90,756	11,130	11,558	199.4	15.8	11.2	10.4
1969	94,642	10,993	11,633[c]	199.8	15.5	11.1	10.6
1970	97,605[b]	10,915	11,938[c]	199.7	10.0	11.2	10.6
1971	97,411[c]	11,356	12,497[c]	192.1	10.1	11.4	10.6
1972	106,358	12,086	13,911[c]	199.5	10.7	12.3	11.0
1973	102,078	12,236	14,840[c]	186.3	10.8	12.9	10.9
1974	103,287	12,489	15,164[c]	180.3	10.5	12.9	10.5
1975	101,559	12,688	14,858[c]	171.6	15.6	12.4	10.1
1976	99,722	13,104	14,693	163.5	15.8	11.9	10.0
1977	103,706	13,691	15,098	163.8	16.0	11.9	10.1

Table 7 (continued)

Year	Number of Marriages			Marriage Rate per 1,000 Population			
	Nevada	Idaho	Utah	Nevada	Idaho	Utah	United States[a]
1978	114,646	13,570	16,365	172.1	15.4	12.4	10.5
1979	103,462	13,429	16,699	147.4	14.8	12.2	10.6
1980	115,411	13,084	17,074	144.4	13.9	11.7	10.9

a. Estimated

b. Excluding non-reporting counties

c. Totals are transcripts received

d. Incomplete

Sources: National Center for Health Statistics, Monthly Vital Statistics Report, Advance Report, Final Marriage Statistics, 1975. Hyattsville, MD: 1977.
National Center for Health Statistics, Monthly Vital Statistics Report, Annual Summary for the U.S., 1976. Tables 1 and 3. Hyattsville, Md: 1977.
National Center for Health Statistics, Monthly Vital Statistics Report, Advance Report, Final Marriage Statistics, 1977. Hyattsville, Md.: 1981.
National Center for Health Statistics, Vital Statistics of the United States 1960, Vol III-Marriage and Divorce. Tables 1-D and 3-B. Hyattsville, Md: 1964.
National Center for Health Statistics, Vital Statistics of the United States 1965, Vol III-Marriage and Divorce. Table 1-8. Hyattsville, Md: 1968.
National Center for Health Statistics, Vital Statistics of the United States.1974, Vol III-Marriage and Divorce. Tables 1-5, 2-2, and 2-6. Hyattsville, Md: 1977.
National Center for Health Statistics, 100 Years of Marriage and Divorce Statistics: United States, 1867-1967. Tables 1, 7, and 9. Hyattsville, Md.: 1973.
National Center for Health Statistics, Monthly Vital Statistics Report, Births, Marriages, Divorces and Deaths for 1980. Hyattsville, Md: 1981.
U.S. Bureau of the Census, 1980 Census of Population and Housing, U.S. Summary, Final Population and Housing Counts. Washington, D.C.: 1982.

state-national differences may be more accurately highlighted if a more appropriate base is used in computing the indexes. When refined or general marriage rates are computed using unmarried women 15 years old and over as a base (see Table 8),[9] we find that while Utah's marriage rates are higher than the nation's, since 1940 they have been consistently lower than the rates for Idaho and Nevada.

For Nevada and Idaho, the refined marriage rates show trend patterns similar to crude marriage rates. Nevada's refined marriage rates were below those for the nation only in 1890. Since that time, refined marriage rates for Nevada women have been much higher than comparable rates for the nation, ranging up to 42.3 times as high as the U.S. rate in 1940.

The refined marriage rates for women in Idaho have been lower than those of Nevada, but have followed similar trends. Unmarried Idaho women have married at higher rates than women generally for each year recorded in Table 8. The Idaho rates range from 1.5 times higher than U.S. rates in 1930 to 2.4 times higher in 1960. The 1970 figures reveal that rates in all three states continue well above the national rates despite declines in the most recent years.

Median duration of marriage. Before discussing divorce in Nevada, Idaho, and Utah, let us consider a final marriage statistic—median duration of marriage before divorce. Data on the median duration of marriage before divorce are only available for Nevada for five different years between 1880 and 1930. In each of those years, marriages that ended in divorce in Nevada were of longer duration than those in the nation as a whole (see Table 9). Obviously, these data are old and may not reflect current trends.

Information on duration of marriage before divorce is more complete from Idaho, where it is available since 1900. Between 1900 and 1922 there was little difference between Idaho and the nation in the average duration of marriages ending in divorce. However, since 1930, Idaho marriages that ended in divorce have consistently been briefer than marriages in other states which terminated in divorce. In 1979, the median duration of marriages dissolved in Idaho was 5.0 years, well below the U.S. average of 6.8 years.

From 1900 until 1960, Utah marriages that ended in divorce were of shorter duration than those in Idaho, Nevada, or the United States in general. However, in 1970 and 1975, the median duration of dissolved marriages in Utah was slightly longer than for Idaho, although still well below the national average. In 1979 the duration of marriage in Utah again dropped below Idaho's figure and tied with Wyoming as being the lowest of all 30 states in the Divorce Reporting Area (DRA) at 4.8 years.[10]

Divorce in Nevada, Idaho, and Utah

For the past century, Nevada has consistently had significantly higher than national divorce rates. Nevada's high divorce rates are generally attributed to

Table 8
Marriage Rates per 1,000 Unmarried Women Aged 15 and Over, Nevada, Idaho, Utah, and U.S., 1890-1970

	Nevada	Idaho	Utah	United States
1890	58.7 [a]	122.2 [b]	107.8 [b]	67.4
1900	141.3 [a]	110.0	84.7 [b]	68.2
1930	687.8	101.6	95.7	67.8
1940	3,503.3	160.6	122.6	82.8
1950	3,482.7 [c]	168.1	108.9 [c]	90.2
1960	2,366.7 [c]	175.7	85.3	73.5
1970	1,696.2	124.1	85.3	71.5

a. Estimated

b. Incomplete

c. Marriage Licenses

Sources: National Center for Health Statistics, 100 Years of Marriage and Divorce Statistics, U.S., 1867-1967, Table 8. Hyattsville, Md.: 1973.
National Center for Health Statistics, Vital Statistics of the United States 1970, Vol.III, Marriage and Divorce. Table 1-7. Hyattsville, Md.: 1974.

Table 9
Median Duration of Marriage Before Divorce for Nevada, Idaho, Utah, and U.S., 1880-1979

	Nevada	Idaho	Utah	U.S.
1880	7.7	( )[c]	7.0	7.9
1890	9.0	( )[c]	9.4	8.2
1900	( )[c]	8.4	8.1	8.3
1906	9.8	8.2	6.8	7.9
1922	8.1	6.6	5.9	6.6
1930	9.1[b]	6.3[b]	5.9[b]	6.9
1950		4.2	d	5.8[a]
1960		4.8	4.7	7.2
1970		4.6	5.3	6.7
1975		4.8	4.9	6.5
1979		5.0	4.8	6.8

a. DRA in 1967, all reporting states in 1950.   c. Less than 50 cases.
b. Computed from group data.   d. Not available.

Sources: National Center for Health Statistics, 100 Years of Marriage and Divorce Statistics. Table 13. Hyattsville, Md.: 1973.
National Center for Health Statistics, Vital Statistics of the U.S., 1970. Vol. III-Marriage and Divorce. Table 2-6. Hyattsville, Md: 1973.
National Center for Health Statistics, Monthly Vital Statistics Report, Advance Report, Final Divorce Statistics, 1975. Table 3. Hyattsville, Md.: 1978.
National Center for Health Statistics, Monthly Vital Statistics Report, Advance Report, Final Divorce Statistics, 1979. Table 3. Hyattsville, Md.: 1981.

lenient legal statutues, which are discussed later in the chapter. In 1946, Nevada's crude divorce rate of 143.9 divorces per 1,000 population was 33.5 times as great as the U.S. rate (4.3). However, for the last three decades, Nevada's divorce rates generally have been on the decline while U.S. rates have been increasing. As may be seen in Table 10 and Figure 2, in 1980 Nevada's crude divorce rate was only 3.2 times as high as the U.S. rate (17.1 compared with 5.3).

With the exception of 1890, when both Idaho and the United States had 0.5 divorces per 1,000 population, crude divorce rates in Idaho have been higher than rates for the rest of the nation every year since 1870 (see Table 10). Idaho divorce rates increased slowly from the late 1800s until about 1940 when they rose dramatically, peaking in 1946 at the end of World War II. In that year, Idaho's rate was twice that of the rest of the nation (8.8 versus 4.3 for the U.S.).

Table 10
Divorce Statistics for Nevada, Idaho, Utah, and the U.S., 1870-1980

Year	Number of Divorces			Divorce Rate per 1,000 Population			
	Nevada	Idaho	Utah	Nevada	Idaho	Utah	United States[a]
1870	28	9	82	0.8[b]	0.9[a]	0.9	0.3
1880	64	23	115	1.0[c]	1.0[a]	0.8	0.4
1890			152	1.2[c]	0.5	0.7	0.5
1900			273	1.0[c]	1.3	1.0	0.7
1916			387	8.2	2.3	1.2	1.1
1930			661	28.7	2.2	1.6	1.6
1939			1,016	NA	NA	2.0	1.9
1940	5,533[a]	1,644[a]	1,500	47.1[a]	3.2[a]	2.7	2.0
1941	6,433[a]	1,900[a]	1,360	53.6[a]	3.8[a]	2.4	2.2
1942	8,604[a]	2,200[a]	1,433	62.8[a]	4.6[a]	2.2	2.4
1943	11,113[a]	2,500[a]	1,982	73.6[a]	5.0[a]	3.2	2.6
1944	12,768	2,700	2,995	83.5	5.1	3.2	2.9
1945	15,019	3,300	2,651	100.8	6.5	4.2	3.5
1946	20,572	4,500	3,434	143.9	8.8	5.4	4.3
1947	13,747	3,600	2,927	92.3	6.5	4.5	3.4
1948	11,000	3,190	2,199	70.5	5.8	3.3	2.8
1949	10,800	2,773	2,166	68.8	4.9	3.2	2.7
1950	8,909	2,696	2,107	55.6	4.6	3.0	2.6
1951	9,298	2,569	2,271	56.2	4.4	3.2	2.5
1952	9,841	2,586	2,331	55.9	4.4	3.2	2.5
1953	9,669	2,584	2,433	52.4	4.4	3.2	2.5
1954	9,586	2,523	2,140	48.0	4.2	2.8	2.4
1955	9,559	2,414	2,059	43.4	3.9	2.6	2.3
1956	9,141	2,214	2,189	38.1	3.6	2.7	2.3
1957	9,249	2,360	1,565	37.1	3.7	1.9	2.2
1958	9,409	2,372	2,002	36.3	3.7	2.3	2.2
1959	9,509	2,652	2,179	34.3	4.0	2.5	2.2
1960	8,455	2,592	2,167	29.6	3.9	2.4	2.2
1961	8,223	2,685	2,360	26.4	3.9	2.5	2.3
1962	9,415	2,547	2,480	27.1	3.7	2.6	2.2
1963	9,682	2,798	2,659	24.8	4.1	2.7	2.3
1964	11,849	2,876	2,895	28.3	4.2	3.0	2.4
1965	9,996	2,874	2,872	23.0	4.1	2.9	2.5
1966	9,733	3,062	3,090	21.4	4.4	3.0	2.5
1967	9,708	3,183	3,288	22.3	4.5	3.2	2.6
1968	10,103	3,278	3,390	22.5	4.7	3.3	2.9
1969	10,951	3,506	3,841	24.0	4.9	3.7	3.2
1970	9,138	3,612	3,912	18.7	5.1	3.7	3.5
1971	1,474	3,664	4,419	18.5	5.0	3.8	3.7
1972	11,560	3,847	4,876[c]	21.9	5.1	4.2	4.0
1973	9,975	4,341	5,137[c]	18.2	5.6	4.5	4.4
1974	10,045	4,808	5,670	17.5	6.0	4.8	4.6
1976	10,542	5,203	6,131	17.8	6.3	5.1	4.9
1976	10,151	5,699	6,170	16.9	6.9	5.0	5.0
1977	10,280	6,013	6,947	16.2	7.0	5.5	5.0
1978	11,213	6,356	7,128	16.8	7.2	5.4	5.2
1979	11,787	6,449	7,594	16.8[d]	7.1[d]	5.6[d]	5.4[e]
1980	13,659	6,643	7,957	17.1[d]	7.0[d]	5.4[d]	5.3[e]

a. Estimated

b. Excluding non-reporting counties

c. Totals are transcripts received

d. Computed

e. Preliminary

Sources: National Center for Health Statistics, United States. Table 5.
Hyattsville, Md.: 1978.
National Center for Health Statistics, Monthly Vital Statistics
Report, Annual Summary for the U.S., 1976. Tables 1 and 3.
Hyattsville, Md.: 1977.
National Center for Health Statistics, Monthly Vital Statistics
Report, Advance Report, Final Divorce Statistics, 1979.
Hyattsville, Md.: 1981.
National Center for Health Statistics, Vital Statistics of the
United States 1960, Vol III-Marriage and Divorce. Tables 1-D and
3-B. Hyattsville, Md.: 1964.
National Center for Health Statistics, Vital Statistics of the
United States 1965, Vol III-Marriage and Divorce. Table 1-8.
Hyattsville, Md.: 1977.
National Center for Health Statistics, Vital Statistics of the
United States 1974, Vol III-Marriage and Divorce. Tables 1-5,
2-2, and 2-6. Hyattsville, Md.: 1977.
National Center for Health Statistics, 100 Years of Marriage and
Divorce Statistics: United States, 1867-1967. Tables 1, 7, and
9. Hyattsville, Md.: 1973.
National Center for Health Statistics, Monthly Vital Statistics
Report, Births, Marriages, Divorces and Deaths for 1980.
Hyattsville, Md.: 1981.
U.S. Bureau of the Census, 1980 Census of Population and Housing,
U.S. Summary, Final Population and Housing Counts. Washington,
D.C.: 1982.

Figure 2

Divorce Rates per 1,000 Population for Nevada, Idaho, Utah, and the U.S., 1870-1980

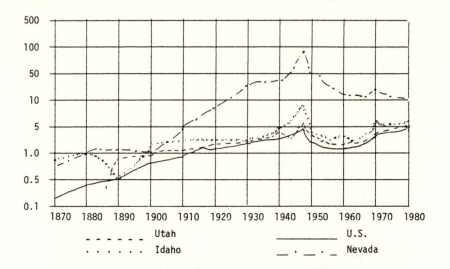

Utah · · · · · Idaho   _____ U.S.   _ . _ . _ Nevada

Sources: National Center for Health Statistics, United States. Table 5.
Hyattsville, MD: 1978.
National Center for Health Statistics, Monthly Vital Statistics Report,
Annual Summary for the U.S., 1976. Tables 1 and 3. Hyattsville, MD: 1977.
National Center for Health Statistics, Monthly Vital Statistics Report,
Advance Report, Final Divorce Statistics, 1979. Hyattsville, MD: 1981.
National Center for Health Statistics, Vital Statistics of the United
States 1960, Vol. III-Marriage and Divorce. Tables 1-D and 3-B.
Hyattsville, MD: 1964.
National Center for Health Statistics, Vital Statistics of the United
States 1965, Vol. III-Marriage and Divorce. Table 1-8. Hyattsville,
MD: 1977.
National Center for Health Statistics, Vital Statistics of the United
States 1974, Vol. III-Marriage and Divorce. Tables 1-5, 2-2, and 2-6.
Hyattsville, MD: 1977.
National Center for Health Statistics, 100 Years of Marriage and Divorce
Statistics: United States, 1867-1967. Tables 1, 7, and 9.
Hyattsville, MD: 1973.
National Center for Health Statistics, Monthly Vital Statistics Report,
Births, Marriages, Divorces and Deaths for 1980. Hyattsville, MD: 1981.
U.S. Bureau of the Census, 1980 Census of Population and Housing, U.S.
Summary, Final Population and Housing Counts. Washington, D.C: 1982.

The divorce rates went down after 1946, then gradually rose again in the early 1960s in an upward trend that still continues. Figures for 1980 show Idaho with 7.0 divorces per 1,000 population, higher than the 5.3 divorces per 1,000 population in the United States as a whole.

Utah's divorce rates have also consistently been higher than the U.S. rates. Since 1890 there have been only three years that were exceptions: in 1941 Utah had 2.2 divorces per 1,000 population while the U.S. rate was 2.4; in 1957 Utah's rate was 1.9 and the U.S. rate was 2.2; and in 1976 Utahns experienced 5.0 divorces per 1,000 population, the same rate as the nation.

Refined divorce rates. A better picture of divorce in the three states is available from the use of refined divorce rates (the number of divorces per 1,000 married women) in place of the crude rates described above. The refined divorce rate is subject to fewer biases than the crude rate, since its base includes only the population at risk, that is, married people. The refined divorce rates for Nevada, Idaho, Utah, and the United States for 1890-1979 are shown in Table 11. Inspection of the series of refined rates reveals that, as with the crude rates, Nevada's divorce rates are considerably higher than for the United States as a whole, ranging from 2.9 times higher than the nation in 1890 to 23.1 times higher in 1940, when Nevada had 203.4 divorces per 1,000 married women, and the U.S. rate was 8.8. As with the marriage rates, both crude and refined, divorce rates in Nevada began rising after 1900, jumped after the 1930 legal changes, and peaked after World War II. Between 1960 and 1970, the divorce rate per 1,000 married women in Nevada *decreased* by 35.5 percent while the U.S. rate *increased* by 62 percent. By 1970, refined divorce rates in Nevada were only 5.2 times as high as the U.S. rates. Only one other state, Alabama, had a decrease in its divorce rate during this period. The change that occurred in Nevada, however, is not an indication of fewer Nevadans getting divorced but, rather, is an indication of fewer people coming from other states *to* Nevada to be divorced.

Idaho's refined divorce rates have always been higher than the national rates, typically about one and a half times as high (see Table 11). Despite the difference in magnitude, Idaho rates have not increased as quickly as U.S. rates in recent years. The increase from 1960 to 1970 in Idaho was less than half of the increase in U.S. divorce rates, 28.7 percent compared with 62 percent.

Although not so high as Idaho or Nevada rates, refined divorce rates for Utah have been higher than those for the country as a whole since 1890. Utah's rates increased by 52.3 percent between 1960 and 1970 while rates in the United States rose 62 percent. Increases from 1970 to 1979 were not quite so dramatic—Utah's refined divorce rate rose 50 percent from 16.6 to 24.9 and the U.S. rate increased only slightly more, 53 percent, from 14.9 to 22.8 divorces per 1,000 married women.

Age-specific divorce rates. The use of age-specific divorce rates for men and women makes differences between state and national figures more meaningful because they allow for variations in the age composition of the population which may artificially inflate or depress crude rates. The age-specific data for computing these rates are not available for Nevada, but a comparison of age-specific divorce for Idaho, Utah, and the nation for 1970 is possible. As may be seen in Table 12, divorce rates are substantially higher in Idaho than in the United States for both sexes in all age groups, with the exception of Idaho men aged 60-64, who have a slightly lower divorce rate than U.S. men in the same age category. The divorce rate for Idaho men aged 14-19 is four times higher than the U.S. rate (61.5 compared with 15.1), and the age-specific divorce rate for Idaho women aged 14-19 is twice as high as the national rate (54.4 versus 26.9). Men and women aged 20-24 in Idaho have divorce rates that are not quite twice as high

Table 11

Refined Divorce Rates per 1,000 Married Women, Nevada, Idaho, Utah, and the U.S., 1890-1979

	Nevada	Idaho	Utah	U.S.
1890	8.8[a]	3.3	4.5	3.0
1900	7.4[a]	7.6	5.8	4.1
1930	143.1	10.9	10.2	7.5
1940	203.4	14.0	12.5[a]	8.8
1950	220.5	18.7	12.9	10.3
1960	121.0	16.4	10.9	9.2
1970	78.9	21.1	16.6	14.9
1979	---	---	24.9	22.8

a. Incomplete

Sources: National Center for Health Statistics, 100 Years of Marriage and Divorce Statistics, United States, 1867-1967. Table 10. Hyattsville, Maryland: 1973.
National Center for Health Statistics, Divorce and Divorce Rates, United States. Table 4. Hyattsville, Md: 1978.
National Center for Health Statistics, Monthly Vital Statistics Report, Advance Report, Final Divorce Statistics, 1979. Table 3. Hyattsville, Md: 1981.
Utah Bureau of Health Statistics, Marriage and Divorce 1979. Table A. Salt Lake City, Utah: 1981.

as comparable U.S. divorce rates for the same age group. Although Idaho rates are higher than national rates in the remaining categories, the differences are not as marked as in the teenage and young adult categories.

For most of the specific age groups in Utah, divorce rates are as high or higher than rates for comparable age and sex categories in the United States but considerably lower than for Idaho. Only in the category of men aged 60-64 are Utah rates higher than Idaho rates.

Remarriage in Nevada, Idaho, and Utah

Table 13 shows that for the past two decades remarriages account for a higher proportion of marriages in Idaho than in the nation in general. Figures for 1977 reveal that 42.5 percent of Idaho brides and 42.3 percent of Idaho grooms were entering a remarriage. Comparable U.S. figures are 28.2 and 30.0 percent, respectively. Probabilities of remarriages in Utah are lower than in the rest of the nation, and are considerably lower than in Idaho. For the most recent year shown, only 17.8 percent of Utah brides and 18.8 of Utah grooms were entering a remarriage.

Table 12
Age-Specific Divorce Rates by Age of Husband and Wife at Time of Decree, Idaho, Utah, and the U.S., 1970

Age	Idaho		Utah		U.S.[a]	
	Husbands	Wives	Husbands	Wives	Husbands	Wives
14-19	61.5	54.4	21.0	27.8	15.1	26.9
20-24	65.2	59.4	38.6	34.7	33.6	33.3
25-29	41.2	32.7	29.6	26.4	30.0	25.7
30-34	30.6	25.0	22.4	17.5	22.3	18.9
35-39	22.9	18.7	15.0	16.3	17.9	14.8
40-44	18.4	14.1	13.1	10.6	13.8	11.9
45-49	16.3	12.2	9.3	7.3	10.7	8.5
50-54	10.7	9.7	8.8	6.6	7.6	5.6
55-59	7.7	3.8	4.8	3.4	5.1	3.5
60-64	3.3	3.9	3.7	2.0	3.4	2.3
65+	2.7	1.6	1.9	1.4	1.9	1.3
TOTAL	21.0	20.8	15.5	15.4	14.2	14.0

a. U.S. includes 29 states in the DRA

Source: National Center for Health Statistics, Divorces and Divorce Rates, United States. Table 8. Hyattsville, Md: 1978.

The proportions of remarriages are more meaningful when placed in the context of the population available for remarriage. Remarriage rates are computed by dividing the total number of widowed and divorced people by the number of widowed and divorced people who remarry in a specified year.

Rates for all remarriages and for widowed and divorced persons are shown in Table 13 for Idaho, Utah, and the United States in 1970. Remarriage rates are three times as high for Idaho brides as U.S. brides, and twice as high for grooms. For example, Idaho women whose previous marriage ended in divorce remarried in 1970 at a rate of 375.1 per 1,000 divorcees 14 years and older. U.S. divorcees remarried at a 123.3 rate. Rates for Idaho and U.S. men were 422.2 and 204.5, respectively.

Just as Utah's proportion of marriages is low, rates of remarriage there are also low in comparison. Table 13 shows that in 1970, about 95 out of 1,000 divorced women in Utah remarried, while about 123 out of 1,000 divorced U.S. women remarried.

Table 13
Remarriage Rates per 1,000 Previously Married Population 14 Years and Older, Idaho, Utah, and the U.S., 1970

	Idaho[a]		Utah[a]		U.S.	
	Women	Men	Women	Men	Women	Men
All marriages	124.1	129.2	85.3	97.7	64.8	80.8
First marriages	130.0	97.8	108.5	95.6	82.9	72.1
Remarriages	114.1	274.3	36.0	106.1	36.6	116.5
Widowed	27.5	65.4	8.9	48.9	10.9	40.6
Divorced	375.1	422.2	94.9	138.6	123.3	204.5

a. Computed

Sources: National Center for Health Statistics, Vital Statistics of the
           United States 1970, Vol. III-Marriage and Divorce. Tables 1-20 and
           1-42. Hyattsville, Md: 1974.
           U.S. Bureau of the Census, Census of Population: 1970, Vol. 1-
           Characteristics of the Population. Part 14 and Part 46: Table
           152. Washington, D.C.: U.S. Government Printing Office, 1973.

Data are not available to compute remarriage rates for Nevada, but it is assumed that the rates are higher than rates of remarriage in Idaho or Utah.

Historical patterns of marriage and divorce have helped to shape the current status of marital statistics for the mountain states and the nation. We have documented Nevada's extremely high marriage and divorce rates and postulated that high remarriage rates contribute to the overall marriage picture in the state. Although not so high as in Nevada, rates of marriage, divorce, and remarriage in Idaho are higher than comparable statistics in the United States, Utah's position is one of currently higher-than-national marriage and divorce rates. However, both rates of marriage and of divorce are relatively low when compared with other mountain states. Finally, there is less remarriage in Utah than in surrounding states or in the country as a whole.

Correlates of Divorce

The correlates of divorce, factors which appear to facilitate or inhibit the dissolution of marriage, include the personal characteristics of individuals, the dynamics of particular relationships, and cultural or societal influences. In this section we discuss the demographic and societal variables which may affect the divorce rate nationally.[11]

Price-Bonham and Balswick[12] and Kitson and Raschke[13] provide an inventory of research on variables related to divorce. Among the factors identified which have either positive or negative influence on marital dissolution are legal statutes, age at marriage, religion, education, economic factors, employment of women, children, premarital pregnancy, race, migration, intergenerational transmission of divorce-proneness, and remarriage. Each of these factors will be examined using available state-level data for Nevada, Idaho, and Utah with comparisons for the United States. Several of these variables receive additional attention in later chapters as the data from the Intermountain Divorce Study are presented.

Laws about marriage and divorce. In *The Road to Reno*, Nelson M. Blake[14] traces the history of American divorce from colonial roots through the 1950s. He notes that differences in state laws and practices have ranged from allowing no divorce at all (South Carolina until 1948) to almost "free divorce" in some early western territories. Where divorce has been legally uncomplicated, divorce rates have been high. Where legal statutes have made divorce difficult by allowing only a few specific grounds for marital dissolution, or requiring lengthy proofs of alleged fault behavior, divorce rates have been low. These rates, however, may be misleading and not reflect the true marital experiences of a population. For example, where divorce is difficult to obtain, the rates of annulments and separations are high and many residents go out of state to divorce. Marital dissolutions take place, but they are officially recorded in other jurisdictions. Thus states where rates appear to be high may be accepting the divorce trade from states with stricter laws. The situation in which a person establishes residence in another area for the particular purpose of avoiding the divorce laws of his or her own state has been referred to as "migratory divorce."

Among the most powerful factors affecting a state's divorce rate are its residency requirements and the leniency of its divorce laws. When the mountain states were frontier territories, their legislators enacted laws that required only a brief stay in the state before legal residency could be granted. These laws were designed to enable migrants from the East to vote. To qualify for statehood, western states needed to claim as large a population as possible, and the lenient residency requirements facilitated this end.[15] Another, perhaps unintended, consequence of the short-term residency requirement was that it made it easy for migrants from states having less liberal divorce laws to qualify for divorce.

Besides the residency issue, some states were very liberal about grounds for divorce. An 1867 California law allowed six grounds for divorce: adultery, cruelty, desertion, non-support, alcoholism, and a felony conviction. The California law served as a model for divorce statutes in Nevada (1875), Idaho (1887), and Montana (1895).[16] These grounds, considered fairly liberal at the time, combined with the short residency requirements to make the western states attractive to persons seeking divorce.

An enterprising New York lawyer saw advantages to the system in Nevada and set up an office in Reno in 1907. He published and circulated in New York a pamphlet entitled, "Divorce Practice and Procedure," which expounded the virtues of Nevada law, in particular the provisions for divorce, and modestly advertised his own legal services. According to the booklet, one only had to live in the state for six months to claim Nevada residency, and the grounds for divorce included "extreme cruelty," which was easy to prove.

In 1913, conservatives and moralists, hoping to stem the inflow of divorce-seeking migrants, convinced the Nevada legislature to change the residency requirement to one year. But in 1915 the businessmen prevailed and the required period of residency was changed back to six months. In 1927 it was further reduced, this time to three months.[17] Early in 1931, the Idaho and Arkansas legislatures lowered their residency requirements to three months. Nevada responded with a statute reducing the minimum residency to only six weeks. Idaho was still interested in a share of the divorce trade, and its residency requirement was lowered to six weeks in 1937. However, despite short residency and fairly lenient grounds for divorce, Idaho has never had the attraction of Nevada's gambling and glitter, and divorce is not as frequent as in Nevada. In both states, however, fluctuations in the divorce rate have followed changes in the law.

Through the years Utah has experienced fewer changes in the laws affecting marriage and divorce. Statutory grounds for divorce and residency requirements in Utah, although not as lenient as those in Nevada and Idaho, have been fairly liberal compared to those of many states. Thus, migratory divorce accounts for some of Utah's divorce trade.

Stetson and Wright[18] demonstrated that in 1960, before any states had enacted no-fault divorce laws, the permissiveness of the law had a substantial effect on divorce rates in a state. They ranked Idaho and Utah high on both liberality and leniency of implementation of divorce laws. Had Nevada been included in their analysis, it presumably would have ranked at the top of the list.

In a later analysis of the impact of the no-fault divorce laws enacted by many states after 1970, Wright and Stetson[19] found that divorce rates in states that had liberalized their laws differed little from rates in states that had not made legal changes. Freed and Foster[20] describe the prevailing patterns of divorce legislation and note that only three states (Illinois, Pennsylvania, and South Dakota) still retain fault-only grounds for divorce. No-fault grounds accepted by Idaho and Nevada include incompatability or irreconcilable differences, and Utah allows three years of living apart with a court decree of separate maintenance. There has also been an increase in the number and types of accepted grounds for divorce, making divorce still easier. For example, in Utah, the most often used ground for divorce is mental cruelty, traditionally a fault ground, but easier to prove than incompatability in many states.

Age at marriage. One of the best predictors of marital stability is age at marriage. Researchers have consistently found that couples who marry at an early age are more prone to divorce than those who marry later.[21] Unfortunately, data are not available on age at marriage in Nevada, but that state's legal minimum age requirement with parental consent has been fairly high compared with other mountain states (see Table 14). The minimum age has recently been lowered such that males and females must be 16 years old before a marriage license can be issued in Nevada.

The legal minimum age for marriage in Idaho is now 16 for both males and females with parental consent, up from 15 in 1958. This requirement is similar to that in most of the mountain states. Idaho reports median ages at first marriages for brides and grooms that have been comparable to median ages in the nation as a whole.[22] But the proportion of teenage marriages in the state is higher than for the United States as a whole: for example, in 1974, 33.8 percent of all Idaho brides were under age 20, as compared with 30.7 percent of the nation's brides.[23] The proportion of teenage brides in Idaho and the United States has been decreasing for the past few years. In 1979, 28.7 percent of Idaho brides and 22.5 percent of U.S. brides were under 20 years of age.[24]

For at least the last two decades the minimum age at which Utahns may legally marry with parental consent has been lower than in other mountain states. Table 14 shows that in 1958, with parental consent, Utah males could marry at age 16 and females at age 14. The legal age for males was eventually dropped to 14. Most other mountain states required males to be at least 18 years and females to be at least 16 years. The exceptions are Idaho, where the minimum age was 15 years for both males and females, and Colorado, where both parties must be 16 years old. All states except Colorado and Idaho reduced their legal minimum age before 1981, but Utah still has the lowest legal age: males and females must be only 14 to marry with parental consent.

Utah brides and grooms have generally been younger than those in the nation as a whole. In 1978, the median age at first marriage for Utah brides was 20.5, and for grooms it was 22.5, in contrast with 21.4 and 23.2 respectively, for brides and grooms nationwide.[25]

Using the proportion of teenage brides as an indicator of youthful marriages, we find that in 1979, 36 percent of Utah brides were under age 20, down from 40.5 percent in 1974. The 1979 figure compares with 22.5 percent of teenage brides in the nation.[26] Thus, both indicators—median age at marriage and proportion of teenage brides—show Utahns to marry younger than do Americans generally.

Church membership. Carter and Glick,[27] among others, have noted lower divorce rates in areas where there is a high rate of membership in the Catholic church, and conversely, higher divorce rates where there are fewer Catholics. Viewing the same phenomenon differently, Coombs and Zumeta [28] found lower divorce rates among Catholics than Protestants, and Thornton [29] found less divorce among Catholics and those listing "other" as religious preference than among Fundamentalists or Baptists. Fenelon[30] took a broader view and posited higher divorce among those with no religious preference because of the higher social costs of divorce for those with membership in any church. Although it is

Table 14

Legal Minimum Age at Marriage for the Mountain States, August 1958 and March 1981

	With Parental Consent				Without Parental Consent			
	1958		1981		1958		1981	
	Male	Female	Male	Female	Male	Female	Male	Female
Arizona	18	16	16[a]	16	21	18	18	18
Colorado	16	16	16	16	21	18	18	18
Idaho	15	15	16	16	18	18	18	18
Montana	18	16	15	15	21	21	18	18
Nevada	18	16	16	16	21	18	18	18
New Mexico	18	16	16	16	21	18	18	18
Utah	16	14	14	14	21	18	18	18
Wyoming	18	16	16	16	21	21	19	19

a. Statute provides for obtaining license with parental or court consent with no state minimum age.

Sources: Paul H. Jacobson, American Marriage and Divorce. New York: Rhinehard and Co. Inc., 1959.
William E. Mariano, in The World Almanac and Book of Facts 1982: Jane D. Flatt (ed.) New York: Newspaper Enterprise Association, Inc., 1982.

not clear that those who do not belong in some church are the ones who divorce, the correlation between no-preference church identity and high divorce rates has consistently been found.[31]

Relatively few of Nevada's residents claim church membership. In the state, 37.8 percent of the total population are affiliated with some church, and only four states (Alaska, Washington, Oregon, and California) and the District of Columbia have lower proportions of church membership.[32] Despite low levels of church membership, half of those professing some church affiliation in Nevada are Catholics whose official church doctrine traditionally rejects divorce.[33]

In Idaho the "churched" population is higher. Over half of the population (53.6 percent) claim membership in some church. Of all adherents, 15.5 percent are Catholic and 50.7 percent are members of the Church of Jesus Christ of Latter-Day Saints, or the Mormon church. The Mormon church also has strong sanctions against divorce and a distinct doctrinal emphasis upon family solidarity.[34]

Most of Utah's population claims some religious affiliation (83.6 percent in 1971), making it the most "churched" state in the nation. That Utah is atypical in this respect is apparent in the sizable gap in church affiliation rates between it and the next most "churched" state, North Dakota, where 76.6 percent of the population claim a religious affiliation. Additionally, the Utah population is religiously homogeneous; the majority (89.2 percent) of all who claim religious affiliation belong to the Mormon church.[35]

Religious homogamy. Related to a population's religious composition is the incidence of interfaith marriages. States with homogeneous populations with respect to religion are more likely to have more same-faith marriages than populations that are more mixed, since the field of same-faith eligibles is greater for members of a dominant faith. Researchers interested in marital stability in interfaith marriages have consistently found higher rates of divorce among couples who do not share the same religious preference.[36]

The subject of religious homogamy will be treated in greater detail elsewhere in this book; however, a few general statements appear appropriate here. Data from the 1957 Current Population Survey showed that 9.6 percent of marriages nationally were between members of different faiths.[37] A more recent estimate by Bumpass[38] held that 14 percent of U.S. marriages to white women married between 1960 and 1965 had been "interfaith" marriages in the sense that a person in one of the broad religions had married someone in a different major category.

Information on the religious composition of existing marriages is not available for Nevada, Idaho, or Utah, but we do have estimates of interfaith marriage from the survey data we collected. When the broad categories of Catholic, Protestant, and Mormon are used, Nevada residents have more interfaith marriages than couples nationally (21.0 percent) and Idaho residents have slightly fewer (14.7 percent). The data for Utah reveal a much lower incidence of interfaith marriages (6.7 percent).

Type of marriage ceremony. Carter and Glick[39] indicate that divorce rates may be influenced by another religious factor—religious marriage ceremonies. Marriages commenced with a ceremony officiated by a religious authority are more stable than those begun with a civil ceremony. Information is not available from Nevada, but 1977 data from Idaho show that 85.3 percent of first marriages and 76.3 percent of remarriages for brides in Idaho began with religious ceremonies. Comparable figures for Utah are 85.3 and 68.2 percent. In the United States, 79.2 percent of first marriages and 60.6 percent of remarriages were religious.[40]

Education. Research findings on the relationship between education and divorce are not consistent. Early studies generally found a negative relationship showing that as educational attainment increased in a population, the probability of divorce generally declined.[41] More recent analyses have shown that the negative relationship between education and marital stability is weakened when other factors such as age at marriage, race, and religion are taken into account.[42]

Another interesting finding by Carter and Glick[43] is that divorce is more prevalent among people who begin an educational program, either high school or college, and drop out, than it is among those who graduate.

One measure of education, the median number of years of school completed, is available for Nevada, Idaho, Utah, and the United States. This figure has been increasing for the past several decades in all areas, with persons in the three mountain states continuing to complete more years of school than those in the rest of the United States. Data from 1976 show that Nevadans and Idahoans completed a median of 12.6 years of school, Utahns completed a median of 12.8 years, while the national figure was 12.5 years.[44]

Employment of women. The correlation between women's employment and divorce is positive: where employment rates for women are high, divorce rates are also high. Employed women are more likely to divorce, but the direction of the relationship—whether women's employment leads to divorce or divorce necessitates employment—is not clear.[45] Suggested reasons for the relationship include: the level of marital satisfaction as related to role expectations,[46] power conflicts between husbands and wives,[47] and the fact that an employed woman may be able to support herself without a spouse.[48]

Since at least 1950, Nevada has had a higher proportion of women in the labor force than the nation as a whole. In 1970, 45 percent of Nevada women 14 years and older were in the labor force. That same year 41.4 percent of U.S. women were employed.[49] By 1979, women's employment had increased in the state and in the nation, with Nevada still having the higher proportion of employed women 16 years and older, 57.4 percent compared with 51.5 percent.[50]

Until recently, Idaho had lower than national rates of female employment. In 1970, 37.3 percent of women 14 years and older in Idaho were in the labor force, compared with 41.4 percent of women nationally.[51] By 1979, the women in Idaho were more apt to be employed than women in the United States generally, 51.9 percent of Idaho women 16 years and older were in the labor force, compared to the U.S. figure of 51.5 percent.[52]

Women's labor force participation in Utah has generally been lower than that for women in the rest of the nation. In 1970, however, the percentage of Utah women in the labor force was on a par with that for U.S. women, at 41.5 percent. [53] After 1970, employment rates for women in Utah continued lower than national rates such that in 1979, 50.4 percent of Utah women 16 years and older were employed and 51.5 percent of women in the U.S. as a whole were in the labor force.[54]

Economic factors. Even in families where wives are employed, income levels may be relatively low. A common theme in research has been that where incomes are low, divorce is high.[55] However, it may be changes in income rather than their absolute level that contribute to high divorce rates.[56] Welfare may also have an impact on marital stability, but researchers disagree about the direction. Cutright and Scanzoni[57] concluded that welfare in the form of Aid to Families with Dependent Children (AFDC) had not contributed to family instability among their sample. In contrast, Bahr[58] found that families receiving welfare were more likely to divorce, and Hannan *et al.*[59] reported that higher subsidies did increase the rate of divorce among families in income maintenance experiments.

Table 15 shows three indicators of the 1979 economic situation in Nevada, Idaho, and Utah. As can be seen in the table, Nevadans have a very high per capita income relative to the rest of the United States. In 1979, the amount of per capita income in Nevada was ranked number two in the nation; only Connecticut's was higher. On the average, Nevadans earned $1,500 more than Americans in general. Unemployment rates were also lower than in the rest of the country, 4.7 for Nevada men compared with 5.1 for U.S. men. For those who did receive welfare, average monthly AFDC payments were lower in Nevada than in the nation, $193 and $263 respectively.

1979 per capita income in Idaho was lower than the national average, $7,446 compared with $8,706. Unemployment for men was on a par with the rest of the nation (5.1), and AFDC payments were also equal ($263 per month).

Although Utah's median family income was comparable to U.S. levels, per capita family income was over $1,500 lower due to larger family sizes in Utah. Only five states had lower per capita incomes than Utah: Maine, South Carolina, Alabama, Mississippi, and Arkansas. For Utah families receiving AFDC, the average payment of $282 per month was $19 higher than average U.S. payments.[60]

Children. Conventional wisdom has it that couples with no children are more likely to divorce than those with children. This is only partially supported in the literature. Bumpass and Sweet[61] found that childless women were more likely to divorce than women with children and Walker and Whitney[62] reported that couples with few or no children divorce at a higher rate than couples with large families. However, Chester's[63] research showed that couples who divorced had more children than those who did not and Thornton[64] showed that couples with moderate-sized families were more likely to divorce or separate than those with no children or with large families.

Families in Nevada are typically smaller than U.S. families, while Idaho and Utah couples have larger families. The 1970 Census lists the average number of children ever born to ever-married women aged 35 to 44 as 2.9 in Nevada, 3.6 in Idaho, and 3.9 in Utah. The comparable figure for American women in general was 3.1 children.[65]

More current information is available for Idaho and Utah in the form of fertility rates—the number of births in a given year per 1,000 women aged 15-44. In 1973, the fertility rate for Idaho women was 98.8 and for Utah women it was 127.4, more than twice as high as the national fertility rate of 66.4 births per 1,000 women aged 15-44.[66]

The relatively low fertility of Nevada families and the high fertility in Idaho and Utah are reflected in data about children involved in divorce. Child involvement in divorce is measured in three ways: (1) the mean number of children per divorce, that is, the total number of children affected divided by the total number of all divorces; (2) the mean number of children per divorce with children

Table 15
Economic Indicators for Nevada, Idaho, Utah, and the U.S., 1979

	Per Capita Income		Unemployment Rate		
	Total Dollars	Rank	Male	Female	Average Monthly AFDC Payments
United States	$8,706	X	5.1	6.8	$263
Nevada	10,204	2	4.7	5.7	193
Idaho	7,446	37	5.1	6.5	263
Utah	7,185	45	3.6	5.3	282

Source: U.S. Bureau of the Census, Statistical Abstract of the United States, 1980 (101st Edition). Tables 740, 684 and 573. Washington, DC: U.S. Government Printing Office, 1980.

reported, that is, the total number of children affected divided only by the number of divorces where children were involved; and (3) the involvement rate of children generally, that is, the number of children whose parents divorce per 1,000 population under 18 years of age. The mean number of children per divorce depends on the family size of the divorcing family, such that as family size increases, the child-per-divorce ratio also increases.

Data on children affected by divorce in Nevada are only available for the period between 1870 and 1930 (see Table 16). In 1870 the mean number of children per divorce with children reported in Nevada was higher than the nation as a whole, but from 1880 through 1930 fewer children have been involved in divorce in Nevada than in the rest of the states. If the trend has continued, the number of Nevada families disrupted by divorce is still smaller than the number of families residing elsewhere ending in divorce.

For the past several years, over half the divorces in Idaho generally have involved more children than divorces in the nation as a whole. The only exception to the pattern is that in 1967 Idaho divorces with children reported involved an average of 2.12 children, less than the U.S. figure of 2.18 children per divorce. More recent measures of the number of children per divorce (all divorces) shown in Table 17 reveal the same pattern; only in 1970 did Idaho divorces involve fewer children than the nation as a whole, 1.20 compared with 1.23 children per divorce.

The third measure, the rate of child involvement in divorce, is computed as the number of children under 18 years old whose parents divorce in a given year per 1,000 population under 18 years of age. For all available years, this child involvement rate has been increasing for both Idaho and the nation, with figures consistently higher for Idaho. This indicates that a higher proportion of children

Table 16
Mean Number of Children per Divorce with Children Reported for Nevada, Idaho, Utah, and the U.S., 1870-1977

Year	Children per Divorce with Children Reported			
	Nevada	Idaho	Utah	U.S.
1870	2.63[a]	1.67[a]	3.00[a]	2.10
1880	1.86[a]	2.73	1.13	2.06
1890	1.71[a]	2.19	2.13	1.90
1900	1.68[a]	2.23	2.17	1.87
1922	1.70	2.02	1.87	1.84
1930	1.63	1.95	1.99	1.78
1952	--	1.86	--	1.82[b]
1960	--	2.11	2.12	2.08
1967	--	2.12	2.40	2.18[c]
1977	--	1.85[d]	1.96[d]	1.82[d]

a. Less than 50 divorced couples with children.

b. All reporting states.

c. DRA

d. Computed

Sources: National Center for Health Statistics, 100 Years of Marriage and Divorce Statistics: United States, 1867-1967. Table 19. Hyattsville, Md: 1973.
National Center for Health Statistics, Monthly Vital Statistics Report, Advance Report, Final Divorce Statistics, 1976. Table 4. Hyattsville, Md: 1978.
Utah Bureau of Health Statistics, Utah Marriage and Divorce 1976. Table U. Salt Lake City, Utah: 1977
Utah Bureau of Health Statistics, Utah Marriage and Divorce 1978. Table U. Salt Lake City, Utah: 1979.
Idaho Department of Health and Welfare, 1979 Annual Summary of Vital Statistics. Boise, Idaho: 1980.

are affected by divorce in Idaho than in the United States generally, 21.7 per 1,000 in Idaho but only 16.0 per 1,000 in the nation in 1979. It appears that the size of families broken by divorce in Idaho is slightly larger than families broken by divorce in the rest of the country (children per divorce), and because divorce is more frequent (higher divorce rates), a higher proportion of children are affected by divorce in that state.

Table 17

Mean Number of Children per Divorce and Child Involvement Rate per 1,000 Population Under 18 Years, Idaho, Utah, and the U.S., 1950–1979

Year	Idaho		Utah		U.S.	
	Children per divorce	Child involve-ment rate	Children per divorce	Child involve-ment rate	Children per divorce	Child involve-ment rate
1950	0.96	12.4[a]	--	--	0.78	6.3
1960	1.23	12.4[a]	1.34	7.1	1.18	7.2
1970	1.20	16.3	1.43	12.3	1.22	12.5
1979	1.01	21.7	1.17	17.2	1.00	16.0

a. Computed

Sources: National Center for Health Statistics, Children of Divorcing Couples: U.S. Selected Years. Table 10. Hyattsville, Md: 1970.
National Center for Health Statistics, Vital Statistics of the United States, 1970 Vol.III-Marriage and Divorce. Table 2-8. Hyattsville, Md: 1974.
National Center for Health Statistics, Vital Statistics of the United States, 1977, Vol.III-Marriage and Divorce. Table 2-7. Hyattsville, Md: 1981.
U.S. Bureau of the Census, Census of Population 1970: Vol.1-Characteristics of the Population. Part 14. Idaho: Table 21. Washington, DC: U.S. Government Printing Office, 1973.

Since 1890, Utah divorces with children reported have consistently involved more children than U.S. divorces with children reported (see Table 16). Using a second measure of child involvement (Table 17), in 1970 the mean number of children per divorce (all divorces) for Utah was 1.43; for the nation it was 1.22. Comparable figures for 1979 are 1.17 and 1.00 respectively.

In 1970, 12.3 children out of 1,000 children in Utah had parents who divorced that year, compared to 12.5 in the United States. In 1979, 17.2 out of 1,000 Utah children and 16.0 out of 1,000 of the nation's children were involved in a divorce. Plainly, people who divorce in Utah have larger families than do the divorced in the nation as a whole, and a Utah divorce is likely to involve more children than a non-Utah divorce. But because intact Utah families also have high fertility, the involvement rates of children (number experiencing a parental divorce per 1,000 children) in Utah are lower than the national rate.

Premarital pregnancy. There is substantial consensus about the relationship between premarital pregnancy and divorce: when a premarital conception has occurred, divorce is more likely.[67] Since the majority of pregnant brides are young, lack of preparation for marriage, including economic problems and the interruption of schooling, are strongly implicated.[68]

Data on premarital pregnancies in Nevada and Idaho are not available. However, a recent publication from the Utah Bureau of Health Statistics gives some estimates for Utah. Approximately 40 percent of births to adolescents in the nation are illegitimate; the rate in Utah is 20 percent. In 1975, researchers estimated that 60 percent of all first births to teenagers in Utah were premarital conceptions, similar to proportions in other states. The difference in illegitimacy rates results because more Utah teens marry before the baby is born. For example, in 1975, two out of ten births to teens in Utah were out of wedlock, four out of ten teenaged mothers married before the birth of the child, and four out of ten babies were conceived after marriage.[69]

Race and migration. Most research has shown that blacks (and some other non-whites) are more likely to divorce than whites.[70] Additionally, Fenelon[71] found that states with high proportions of non-whites typically had high divorce rates.

Data are not available to show divorce rates by race because populations of non-whites are so small in the mountain states. However, 1980 Census data are available which show the proportion of non-whites in each state. Nevada had 12.5 percent non-whites, Idaho had 4.5 percent and Utah had 5.0 percent, all increases from 1970 figures. In the nation in 1980, 16.8 percent of the population was non-white.[72]

Fenelon[73] also discussed the relationship between migration and divorce, suggesting that states with high migration rates also had high divorce rates. The situation in Nevada illustrates this point well. Only 59.8 percent of all Nevada residents lived in the same county in 1970 and in 1965. In the nation as a whole 76 percent of the population lived in the same county as five years earlier.[74]

Thus, Nevada had almost 1.3 times as many movers as the rest of the nation, possibly giving additional support to the idea that migratory divorce accounts for some of the divorces granted in Nevada.

Idaho experiences only slightly higher amounts of migration than the nation generally, and Utah's migration rate is comparable to the national rate. In 1970, 70 percent of Idahoans lived in the same county as 1965.[75] Utah was slightly more stable with approximately 75 percent of the residents in 1970 living in the same county as they had in 1965.[76]

Transmission of instability. Another interesting correlate of marital disruption is the idea that divorce-proneness can be transmitted from parents to children. Empirical support for this idea has been put forth by Bumpass and Sweet,[77] Pope and Mueller,[78] Mott and Moore,[79] and others, although differences are often small between people who experienced a parental divorce and those who did not.

Data on divorce transmission are not available for Nevada or Idaho from state sources. Although the question has been asked on divorce certificates in Utah, non-response has been so frequent on the item that the answers have not been published. A question about parental divorce was included in the Intermountain Divorce Study; our results are reported later.

Extent of remarriage. A final correlate of divorce to be discussed is the extent of remarriage in a state. Given the dramatic historical decline in the proportion of marriages disrupted by death, most marital dissolutions are now a result of divorce, not bereavement. Statistically, divorcees are more likely to remarry than widows, so more second, third, or higher order marriages are being contracted than ever before. Such remarriages have been shown to end in divorce more often than first marriages.[80]

In Nevada, the proportions of marriages that are remarriages are not available from vital statistics reports, but census reports include information on whether respondents had been married more than once. Data from the 1970 Census show that 28.9 percent of the ever-married Nevada males and 31.2 percent of the ever-married Nevada females had been married more than once.[81] Comparable U.S. figures are 14.5 and 14.8 respectively.[82]

Idaho also has a high proportion of remarried persons—18.1 percent of the ever-married males and 19.1 percent of the ever-married females in 1970 had been married more than once.[83] In 1969 Idaho ranked number one out of 40 states in the MRA with the highest percentage of marriages that were remarriages for brides—41.9 percent.[84] In 1977, 42.5 percent of all marriages for brides were remarriages, giving the state a rank of four out of the 40 states in the MRA (Wyoming was ranked number two in 1969 and number one in 1977). For the nation as a whole, only 28.2 percent of the brides were reentering matrimony (see Table 6).

For Utah in 1969, 14.1 percent of the brides were entering a remarriage. Only one state, Wisconsin, had lower proportions of remarrying brides.[85] In 1977,

Utah had the lowest percent of remarriages for brides in the MRA with 17.8 percent contracting second or higher order marriages (see Table 6).

Correlates of Remarriage

Many of the social and demographic factors that influence divorce are also related to probabilities of remarriage. Price-Bonham and Balswick's[86] inventory lists several correlates of remarriage, but there has been little empirical work on the topic. Correlates of remarriage that will be discussed briefly here include: sex, previous marital status, race, laws about divorce and remarriage, age at divorce, duration of first marriage, children, education, and economic factors. Where available, relevant information from Nevada, Idaho, and Utah will be presented.

Sex. Historically, men have had higher rates of remarriage than women and this trend is continuing in the United States today. [87] Nevada remarriage rates are not available. Idaho men remarry at a rate almost two and a half times higher than the rate for women—274.3 compared with 114.1 (see Table 12). In Utah the difference is even greater (106.1 remarriages per 1,000 for men compared with 36.0 for women).

Previous marital status. Carter and Glick[88] have documented higher remarriage rates for previously divorced persons than for the widowed. Trend data show that remarriage rates for widows and widowers have remained fairly constant over the past two decades while rates for divorced men and women have increased.[89] Rates of remarriage for widows and widowers in Idaho were 27.5 and 65.4 respectively in 1970. That same year divorced women and divorced men remarried at rates of 375.1 and 422.2 (see Table 12). Although rates were lower, the pattern was similar for Utah. Widows' remarriage rate was 8.9 compared with a rate of 94.9 for divorcees. Widowers also remarried at a lower rate than divorced men—48.9 and 138.6 per 1,000 previously married men 14 years and older.

Race. Whites have consistently had a higher probability of remarriage than blacks, particularly in the five years following divorce.[90] The number of blacks is so low in Idaho and Utah that reliable remarriage rates by race cannot be computed for these states. Information on race for Nevada is not available.

Laws about divorce and remarriage. Williams and Kuhn[91] have suggested that variations in state laws related to divorce and remarriage may account for some of the variation between states in remarriage rates. As mentioned earlier, legal statutes in both Nevada and Idaho about marriage and divorce have been very lenient. After a divorce decree is final in Nevada or Idaho, either party may remarry without a waiting period. Utah requires prospective brides and grooms to wait for three months after the dissolution by divorce of a previous marriage.

Age at divorce. Younger age at marriage is positively related to divorce and younger age at divorce is positively related to the probability of remarriage.[92] In 1977 the median age at divorce for women in Idaho was 28.4 years, lower than the median age of 29.9 years for women in the nation as a whole. Idaho men who divorced were also younger, 30.8 years compared with 32.4 years for U.S. men. Utah women had the same median age at divorce as Idaho women (28.4) and a slightly lower median age for men (30.6). Both divorcing men and women in Utah were younger than divorcing men and women in the nation. Data by age are not available for Nevada.

Duration of marriage. Using data from the 1967 Survey of Economic Opportunity, Becker, Landes, and Michael[93] found that divorced persons who had longer durations of marriage before divorce were more likely to remarry than those who had shorter durations. Analyzing data from the National Survey of Family Growth, Eckhardt et al.[94] discovered the opposite, that those with shorter durations of previous marriages were more likely to remarry. However, when other factors were controlled, the differences were non-significant.

Children. Findings about the effect of children on probabilities of remarriage are not consistent. Becker et al.[95] assert that women with fewer children have a higher probability of remarriage than those with many. Eckhardt et al.[96] found that differences were not significant even though women with no children or only one child were slightly more likely to remarry than those with many children.

Education. With respect to the effect of educational attainment on probabilities of remarriage, there is also disagreement. Becker et al.[97] found no relation, but Glick[98] reported that women with lower levels of educational attainment were more likely to remarry than women who had more years of schooling. From information presented earlier, it is clear that women (and men) in Nevada, Idaho, and Utah have higher levels of education than their counterparts in the nation as a whole.

Economic factors. Falasco[99] identified economic factors related to probabilities of remarriage for divorced women. The level of female earnings and welfare payments were found to be negatively related to remarriage [100] while poverty rates for female-headed families and rates of labor force participation of divorced women were positively related to remarriage. Bahr[101] reported that women who did not receive AFDC were more likely to remarry than those who did receive this form of welfare.

Levels of female earnings were higher in Nevada than in the United States in 1975 [102] and levels of welfare payments were lower (see Table 15). Divorced women made up a much higher percentage of the female labor force in Nevada than in the country as a whole, 14.6 percent compared with 8.5 percent.[103] Poverty rates for female-headed families are not available by state.

In Idaho levels of female earnings and AFDC welfare payments were lower than in the states generally (see Table 15).[104] A higher-than-national percentage of female workers were divorced in Idaho in 1975, 9.2 compared with 8.5 percent for the nation.[105]

Female workers in Utah made less money than the national average,[106] but families receiving AFDC received higher-than-national payments (see Table 15). Divorced women in Utah made up 8.9 percent of the female labor force, slightly more than in the United States [107]

Summary

Table 18 is a summary of the correlates of divorce discussed in this chapter and the state data relevant to each correlate. The state-level findings which are thought to contribute to higher-than-national divorce rates are indicated by an asterisk.

In Nevada, the factors which may contribute most heavily to high divorce rates are the lenient divorce laws combined with high migration, low levels of church membership, high rates of religious intermarriage, and higher proportions of remarried persons. All of these factors are positively related to divorce.

The factors having the most effect on increasing divorce in Idaho are permissive laws combined with relatively high migration, young age at marriage, income levels lower than the national average, and high rates of remarriage.

Utah's divorce rates are positively affected by relatively permissive laws, young age at marriage, low income, and high welfare payments. Although Utah's divorce rates are higher than the national average, they are the lowest of the intermountain states. Factors which may act to depress Utah's divorce rates are high levels of church membership, low levels of interfaith marriage, a high incidence of religious marriage ceremonies, historically lower-than-national rates of female employment, and fewer remarriages than other states.

A summary of the correlates of remarriage and relevant state data are shown in Table 19. Nevadans and Idahoans were found to experience more remarriage than Utahns. Factors in each state related to an increase in remarriage are marked with the letter a.

Although data are limited from Nevada, a factor which clearly would act to increase remarriage is the lenient legal situation. Lower-than-national welfare payments and higher-than-national proportions of employed divorced women may also contribute to high remarriage in the state.

Idaho also has lenient laws and a high proportion of divorced women in the labor force. Additionally, female earnings are lower than in other states and people who divorce do so at a younger age, thus increasing their chances of remarriage.

The same factors thought to have a positive effect on remarriage in Idaho are present in Utah, but not to the same degree because Utah's remarriage rates are lower than Idaho, Nevada, or the rest of the United States. Other inhibiting factors must be operating to keep the number of remarriages low.

Although this chapter focused on only Nevada, Idaho, and Utah, the other states in the intermountain region have similar patterns and contribute to the unique regional picture of marriage and divorce. Historically these states have

Table 18
Correlates of Divorce

Correlate	Research Findings	State Data		
		Nevada	Idaho	Utah
Laws	permissive laws positively related to divorce no-fault changes had little effect	historically permissive laws[a] no-fault ground is irreconcilable differences[a]	historically permissive laws[a] no-fault ground is incompatability[a]	relatively permissive laws[a] no-fault ground is living apart 3 years
Age at marriage	young age at marriage positively related to divorce	historically high legal minimum age at marriage	low age at marriage[a] higher than national proportion teen brides[a]	low age at marriage[a] higher than national proportion teen brides[a]
Church membership	church membership negatively related to divorce Catholics (Mormons) have lower divorce	low levels of church membership, half are Catholic	moderate levels of church membership, half are Mormons	high levels of church membership, most are Mormons
Religious homogamy	interfaith marriage positively related to divorce	more interfaith marriages than U.S.[a]	slightly less interfaith marriages than U.S.	much less interfaith marriages than in U.S.
Marriage ceremony	religious marriage ceremonies negatively related to divorce	- - - - - - - -	more religious ceremonies than in U.S.	more religious ceremonies than in U.S.

Correlate	Research Findings	State Data		
		Nevada	Idaho	Utah
Education	level of education generally negatively related to divorce	slightly more years of school completed than in U.S.	slightly more years of school completed than in U.S.	more years of school completed than in U.S.
Women's employment	employment of women positively related to divorce	historically higher than national rates of female employment[a]	historically lower female employment rates, current rates slightly higher than U.S.	historically lower than national female employment rates
Economic factors	income negatively related to divorce unemployment positively related to divorce effect of AFDC questionable	income higher than U.S. average unemployment lower than U.S. AFDC payments lower than U.S.	income lower than U.S. average[a] unemployment equal to U.S. AFDC payments equal to U.S.	income much lower than U.S.[a] unemployment lower than U.S. AFDC payments higher than U.S.
Children	number of children negatively related to divorce or positively related to divorce	lower fertility than in U.S. fewer children per divorce	higher fertility than in U.S. more children per divorce higher child involvement rate than U.S.	much larger families than U.S. more children per divorce lower child involvement rate than U.S.
Premarital pregnancy	Premarital pregnancy positively related to divorce	- - - - - -	- - - - - - -	equal to or lower than national rates for teenagers

65

Table 18 (continued)

Correlate	Research Findings	State Data			
		Nevada	Idaho	Utah	
Race	non-white ethnic status positively related to divorce	low proportions of non-whites	very low proportions of non-whites	very low proportions of non-whites	
Migration	migration positively related to divorce	higher than national migration rates[a]	slightly higher than national migration rates[a]	migration rates comparable to U.S.	
Intergenerational transmission	parental divorce positively related to divorce of children				
Remarriage	remarriage positively related to divorce	higher than U.S. proportion of remarried people[a]	more remarriages than in U.S.	fewer remarriages than in U.S.	

a. Higher-than-national divorce rates.

Table 19
Correlates of Remarriage

Correlate	Research Findings	State Data — Nevada	State Data — Idaho	State Data — Utah
Sex	men more likely to remarry than women	- - - -	higher remarriage rates for men	higher remarriage rates for men
Previous marital status	divorced more likely to remarry than widowed	- - - -	higher remarriage rates for divorced	higher remarriage rates for divorced
Race	whites more likely to remarry than blacks	- - - -	- - - -	- - - -
Laws	permissive laws positively related to remarriage	very lenient laws[a]	very lenient laws[a]	moderately lenient laws[a]
Age at divorce	younger age at divorce more likely to remarry	- - - -	younger age at divorce than U.S.[a]	younger age at divorce than U.S.[a]
Duration of marriage	longer duration of marriage likely to divorce or no significant differences	- - - -	shorter than U.S. duration of marriage before divorce	shorter than U.S. duration of marriage before divorce
Children	fewer children more likely to remarry or no relationship	- - - -	more children than U.S. average	more children than U.S. average
Education	lower educational attainment more likely to remarry or no relationship	higher than national levels of education	higher than national levels of education	higher than national levels of education

67

Table 19 (continued)

Correlate	Research Findings	State Data		
		Nevada	Idaho	Utah
Religion	no significant difference between Catholics and Protestants	low levels of church membership	moderate levels of church membership, half are Mormons	high levels of church membership, most are Mormons
Economic factors	female earnings and welfare negatively related to remarriage, labor force participation of divorced women positively related to remarriage	female earnings higher than U.S. welfare payments lower than U.S.[a] more divorced women in labor force[a]	female earnings lower than U.S.[a] welfare equal to U.S. more divorced women in labor force[a]	female earnings lower than U.S.[a] welfare higher slightly more women in labor force[a]

a. Higher-than-national remarriage rates.

had higher-than-national divorce rates and most have high rates of remarriage as well. Many of the correlates positively related to divorce and remarriage discussed in the literature are documented with state-level data in the intermountain states and contribute to the distinctivene of this region. The next chapters discuss more of the details of divorce and remarriage from our empirical research.

Notes

1. Hugh Carter and Paul C. Glick, *Marriage and Divorce: A Social and Economic Study* (Cambridge, Mass.: Harvard University Press, 1976).

2. National Center for Health Statistics, *Monthly Vital Statistics Report, Births, Marriages, Divorces and Deaths for 1980* (Hyattsville, Md.: 1981).

3. National Center for Health Statistics, *Monthly Vital Statistics Report*, 1981.

4. Arthur J. Norton and Paul C. Glick, "Marital Instability in America: Past, Present, and Future," in George Levinger and Oliver C. Moles (eds.), *Divorce and Separation: Context, Causes, and Consequences* (New York: Basic Books, 1979).

5. Information for the United States is taken from the Marriage Registration Area (MRA) which consists of states and independent areas that meet strict requirements established by the National Center for Health Statistics for completeness, accuracy, and timely reporting of marriage information. New states are continually being added to the MRA and in 1979 only 8 states were not included: Arizona, Arkansas, Nevada, New Mexico, North Dakota, Oklahoma, Texas, and Washington. Idaho joined the MRA in 1907, Utah in 1919, Wyoming in 1941, Montana in 1943, and Colorado in 1979.

6. Norton and Glick, "Marital Instability in America."

7. The difference in magnitude of marriage and divorce rates for Nevada compared with those for Idaho, Utah, and the United States is best shown using a log-normal plot. The log-normal plot is not only able to show similar patterns but also reveals the relative magnitude of rates in Nevada and other states.

8. William E. Mariano, "Marriage Information," in Jane D. Flatt (ed.), *The World Almanac and Book of Facts* (New York: Newspaper Enterprise Association, Inc., 1982).

9. "When observing trends in marital behavior over an extended period of years, rates for women are generally used because they present a more consistent population base, less affected than rates for men by fluctuations in service in the armed forces" (Norton and Glick, "Marital Instability in America," p. 8).

10. Like the MRA, the Divorce Reporting Area (DRA) consists of states and areas that meet strict requirements for completeness, accuracy, and timely reporting of divorce information. Wyoming joined the DRA in 1941, Montana joined in 1943, Idaho in 1947, and Utah in 1954. There are currently 30 states in the DRA.

11. For a review of research related to the quality of marital relationships, see Graham B. Spanier and Robert A. Lewis, "Marital Quality: A Review of the Seventies," *Journal of Marriage and the Family* 42 (November 1980): 825-39.

12. Sharon Price-Bonham and Jack O. Balswick, "The Noninstitutions: Divorce, Desertion, and Remarriage," *Journal of Marriage and the Family* 42 (November 1980): 959-72.

13. Gay C. Kitson and Helen J. Raschke, "Divorce Research: What We Know; What We Need to Know," *Journal of Divorce* 4 (Spring 1981): 1-37.

14. Nelson M. Blake, *The Road to Reno: A History of Divorce in the United States* (New York: Macmillan, 1962).

15. Carter and Glick, *Marriage and Divorce*.

16. Blake, *The Road to Reno*.

17. Ibid.

18. Dorothy M. Stetson and Gerald C. Wright, Jr., "The Effects of Laws on Divorce in American States," *Journal of Marriage and the Family* 37 (August 1975).

19. Gerald C. Wright, Jr. and Dorothy M. Stetson, "The Impact of No-Fault Divorce Law Reform on Divorce in American States," *Journal of Marriage and the Family* 40 (1978): 575-80.

20. Doris Jonas Freed and Henry H. Foster, Jr., "Divorce in the Fifty States: An Overview," unpublished manuscript obtained from Doris Jonas Freed, 60 East 42nd Street, Suite 2022, New York, NY 10017, 1978.

21. Larry L. Bumpass and James A. Sweet, "Differentials in Marital Instability: 1970," *American Sociological Review* 37 (December 1972): 754-66; Carter and Glick, *Marriage and Divorce*.

22. National Center for Health Statistics, *100 Years of Marriage and Divorce Statistics: United States, 1867-1967*, Table 23 (Hyattsville, Md.: 1973).

23. National Center for Health Statistics, *Monthly Vital Statistics Report, Advance Report, Final Marriage Statistics, 1975*, Tables 1-15 and 1-18 (Hyattsville, Md.: 1977).

24. Idaho Bureau of Vital Statistics, *Annual Summary of Vital Statistics, 1979* (Boise, Idaho: Idaho Department of Health and Welfare, 1981), p. 74; National Center for Health Statistics, *Monthly Vital Statistics Report, Births, Marriages, Divorces and Deaths for 1980*.

25. Utah Bureau of Health Statistics, *Utah Marriage & Divorce, 1972-1979*, Table D (Salt Lake City, Utah: 1981).

26. Ibid., Table 3.

27. Carter and Glick, *Marriage and Divorce*.

28. L. C. Coombs and Z. Zumeta, "Correlates of Marital Dissolution in a Prospective Fertility Study: A Research Note," *Social Problems* 18 (Summer 1970): 92-102.

29. A. Thornton, "Marital Instability Differentials and Interactions: Insights from Multivariate Contingency Table Analysis," *Sociology and Social Research* 62 (July 1978): 572-95.

30. Bill Fenelon, "State Variations in United States Divorce Rates," *Journal of Marriage and the Family* 33 (no. 2, 1971): 321-27.

31. Patrick C. McKenry, Priscilla N. White, and Sharon Price-Bonham, "The Fractured Conjugal Family: A Comparison of Married and Divorced Dyads," *Journal of Divorce* 1 (Summer 1978): 329-39.

32. Douglas W. Johnson, Paul R. Picard, and Bernard Quinn, *Churches and Church Membership in the United States: 1971* (Washington, D.C.: Glenmary Research Center, 1974).

33. R. Dailey, "Divorce (Moral Aspect)," in *New Catholic Encyclopedia*, Vol. IV (New York: McGraw-Hill, 1967), p. 931.

34. Spencer W. Kimball, *Marriage and Divorce* (Salt Lake City, Utah: Deseret Book, 1976).

35. Johnson, *et al.*, *Churches and Church Membership in the U.S.*, p. 8.

36. Barbara Thornes and Jean Collard, *Who Divorces*? (London: Routledge and Kegan Paul, 1979); A. S. Moller, "Jewish-Gentile Divorce in California," *Jewish Social Studies* 37 (Summer 1975): 279-90; Bumpass and Sweet, "Differentials in Marital Instability."

37. U.S. Bureau of the Census, *Statistical Abstract of the United States, 1957* (Washington, D.C.: U.S. Government Printing Office, 1957).

38. Larry Bumpass, "The Trend of Interfaith Marriage in the United States," *Social Biology* 17 (1970): 253-59.

39. Carter and Glick, *Marriage and Divorce*.

40. National Center for Health Statistics, *Vital Statistics of the United States 1977, Vol. III—Marriage and Divorce*, Table 1-15 (Hyattsville, Md.: 1981).

41. Phillips Cutright, "Income and Family Events: Marital Instability," *Journal of Marriage and the Family* 31 (May 1971): 291-306.

42. Thornton, "Marital Instability Differentials and Interactions."

43. Carter and Glick, *Marriage and Divorce*.

44. U.S. Bureau of the Census, *Statistical Abstract of the United States, 1979* (100th ed.), Table 235 (Washington, D.C.: U.S. Government Printing Office, 1979).

45. Norton and Glick, "Marital Instability in America."

46. Stephen J. Bahr and Randal D. Day, "Sex Role Attitudes, Female Employment, and Marital Satisfaction," *Journal of Comparative Family Studies* 9 (no. 1, 1978): 53-67.

47. Letha Scanzoni and John Scanzoni, *Men, Women, and Change: A Sociology of Marriage and the Family* (New York: McGraw-Hill, 1976).

48. Andrew Cherlin, "Work Life and Marital Dissolution," in George Levinger and Oliver C. Moles (eds.), *Divorce and Separation: Context, Causes, and Consequences*, (New York: Basic Books, 1979).

49. U.S. Bureau of the Census, *Statistical Abstract of the United States*, Part 30, Table 44, and Part 1, Table 215 (Washington, D.C.: U.S. Government Printing Office, 1973).

50. U.S. Bureau of the Census, *Statistical Abstract of the United States, 1980* (101st ed.), Table 654 (Washington, D.C.: U.S. Government Printing Office, 1980).

51. U.S. Bureau of the Census, *Statistical Abstract of the United States*, Part 14, Table 44 and Part 1, Table 75, 1973.

52. U.S. Bureau of the Census, *Statistical Abstract of the United States, 1980*.

53. U.S. Bureau of the Census, *Statistical Abstract of the United States*, Part 44, Table 44 and Part 1, Table 75, 1973.

54. U.S. Bureau of the Census, *Statistical Abstract of the United States, 1980*.

55. Cutright, "Income and Family Events."

56. Heather Ross and Isabel V. Sawhill, *Time of Transition: The Growth of Families Headed by Women* (Washington, D.C.: The Urban Institute, 1975); Cherlin, "Work Life and Marital Dissolution."

57. Phillips Cutright and John Scanzoni, "Income Supplements and the American Family," pp. 54-89 in Joint Economic Committee (eds.), *The Family, Poverty, and Welfare Programs: Factors Influencing Family Instability*, Studies in Public Welfare, Paper No. 12, Part I (Washington, D.C.: U.S. Government Printing Office, 1973).

58. Stephen J. Bahr, "The Effects of Welfare on Marital Stability and Remarriage," *Journal of Marriage and the Family* 41 (August 1979): 553-60.

59. M. T. Hannan, N. B. Tuma, and L. P. Groeneveld, "Income and Marital Events: Evidence from an Income Maintenance Experiment," *American Journal of Sociology* 82 (May 1977): 1186-1211.

60. U.S. Bureau of the Census, *Statistical Abstract of the United States, 1980* (101st ed.), Tables 753, 740, 684, and 573 (Washington, D.C.: U.S. Government Printing Office, 1980).

61. Bumpass and Sweet, "Differentials in Marital Instability."

62. K. Walker and O. Whitney, *The Family and Marriage in a Changing World* (London: Gallancz, 1965).

63. R. Chester, "Is There a Relationship Between Childlessness and Marriage Break-down?" pp. 114-26 in E. Peck and J. Senderowitz (eds.), *Pronatalism: The Myth of Mom and Apple Pie* (New York: Cromwell, 1974).

64. A. Thornton, "Marital Dissolution, Remarriage and Childbearing," *Demography* 15 (1978): 361-80.

65. U.S. Bureau of the Census, *Statistical Abstract of the United States*, Parts 14, 30, and 46, Table 45; Part 1, Table 76, 1973.

66. Idaho Bureau of Business and Economic Research, *Idaho Statistical Abstract*, Table III-10 (Moscow, Idaho: University of Idaho, 1979); Utah Bureau of Health Statistics, *Utah Marriage & Divorce, 1972-1979*, Table 9.

67. Coombs and Zumeta, "Correlates of Marital Dissolution in a Prospective Fertility Study"; Bumpass and Sweet, "Differentials in Marital Instability."

68. Frank F. Furstenberg, "Premarital Pregnancy and Marital Instability," *Journal of Social Issues* 32 (no. 1, 1976): 67-86.

69. Peter C. van Dyck and John E. Brockert, *Adolescent Pregnancy in the 1970s: A Study Comparing Utah and the United States* (Salt Lake City, Utah: Bureau of Health Statistics, 1980).

70. J. Richard Udry, *The Social Context of Marriage* (Philadelphia: J. B. Lippincott, 1966); Norton and Glick, "Marital Instability in America."

71. Fenelon, "State Variations in United States Divorce Rates."

72. U.S. Bureau of the Census, *1980 Census of Population and Housing, U.S. Summary, Final Population and Housing Counts* (Washington, D.C.: U.S. Government Printing Office, 1982).

73. Fenelon, "State Variations in United States Divorce Rates."

74. U.S. Bureau of the Census, *Statistical Abstract of the United States*, Part 30, Table 45; Part 1, Table 72, 1973.

75. Ibid., Part 14, Table 45; Part 1, Table 72, 1973.

76. U.S. Bureau of the Census, *Statistical Abstract of the United States*, Part 46, Table 45, 1973.

77. Bumpass and Sweet, "Differentials in Marital Instability."

78. Hallowell Pope and Charles W. Mueller, "The Intergenerational Transmission of Marital Instability: Comparisons by Race and Sex," *Journal of Social Issues* 32 (no. 1, 1976): 49-66.

79. F. L. Mott and S. F. Moore, "The Causes of Marital Disruption Among Young American Women: An Interdisciplinary Perspective," *Journal of Marriage and the Family* 41 (May 1979): 355-65.

80. Carter and Glick, *Marriage and Divorce*; A. Cherlin, "Remarriage as an Incomplete Institution," *American Journal of Sociology* 84 (November 1978): 634-650.

81. U. S. Bureau of the Census, *Statistical Abstract of the United States*, Part 30,

Table 152, 1973.

82. Ibid., Part 1, Table 203, 1973.

83. Ibid., Part 14, Table 152, 1973.

84. Kristen M. Williams and Russell P. Kuhn, *Remarriages* (U.S. Department of Health, Education, and Welfare, Public Health Service, Hyattsville, Md.: U.S. Government Printing Office, 1973), p. 3.

85. Williams and Kuhn, *Remarriages.*

86. Price-Bonham and Balswick, "The Noninstitutions."

87. Williams and Kuhn, *Remarriages.*

88. Carter and Glick, *Marriage and Divorce.*

89. Williams and Kuhn, *Remarriages.*

90. William R. Grady, *Remarriages of Women 15-44 Years of Age Whose First Marriage Ended in Divorce: United States, 1976* (U.S. Department of Health, Education, and Welfare, Public Health Service, Hyattsville, Md.: U.S. Government Printing Office 1980).

91. Williams and Kuhn, *Remarriages.*

92. Grady, *Remarriages of Women 15-44 Years of Age Whose First Marriage Ended in Divorce.*

93. Gary S. Becker, Elisabeth M. Landes, and Robert T. Michael, "An Economic Analysis of Marital Instability," *Journal of Political Economy* 85 (December 1977): 1141-87.

94. Kenneth W. Eckhardt, William R. Grady, and Gerry E. Hendershot, "Expectations and Probabilities of Remarriage: Findings from the National Survey of Family Growth, Cycle II," paper presented at the meetings of the Population Association of America, Denver, Colo., April 10-12, 1980.

95. Becker, Landes, and Michael, "An Economic Analysis of Marital Instability."

96. Eckhardt, Grady, and Hendershot, "Expectations and Probabilities of Remarriage."

97. Becker, Landes, and Michael, "An Economic Analysis of Marital Instability."

98. Paul C. Glick, "Remarriage: Some Recent Changes and Variations," *Journal of Family Issues* 1 (December 1980): 455-78.

99. Dee Falasco, "A Multivariate Analysis of the Factors Associated With Divorce and Remarriage," paper presented at the meetings of the Population Association of America, Denver, Colo., April 10-12, 1980.

100. Glick, "Remarriage."

101. Bahr, "The Effects of Welfare on Marital Stability and Remarriage."

102. Bureau of Labor Statistics, *Work Experience and Earnings in 1975 by State and Area*, Report 536, Table 5 (Washington, D.C.: U.S. Government Printing Office, 1978).

103. Bureau of Labor Statistics, *Marital and Family Status of Workers by State and Area*, Report 545, Table 2 (Washington, D.C.: U.S. Government Printing Office, 1978).

104. Bureau of Labor Statistics, *Work Experience and Earnings in 1975 by State and Area*, Report 535, Table 5.

105. Bureau of Labor Statistics, *Marital and Family Status of Workers by State and Area*, Report 545, Table 2.

106. Bureau of Labor Statistics, *Work Experience and Earnings in 1975 by State and Area*, Report 536, Table 6.

107. Bureau of Labor Statistics, *Marital and Family Status of Workers by State and Area*, Report 545, Table 2.

Chapter 3

The Divorced
and the Non-Divorced

Introduction

The previous chapter presented a detailed picture of divorce rates and trends in the region where the Intermountain Divorce Study was conducted. In this chapter we want to present a comparative perspective by asking some questions about both the divorced and the non-divorced. Specifically, how are they alike and how are they different? While the following chapters draw primarily from those members of the sample who have experienced a divorce, this chapter uses information obtained in the initial survey of 4,606 respondents. The purpose of the analysis will be to compare the experiences and characteristics of the divorced sample with a much larger group of persons who have not gone through a divorce experience.

As noted in the previous chapter, those factors that facilitate divorce can be divided into two main categories, personal and societal. We have noted major societal trends that tend to contribute to higher divorce rates, including periods of rapid social change that usually accompany urbanization and industrialization and changing legal definitions that either hinder or facilitate the occurrence of divorce. As we compare the divorced and the non-divorced members of our sample, we will concentrate primarily on those characteristics of one group that make them different in some way from the other group.

It is important to begin with the recognition that the similarities between persons who have divorced and persons still in their first marriage are often far more significant than are the differences. For example, the occupation of married and divorced persons does not differ much, particularly if one controls for income.[1] Nevertheless, it is useful to ask whether or not there are some telling differences in the overall characteristics of the two groups.

A large number of personal variables have been identified as important in contributing to "divorce-proneness." Each of these variables can be seen as more likely or less likely to occur in those relationships that have been or will be terminated by divorce than among stable marriages. Among the variables found to be important are the following: (1) marriage at younger ages,[2] (2) marital unhappiness and/or divorce among one's parents,[3] (3) religious factors, including religious identity and activity, and marriage setting,[4] (4) education,[5] and (5) race.[6] These and other factors will be examined in comparing the divorced and the non-divorced in our study.

Looking briefly at the characteristics of the overall sample before comparing the divorced and the non-divorced, we find that 68 percent of our respondents reported that they were presently living together with a spouse in their first marriage. A total of 12 percent of the respondents were living in a remarriage situation—that is, they had been divorced or widowed and then remarried. Five percent were single and had never been married; 6 percent were currently divorced; 7 percent were widowed; 1 percent were permanently separated; and 1 percent reported that they were living together with someone as husband and wife but were not currently married.

A clear majority of all respondents reported that their marriage had occurred in a religious setting. That is, of those who were or had been married, 55 percent reported that their marriage had occurred in a church. In addition, almost 11 percent indicated that their marriage had occurred in a temple (this usually refers to marriages among active members of the Mormon Church whose marriages are solemnized in a church temple "for time and eternity"), 1 percent reported a synagogue marriage, and 6 percent reported a civil marriage followed by a solemnization in a church, temple, or synagogue.

In terms of religious preference, 46 percent of the respondents were Protestant, 21 percent were Mormon, 18 percent were Catholic, 5 percent indicated some other religious preference, and 11 percent indicated no religion. A majority of respondents indicated some religious activity with 51 percent indicating that they attend religious services at least on a monthly basis.

Most respondents were parents—81 percent reported that they had at least one child. Family size varied from none to 14 children, though 86 percent reported four or fewer children. Age at first marriage ranged from 13-64, with a majority of marriages occurring when the respondent was between the ages of 18 and 22. A large majority of respondents came from homes where their parents' marriage had not been broken by divorce (84 percent reported that their own parents had not been divorced).

With this as background, let us now turn to a comparative analysis of the divorced and non-divorced in the study. As will be the case throughout the data presentation, the remarried and the currently divorced segments of our sample are treated separately, primarily because some of the remarried are individuals who have remarried following the death of a spouse rather than following a divorce. Nevertheless, the large majority of the remarried are individuals who have experienced a divorce earlier in their lives. We have also chosen not to treat the permanently separated or the individuals who are living together though they are not married because these segments of the overall sample were very small compared with the other categories.

Age at Marriage

Age at marriage has been found to be a critical determinant of stability of marriage. The evidence indicates that teenage marriages are twice as likely to end in divorce as are marriages that occur when the individual is in his or her twenties.[7] While these findings are often associated with the fact that there is a much higher level of marital instability among women who are premaritally pregnant and teenage women who marry are more likely to be pregnant prior to the marriages than are older women,[8] the relationship holds regardless of the premarital pregnancy.[9]

The other side of the picture is that women who marry for the first time after the age of 30 also tend to have less stable marriages than is true of those who marry in their twenties. According to Glick and Norton,[10] "older" brides are close to half again as likely to end their first marriage within three to five years after the marriage as those who married at an intermediate age. Older brides apparently are more independent and more willing to terminate a bad marriage than is true of those who marry in their twenties.

The same basic pattern also holds for men, except that the optimum age range for a stable marriage for males is 25-29 years of age.[11] This is the age during which most men who are college graduates marry and it has been found that a higher level of education among men contributes to marital stability.

Our data provide strong support for the notion that early marriages are less stable. As the data in Table 20 reveal, while 60 percent of those who married when they were 20 years of age or younger were still in their first marriage, this was true of 77 percent of those who married between the ages of 21 and 25 and of 75 percent of those who married between the ages of 26 and 30. The percentage of those who were either currently divorced or remarried who entered their first marriage at age 17 or younger is twice as high as is the case for those who entered marriage between the age of 21 and 25.

On the other hand, the data reveal that the most stable marriages were those entered into after age 30. A total of 89 percent of these individuals were still in their first marriage and only 6 percent were either currently divorced or remarried. The stability of these marriages is somewhat contrary to national data reported by others. For example, Glick and Norton[12] report a curvilinear relationship between marital stability and age of marriage. Those who enter marriage prior to age 20 have the most unstable marriages but instability also increases if one marries after age 30. An opposing trend, however, is found in the data that reveal that college graduate couples have the most stable marriages and college graduates are most likely to delay marriage. In our data, the contribution

Table 20

Age at First Marriage and Current Marital Status

	Age at First Marriage									
	17 and Under		18-20		21-25		26-30		31+	
Marital Status	N	%	N	%	N	%	N	%	N	%
First Marriage	164	(60)	553	(60)	1461	(77)	410	(75)	458	(89)
Remarriage	60	(22)	193	(21)	210	(11)	58	(11)	15	(3)
Divorced	27	(10)	87	(9)	108	(6)	31	(7)	13	(3)
Widowed	21	(8)	91	(10)	127	(7)	50	(9)	28	(5)
N	272		924		1906		549		514	

of educational level in affecting higher levels of marital stability may counterbalance the influence of marrying at a later age.

Overall, the data reveal that the younger the person at the age of first marriage, the more likely that marriage is to end in divorce. The probability of divorce is particularly high for those marriages contracted when the participants are still teenagers. Age at first marriage constitutes one of the primary factors that distinguishes between stable first marriages and marriages that have been terminated.

Intergenerational Stability and Instability in Marriage

A number of early studies conducted by family sociologists provided evidence that there is some intergenerational transmission of marital instability. That is, marriage failure tends to run in families, in that children whose parents divorce are more likely to divorce themselves. Landis,[13] for example, used family histories prepared by his students to test this hypothesis and found that the divorce rate among the parents and aunts and uncles of his students increased in proportion to the degree of marriage failure among the students' grandparents. The ratio of divorced to non-divorced marriages ranged from 1.0 to 6.8 for those marriages in which neither grandparent family had divorced, to 1.0 to 4.2 if one grandparent family had divorced, to 1.0 to 2.6 if both grandparent families had divorced or separated.

More recent research by Bumpass and Sweet[14] and Pope and Mueller[15] tends to confirm the earlier evidence that broken parental marriages tend to make the marriages of their children more susceptible to basic disrupting influences. Pope and Mueller attribute this, in part, to problems of inadequate role learning. Since sex and marital roles are learned largely in the home through observation and interaction with parents, the child in an unhappy or broken home will be less likely to learn appropriate marital roles as effectively as one in an intact happy home.

When we compare our data from eight Rocky Mountain states with that available from earlier studies, we find some support for the intergenerational transmission hypothesis. The divorced members of our sample were more likely to report that their parents or their spouse's parents were divorced than were respondents who were in their first marriage (see Table 21). Sixty-eight percent of those whose parents were divorced were in their first marriages while 74 percent of those whose parents were not divorced reported that they were in their first marriage. When we examine spouse's parents, the same trend holds, though not quite so strongly. Seventy-one percent of those whose spouse's parents were divorced were in their first marriage compared with 75 percent of those whose spouse's parents were not divorced. While none of these differences are particularly striking, they do indicate some support for the intergenerational transmission of marital instability. The divorced members of our sample were somewhat more likely to come from homes in which their own parents were divorced than was the case for the non-divorced members of our sample.

Religion and Divorce

Studies that have examined the relationship between religion and divorce have usually found that divorce is less frequent when husband and wife share a religious faith than when they do not.[16] In an independent analysis of portions of the data from the Intermountain Divorce Study, Bahr[17] concluded that (1) same-faith marriages are much more stable than interfaith marriages; (2) Catholic and Mormon same-faith marriages are slightly more stable than Protestant same-faith marriages; and (3) interfaith marriages involving Mormons, that is, Catholic-Mormon and Protestant-Mormon marriages are consistently less stable than Catholic-Protestant interfaith marriages.

Denominational identity, however, is only one of several religiosity indicators that may be important in affecting marital stability. For example, previous research has indicated that divorce and marital failure are more likely among persons who do not attend religious services (though some contrary data have recently been reported by Yoder and Nichols).[18] In addition to examining the influence of attending religious services, we will add two additional indicators of religion in comparing the divorced with the non-divorced. First, we will consider the *setting* of the marriage ceremony as another indicator of religiosity. Specifically, we will ask whether or not marriages solemnized in a church setting will be more or less stable than are those presided over by a civil authority. The assumption is that couples who choose to marry in a church are more religiously committed on the whole than are couples who choose a non-church setting for their wedding. Second, we will consider simple *religious identification* of the

Table 21

Relationship between Parents' and Spouse's Parents' Marital Status and Current Marital Status of Respondent

Marital Status	Were Own Parents Divorced				Were Spouse's Parents Divorced			
	Yes		No		Yes		No	
	N	%	N	%	N	%	N	%
First Marriage	441	(68)	2606	(74)	442	(71)	2603	(75)
Remarriage	122	(19)	415	(12)	99	(16)	436	(13)
Divorced	58	(9)	209	(6)	51	(8)	171	(5)
Widowed	32	(5)	285	(8)	32	(5)	275	(8)
N	653		3515		624		3485	

respondent. Since some religious organizations take a stronger stand against the termination of marriage than do others, we would anticipate some relationship between religious identification and divorce-proneness.

Church versus Non-Church Setting. When we compare respondents who married in a church setting with those who did not, there is an immediate and obvious relationship with probability of divorce. Four different marriage settings were considered in the analysis: (1) a non-church or civil setting, (2) marriage in a church or synagogue, (3) marriage in a church temple, and (4) some other setting. Temple weddings are considered independently of other church weddings because of the significant percentage of Mormons in the sample. Highly active and committed members of the Mormon church usually marry in one of the church's several temples. It is assumed that these marriages will be more stable and binding because they are entered into "for time and eternity" rather than just until "death do you part." Thus, one would anticipate lower rates of divorce among Mormons who marry in one of their temples than among other groups, even when these other groups do enter into their marriage in a church setting. One would also anticipate lower divorce rates among temple-married Mormons than among Mormons married in a regular church or a civil setting.

The data in Table 22 indicate a strong relationship between marriage setting and permanence of the marriage. While just 57 percent of those married in a civil setting are still in their first marriage, this is true of 78 percent of those married in a church or synagogue and of 87 percent of those married in a temple. Nine percent of those who had been married civilly were currently divorced and another 26 percent were currently remarried (this includes some widowed persons who have remarried as well as remarriages following divorce). On the other hand, just 5 percent of those married in a church or synagogue were currently

Table 22
Marriage Setting and Current Marital Status

	Marriage Setting							
	Civil		Church or Synagogue		Temple		Other	
Marital Status	N	%	N	%	N	%	N	%
First Marriage	491	(57)	1991	(78)	392	(87)	177	(66)
Remarriage	226	(26)	245	(10)	21	(5)	42	(16)
Divorced	77	(9)	131	(5)	10	(2)	14	(5)
Widowed	64	(7)	184	(7)	30	(7)	35	(13)
N	858		2551		453		268	

divorced with an additional 10 percent remarried, and only 2 percent of the respondents who had been married in a temple were divorced with 5 percent remarried. When we combine the divorced with the remarried, it is obvious that getting married in a church setting has some very direct effect on the permanence of that marriage.

We are not assuming, of course, that the church marriage as such is the key. Rather, more religious persons choose to marry in church settings and this higher degree of religiosity does contribute to a lower level of divorce-proneness.

Religious Identification. Historically, the Catholic and Mormon churches have frowned on divorce more than have many of the Protestant groups, though all of these groups do make some provision for divorce. Nationally, only 4 percent of all Jews divorce, even though this is the group most accepting of divorce.[19] Socioeconomic factors, combined with the high values placed on family stability, account for this low rate. Accordingly, we would expect somewhat lower rates of divorce among Jews, Catholics, and Mormons than among the Protestant faiths or among those that have no religious preference. Table 23 summarizes our findings on this question.

Religious identification per se seems to have much less impact on the stability of a marriage than is true of the other indicators discussed. While there is some relationship between religious identity and marital stability, it is not a strong relationship. Individuals in their first marriage were least likely to be found among those with No Preference, followed by the categories of Protestant, Other, Mormon and Jewish, and Catholic. The status of "currently divorced" was most common among those reporting No Preference, followed by the categories of gories of Other, Jewish, and Protestant. The highest percentage of divorced and

Table 23
Religious Identity and Current Marital Status

Marital Status	Religion										
	Protestant		Catholic		Mormon		Jewish		Other		No Preference
	N	%	N	%	N	%	N	%	N	%	N	%
First Marriage	1375	(70)	586	(79)	680	(76)	35	(76)	109	(73)	297	(68)
Remarriage	273	(14)	55	(7)	105	(12)	3	(7)	18	(12)	83	(19)
Divorced	129	(7)	40	(5)	43	(5)	4	(9)	14	(9)	43	(10)
Widowed	182	(9)	57	(8)	68	(8)	4	(9)	8	(5)	13	(3)
N	1959		738		896		46		149		436	

remarried was found among the No Preference group, followed by Other and Protestant. While these findings tend to be consistent with expectations, it is important to note that there are no major differences among the religions.

The findings reported here are typical of a much larger body of data dealing with the relationship between religion and a variety of other factors. Religious identity is usually a poor predictor of several other types of attitudes and behaviors. This seems to be the case simply because religious *identity* is not a very accurate measure of *religiosity*—it seems to have little to do with commitment, activity, or orthodoxy. Accordingly, one probably should not anticipate that religious identity would strongly affect the quality of one's marriage or its stability. Other religious indicators that actually reflect factors such as commitment, activity, and orthodoxy are much more revealing.

Religious Activity. While the relationship between religious activity and probability of divorce is not as strong as sometimes has been reported in the literature, the data in Table 24 indicate a very clear and consistent pattern. A total of 77 percent of those who attend church services weekly are still in their first marriage. This drops slightly to 74 percent who attend monthly, 73 percent who attend only occasionally or on special occasions, and 68 percent of those who never attend religious services. The percentage of those who are divorced or remarried is just as consistent but in the opposite direction—29 percent of those who never attend religious services fall into these categories, followed by 24 percent of those who attend occasionally, 17 percent of those who attend monthly, and 12 percent of those who attend weekly.

While these percentage differences are not particularly wide, their consistency indicates that religious attendance does contribute to greater marital stability. Combined with the other religious indicators used in the study, the suggestion

Table 24
Religious Activity and Marital Status

	Attendance at Religious Services							
	Weekly		Monthly		Occasionally or on Special Occasions		Never	
Marital Status	N	%	N	%	N	%	N	%
First Marriage	1349	(77)	337	(74)	840	(73)	544	(68)
Remarriage	147	(8)	54	(12)	183	(16)	152	(19)
Divorced	72	(4)	24	(5)	93	(8)	83	(10)
Widowed	186	(11)	39	(9)	38	(3)	25	(3)
N	1754		454		1154		804	

is that religion is still one of the most effective contributors to stable marriage relationships. Much more will be said in chapter six concerning the effect of religion when other factors are considered or controlled for. At this point, it is sufficient to note that religiosity as measured by such things as activity, homogamy, and choosing a religious setting for one's wedding is more characteristic of those who are in their first marriage than of those who are currently divorced or who have been remarried.

Education

National data compiled by Glick and Norton[20] have shown a direct relationship between marital stability and education level, though the relationship is more consistent for men than for women.[21] Because of the high correlation between marital status and age, these researchers limited their analysis to individuals between the ages of 35 and 54. This group includes most of those who will ever divorce but is also young enough to be affected by the recent significant upsurge in divorce rates.

In 1975, the percentage of males between 35 and 54 who had not graduated from high school but who were still in intact first marriages was 64.6 percent. For high school graduates (12 years of education), the percentage still in intact first marriages was 72.2 percent, and for college graduates (16 years of education) it was 78.6 percent. The same percentage for males with 17 or more years of education (at least some graduate education) was 81.8 percent. The clear trend, then, is that the higher one's educational level, the more likely one is not to have had a divorce. The 1975 figures parallel those for 1960, though the percentage still in intact first marriages is lower for all educational levels.

For females in 1975, the percentage still in intact first marriages who had less than a high school education was 57.1 percent. This increases to 66.4 percent of those with a high school degree and 77.3 of those with a college degree. However, the marital stability for women with a graduate degree drops markedly to 63.4 percent still in intact first marriages. This percentage is significantly lower than for those with a college degree and even lower than is true for women with only a high school education. For men, then, the relationship between education and marital stability is consistently positive. For women, the same basic pattern holds until one reaches the highest educational levels and then stability decreases significantly. Several explanations for this have been advanced. For example, Glick and Norton[22] suggest that the highly educated women have many more career options which may conflict with harmonious marriage. They are also likely to have much greater financial independence.

It is important to note in assessing the national data that while college men tend to have the most stable marriages overall, the divorce rates among this group have increased most significantly since 1960. Divorce rates for men with a college education have doubled since 1960. For other educational groups, rates are higher in 1975 than in 1960 but the rate of increase is lower.[23]

Data from the Intermountain Divorce Study tend to parallel the national trends noted above. As Table 25 indicates, the percentage of respondents (both male and female) still in intact first marriages varies from 62 percent for those with less than a completed high school education to 80 percent of those with a graduate education. The percentage of respondents currently divorced is not particularly different among the educational categories. However, when the currently divorced are combined with the remarried, we find the percentages in these two categories ranging from 24 percent with less than a high school education to 15 percent of the college graduates.

If we consider education as our measure of social class, then, we find a direct relationship between class and marital stability. Other indicators of class such as income and occupation are reported to have similar effects on marital stability. That is, the higher one's income, the more stable the marriage and the higher one's occupational status, the more stable the marriage (though the effects of occupation tend to become relatively unimportant when one controls for income level).[24] Comparative data on these other indicators cannot be presented from the Intermountain Divorce Study since income and occupational data were not obtained on the respondent's spouse prior to the divorce for those respondents who were divorced.

Race and Marital Status

National data indicate that black adults are somewhat more likely to be divorced than are white adults.[25] In addition, they are much more likely to be separated. In 1976, the proportion of black adults who were separated was six times the

Table 25
Educational Level and Current Marital Status

Marital Status	Less Than High School Graduation		High School Graduate		Some College		College Graduate		Graduate Degree	
	N	%	N	%	N	%	N	%	N	%
First Marriage	434	(62)	809	(74)	884	(72)	563	(79)	355	(80)
Remarriage	124	(18)	142	(13)	169	(14)	51	(7)	51	(11)
Divorced	40	(6)	63	(6)	87	(7)	55	(8)	23	(5)
Widowed	97	(14)	74	(7)	85	(7)	45	(6)	17	(4)
N	695		1088		1225		714		446	

proportion of separated white adults.[26] However, national divorce statistics are inadequate when one is interested in making valid generalizations regarding the relationship between race and probability of divorce. Figures reflect the marital status of the population only at the time of the census enumeration and so give no real indication of the proportion of each group which has been previously divorced and remarried.[27] In addition, many state reports fail to designate race in their reports on divorce. Because of these data limitations, it is difficult to make valid white/non-white comparisons.

The relative smallness of the non-white groups in the Intermountain Divorce Study also makes questionable any effort on our part to generalize about racial differences in divorce. Nevertheless, the data do reveal some interesting findings. Overall, the lowest percentage still in intact first marriages is found among the *whites* in our population (72 percent). This is followed by American Indians (76 percent still in intact first marriages), blacks (77 percent), other (80 percent), Chicanos (84 percent), and Asian Americans (89 percent). Then we look at the percentage of our sample who report that they are currently divorced, we find the highest percentage among blacks (12 percent), followed by American Indians (8 percent), and whites and other (7 percent). The most stable marriages among members of our sample occur among Asian Americans, followed by Chicanos.

Differences in divorce rates among different racial groups can be attributed to a number of factors. Probably most important are cultural norms relating to divorce and group support. Some cultural and racial groups place much greater stress on the permanence of marriage than do others. Among those groups which place greatest stress on marital permanence, one is also more likely to find strong

Table 26
Race and Marital Status

Marital Status	White		Chicano		Black		Asian American		American Indian		Other	
	N	%	N	%	N	%	N	%	N	%	N	%
First Marriage	2873	(72)	94	(84)	20	(77)	16	(89)	19	(76)	55	(80)
Remarriage	517	(13)	8	(7)	3	(12)	2	(11)	2	(8)	5	(7)
Divorced	258	(7)	6	(5)	3	(12)	0	(0)	2	(8)	5	(7)
Widowed	321	(8)	4	(4)	0	(0)	0	(0)	2	(8)	4	(6)
N	3969		112		26		18		25		69	

group support for resolving marital differences and keeping the marriage intact. Thus, one would expect low divorce rates among Asian Americans as a racial group for basically the same reasons that one finds low divorce rates among Jews as a cultural and religious group.

Comparative Marital Happiness of the Married and the Previously Married

We would expect that persons still in intact first marriages would express much greater satisfaction with those marriages than would persons who had terminated their marriages with divorce. This issue will be dealt with in much greater detail in chapter four where some ideas from exchange theory help explain the decision to divorce. Here we will briefly examine expressed marital happiness and satisfaction of currently married and formerly married respondents.

Two measures of marital happiness and satisfaction were used in the study. The first asked the respondent to compare his or her marriage with that of other couples. The question read: "Compared with other couples you know, how satisfied would you rate your current marriage (or former marriage if divorced or widowed)?" Responses could range from "much less satisfied" to "much more satisfied." The second question asked respondents to compare their marriage with the expectations they held for that marriage before entering into it. The question read as follows: "Compared with your expectations of marriage *before* you were married, how has your current marriage turned out (or last marriage if widowed or divorced)?" Responses could range from "much worse" to "much better than expected."

Data on these two questions are treated somewhat differently than has been the case on previous questions. Specifically, the remarried are responding to this question in terms of their current marriage and not in terms of a prior marriage which has failed. Therefore, their responses should be more similar to those respondents still in intact first marriages than of respondents who are divorced.

Table 27 presents data on the first question comparing marital happiness with perceived marital happiness of others. As would be anticipated, the notable differences are found between the currently married groups (first marriages and remarriages) on the one hand, and the currently divorced respondents on the other. Widowed respondents are much more similar to the currently married groups than to the currently divorced. Both first and remarriages fare very well on a comparative perspective. Forty-four percent of those still in intact first marriages rate their marriage as much better than the marriages of other couples they know. An even higher percentage of the remarried (52 percent) rate their marriage as much better than the marriages of others they know. When the "much better" response is combined with the "somewhat better" response, the percentage of those groups which are willing to rate their marriage as better than other marriages they are familiar with is 65 and 69 percent, respectively. Similarly 59 percent of the widowed respondents rate their former marriage as somewhat better or much better than the marriages of other couples they know. The assumed tendency on the part of persons who have lost a spouse through death to remember only the most positive aspects of that relationship is not evident in these data.

White[28] has reported findings similar to ours indicating that overall, the remarried report more happiness than persons who are in intact first marriages. Of course, this could be a function of the greater propensity of "bad" remarriages to be terminated than is true of "bad" first marriages. Contrary data (indicating greater happiness in intact first marriages) have been reported by Renne[29] and Glenn and Weaver.[30]

Currently divorced respondents present a rather different picture of their former marriages. Only 22 percent of the currently divorced rate their former marriage as somewhat or much better than the marriages of other couples they know. It should be noted that many of these respondents may be comparing their marriage with the marriages of others which have also failed. On the other hand, fully 57 percent of the currently divorced were willing to rate their former marriage as much worse or somewhat worse than the marriages of others. Only 5 percent of those still in intact first marriages rated their marriages as worse than the marriages of other couples they know. Comparative percentages for the remarried and the widowed were 9 percent in both instances.

Table 28 presents data on marital happiness compared with the expectations one had prior to the marriage. In effect, this question asks whether or not the marriage measured up to one's expectations. In this instance, the remarriages come off most favorably of all. Fully 46 percent of the remarried rate their current marriage as much better than they had anticipated it would be. Another

Table 27
Perceived Marital Happiness Compared with Happiness of Others

	Marital Happiness Compared with Others									
	Much Worse		Somewhat Worse		About the Same		Somewhat Better		Much Better		
Marital Status	N	%	N	%	N	%	N	%	N	%	N
First Marriage	49	(2)	98	(3)	896	(31)	595	(21)	1269	(44)	2907
Remarriage	10	(2)	35	(7)	117	(22)	90	(17)	274	(52)	526
Divorced	15	(17)	36	(40)	19	(21)	8	(9)	12	(13)	90
Widowed	7	(3)	15	(6)	89	(33)	49	(18)	110	(41)	270

17 percent report it to be somewhat better than they had expected. Since we are dealing with a group who have already gone through one marriage and since many of these previous marriages have failed, perhaps our married respondents entered into the new relationship with a lower level of expectations than is the case for the first time around. That is, after already having experienced a bad marriage, maybe they did not expect quite so much from another relationship. At any rate, as a group they tend to express a relatively high level of current marital happiness.

One-third of the respondents still in intact first marriages rated these marriages as much better than they had expected them to be and another 19 percent rated their marriages as somewhat better. It should be remembered, of course, that the worst marriages have already been terminated and so would not show up in this category. The widowed are much like those still in their first marriage; 38 percent rated their former marriage as much better than they had expected and another 16 percent rated it as somewhat better.

Divorced respondents, on the other hand, generally indicated that their former marriage had not measured up to their expectations. While 16 percent rated the former marriage as better than expected, fully 75 percent indicated that it had been much worse or somewhat worse than they had expected. While 46 percent of the currently divorced rated their former marriage as *much* worse than they had expected, this was true of only 2 to 3 percent of each of the other three groups.

These findings are generally consistent with those reported in the literature. For example, Hayes, Stinnett, and DeFrain[31] found that fully 25 percent of their divorced respondents felt that their marriage had been a mistake virtually from the start. From the very beginning, then, many of these marriages failed to live up to the expectations the partners held when entering the marriage. Respondents

Table 28
Marital Happiness Compared with Expectations prior to Marriage

Marital Status	Marital Happiness									
	Much Worse		Somewhat Worse		As Expected		Somewhat Better		Much Better	
	N	%	N	%	N	%	N	%	N	%	N
First Marriage	52	(2)	190	(7)	1098	(39)	539	(19)	938	(33)	2817
Remarriage	16	(3)	38	(7)	143	(27)	87	(17)	238	(46)	522
Divorced	48	(46)	30	(29)	10	(9)	7	(7)	10	(9)	105
Widowed	6	(3)	20	(8)	86	(35)	40	(16)	92	(38)	244

who felt that their marriage had been marred by unrealized expectations typically felt that they had not been ready for marriage or that they had married too young. Common reasons for early marriage include escape from an unhappy home environment, premarital pregnancy, or guilt about premarital sex.

We should note, too, that the findings indicating major differences in the perceptions of the currently married and the currently divorced are supported by several other traditions of research. For example, Yoder and Nichols[32] report that married people express a significantly greater degree of overall life satisfaction than do divorced people and that divorced people are much less optimistic about whether life is worthwhile than are the married. Similarly, Glenn[33] found that married persons report higher overall happiness than does any other group. These studies and others provide strong support for the conclusion that one of the most striking differences between those who are divorced and those who have intact marriages is evident in the areas of personal happiness and life satisfaction. In these important regards, the marrieds fare much better.

Summary

In this chapter a number of characteristics were examined that distinguish between the divorced and the non-divorced members of our sample. Specifically, we have sought to determine whether or not these segments of our sample differ on several variables that have been assumed to contribute to "divorce-proneness." These include (1) age at marriage, (2) marital success of parents, (3) religious factors, (4) education, and (5) race. The data have indicated that all of these factors are meaningful in determining success of one's marriage. Specifically, the younger the respondent when married, the more likely the marriage was to have been terminated by divorce. While 60 percent of those who married under the age of 20 were still in intact first marriages, this was true of 89 percent of those who married after the age of 30. Consistent with research, marriages between teenagers are particularly unstable and are twice as likely to be terminated by divorce than are marriages that occur later.

The data reveal some tendency toward the intergenerational transmission of marital instability. Divorced members of our sample were somewhat more likely to come from homes in which their parents had gotten a divorce than was true for non-divorced members of our sample. However, the differences in this instance were not great.

Several religious factors have been found to be important in contributing to marital stability or instability. Those examined specifically in this study included (1) whether the marriage occurred in a church or a non-church setting, (2) the religious identification of the respondent, and (3) religious activity. Marriages that occurred in a church setting were found to be much more stable than marriages that occurred in non-church settings. While 57 percent of those who married in a civil setting were still in intact first marriages, this was true of 78 percent of those who married in a church or synagogue and of 87 percent of those who married in a Mormon temple. The latter marriages, entered into "for time and eternity," were particularly stable. Catholics, Mormons, and Jews were more likely to have stable marriages than were Protestants and those with no religious preference. However, religious identity per se was less important than religious activity. Twelve percent of those who attend church services were either divorced or remarried. However, this was true of 29 percent of those who never attended religious services.

National data have shown a direct relationship between marital stability and educational level, particularly for men. These findings were supported by our data. While 62 percent of those with less than a complete high school education were still in intact first marriages, this was true of 80 percent of those with post-college education. Our findings on the importance of race were rather mixed and must be viewed cautiously because of the relatively small number of non-whites included in the sample. Nevertheless, the data revealed that the most stable marriages were those that occurred among Asian Americans and among Chicanos. Cultural norms that oppose terminating marriage and group support contribute to more stable marriages.

Finally, it was found that the currently married (either first marriages or remarriages) expressed much greater satisfaction with their relationships than did the currently divorced. The first two groups tended to rate their marriages as much happier or much more satisfying than were the marriages of other couples they knew or than they expected them to be prior to entering into the marriage. Widowed persons also tended to rate their former marriage as better than they expected or better than the marriages of others. Currently divorced respondents, on the other hand, rated their former marriages much more negatively on both of these criteria.

Overall, then, the data reveal that there are some differences between the divorced and those still in intact first marriages—the principal ones being age at marriage, whether or not the marriage occurred in a church setting, religious activity of participants, and educational level. The most successful marriages, according to our data, are those that involve partners who are age 20 or older, who have higher levels of education, and who marry in a church setting and maintain their religious activity following marriage.

Notes

1. Phillips Cutright, "Income and Family Events: Marital Stability," *Journal of Marriage and the Family* 33 (May 1971): 291-306.

2. Paul C. Glick, *American Families* (New York: John Wiley, 1957); Paul C. Glick and Arthur J. Norton, "Frequency, Duration, and Probability of Marriage and Divorce," *Journal of Marriage and the Family* 33 (May 1971): 307-17; Larry L. Bumpass and James A. Sweet, "Differentials in Marital Instability: 1970," *American Sociological Review* 37 (December 1972): 754-766.

3. William J. Goode, *After Divorce* (Glencoe, Ill.: Free Press, 1956); Charles W. Mueller and Hallowell Pope, "Marital Instability: A Study of Its Transmission Between Generations," *Journal of Marriage and the Family* 39 (February 1977): 83-92; Bumpass and Sweet, "Differentials in Marital Instability."

4. Judson T. Landis, "Social Correlates of Divorce and Nondivorce Among the Unhappy Married," *Marriage and Family Living* 25 (May 1963): 178-80.

5. Hugh Carter and Paul C. Glick, *Marriage and Divorce: A Social and Economic Study* (Cambridge, Mass.: Harvard University Press, 1976); Paul C. Glick and Arthur J. Norton, "Marrying, Divorcing, and Living Together in the U.S. Today," *Population Bulletin* 32 (October 1977): 1-41.

6. James A. Sweet and Larry L. Bumpass, "Differentials in Marital Instability of the Black Population: 1970," *Phylon* 35 (September 1974): 323-31.

7. Glick and Norton, "Marrying, Divorcing, and Living Together"; Carter and Glick, *Marriage and Divorce*.

8. Frank F. Furstenberg, "Premarital Pregnancy and Marital Instability," *Journal of Social Issues* 32 (no. 1, 1976): 67-86.

9. Jan D. Yoder and Robert C. Nichols, "A Life Perspective Comparison of Married and Divorced Persons," *Journal of Marriage and the Family* 42 (May 1980): 413-19.

10. Glick and Norton, "Marrying, Divorcing, and Living Together."

11. Ibid.

12. Ibid.

13. Judson T. Landis, "The Pattern of Divorce in Three Generations," *Social Forces* 34 (March 1956): 201-7.

14. Bumpass and Sweet, "Differentials in Marital Instability."

15. Hallowell Pope and Charles W. Mueller, "The Intergenerational Transmission of Marital Instability: Comparisons by Race and Sex," *Journal of Social Issues* 32 (1976): 49-66; see also R. A. Kulka and H. Weingarten, "The Long-Term Effects of Parental Divorce in Childhood on Adult Adjustment," *Journal of Social Issues* 35 (1979): 50-78; see also F. L. Mott and S. F. Moore, "The Causes of Marital Disruption Among Young

American Women: An Interdisciplinary Perspective, *Journal of Marriage and the Family* 41 (1979): 355-65.

16. Bumpass and Sweet, "Differentials In Marital Instability"; George Levinger, "Marital Cohesiveness and Dissolution: An Integrative Review," *Journal of Marriage and the Family* 27 (1965): 19-28; Barbara Thornes and Jean Collard, *Who Divorces?* (London: Routledge & Kegan Paul, 1979).

17. Howard M. Bahr, "Religious Intermarriage and Divorce in Utah and the Mountain States," *Journal for the Scientific Study of Religion* 20 (1981): 260.

18. Yoder and Nichols, "Life Perspective Comparison."

19. Lucille Duberman, *Marriage and Other Alternatives* (New York: Praeger, 1977).

20. Glick and Norton, "Marrying, Divorcing, and Living Together."

21. Carter and Glick, "Marriage and Divorce."

22. Glick and Norton, "Marrying, Divorcing, and Living Together."

23. Ibid.

24. Cutright, "Income and Family Events."

25. Carter and Glick, "Marriage and Divorce"; Sweet and Bumpass, "Marital Instability of the Black Population"; A. Thornton, "Marital Instability Differentials and Interactions: Insights from Multivariate Contingency Table Analysis," *Sociology and Social Research* 62 (July 1978): 572-95.

26. Glick and Norton, "Marrying, Divorcing, and Living Together."

27. F. Ivan Nye and Felix M. Berardo, *The Family: Its Structure and Interaction* (New York: Macmillan, 1973).

28. Lynn K. White, "Sex Differentials in the Effect of Remarriage on Global Happiness," *Journal of Marriage and the Family* 41 (November 1979): 869-76.

29. Karen S. Renne, "Health and Marital Experience in an Urban Population," *Journal of Marriage and the Family* 33 (May 1971): 338-50.

30. Norval D. Glenn and Charles N. Weaver, "The Marital Happiness of Remarried Divorced Persons," *Journal of Marriage and the Family* 39 (May 1977): 331-37.

31. Maggie P. Hayes, Nick Stinnett, and John DeFrain, "Learning About Marriage from the Divorced," *Journal of Divorce* 4 (Fall 1980): 23-29.

32. Yoder and Nichols, "Life Perspective Comparison."

33. Norval D. Glenn, "The Contribution of Marriage to Psychological Well-Being of Males and Females," *Journal of Marriage and the Family* 37 (August 1975): 594-600.

Chapter 4

The Decision to Divorce

Introduction

Previous chapters examined trends and patterns in divorce in the United States and in the western region of the country where the Intermountain Divorce Study was conducted. They also examined major differences between persons who have experienced a divorce and those who have not. In this chapter, we begin a more detailed treatment of those members of the study who had personally experienced a divorce. Several issues are treated sequentially, beginning with an analysis of the decision to divorce and examining the types of marital difficulties most likely to culminate in a termination of the marriage, the barriers confronted in reaching a divorce decision, how these barriers are overcome, and so on.

The decision to terminate an unhappy marriage through obtaining a divorce is almost never an easy decision. It is usually reached only after other options and alternatives have been carefully considered and then rejected as non-viable solutions to the problems that have developed between the spouses. As Bernard[1] has noted, despite the increasing frequency of its occurrence, "it is not likely that divorce will ever become matter-of-fact, nor that it will ever become painless or casual or nonchalant. . . .It will probably always be an extremely painful experience for most people, as breaking close ties always is, even outside marriage." From this perspective, our coming to terms with divorce means only that we recognize its inevitability in many cases and try to mitigate some of the worst of its consequences.

First, we review the major theoretical orientations developed in the literature to account for the process through which the individual ultimately decides to seek a divorce. An analysis of the factors that were important in the decision of our respondents will then be presented.

The Decision to Divorce: Considerations of Reward-Cost Outcomes

In assessing the decision to divorce, one acknowledges that the relationship that exists between satisfaction and happiness in a marriage and the stability of that relationship is never a simple or direct one. As Lenthall[2] has noted, "happy" marriages often end in divorce and "unhappy" marriages often endure. Or, as Hicks and Platt[3] conclude after their comprehensive review of the marital satisfaction literature, the factors that make a marriage stable or unstable are much more complicated than just "being happy."

Many researchers, in their efforts to explain the decision to divorce and, more particularly, to clarify the relationship that exists between satisfaction and stability, have adopted a scheme developed a number of years ago by Thibaut and Kelly.[4] Using a social exchange framework similar to that employed by Homans[5] and others, Thibaut and Kelly explain outcomes in social relationships in terms of costs and rewards. More specifically, they propose that the amount of happiness or satisfaction that one attributes to a relationship will be based on the extent to which that relationship measures up to a specified standard that is referred to as the comparison level (CL). Individual comparison levels develop on the basis of personal past experience, observance of the experience of others, and so on. If an individual feels that a relationship he or she is involved with is "better than" the standard (CL), then the individual is likely to feel relative happiness or satisfaction with the relationship.

However, a relationship that is more rewarding to the individual than the comparison level does not have to be a stable relationship. To handle this situation, Thibaut and Kelly[6] introduce what they refer to as a comparison level for alternatives (CL alt). While an existing relationship may be satisfactory on the comparison level criteria, an *alternative* relationship may become available that is even more attractive. In such circumstances, the "happy" relationship may become an unstable relationship. On the other hand, a relationship that does *not* measure up to the comparison level standard may nevertheless remain a stable relationship if only because the alternatives available (CL alt) are even less attractive to the individual involved.

These relationships are summarized in Table 29, which compares individual outcomes from present relationships (O) with comparison level (CL) and the comparison level for alternatives (CL alt).

Relationships of the first type (upper left corner of the table) are both stable and happy because their outcomes are higher than either the comparison level or the comparison level for alternatives. Type 2 relationships, though happy, are unstable because alternatives are available that are more attractive than present outcomes—even though those present outcomes are better than the individual would expect on the basis of the comparison level. Type 3 relationships are stable but unhappy. In this instance, the individual finds himself or herself in a relationship that just does not measure up to what had been expected of it and

Table 29
Relationship between Stability and Happiness in Marital Relationships

Happiness	Stability			
	Stable		Unstable	
Happy	1	$0 \rightarrow CL$ $0 \rightarrow CL_{ALT}$	2	$0 \rightarrow CL$ $0 \leftarrow CL_{ALT}$
Unhappy	3	$0 \leftarrow CL$ $0 \rightarrow CL_{ALT}$	4	$0 \leftarrow CL$ $0 \leftarrow CL_{ALT}$

0   = <u>Present Outcomes</u> associated with one's marriage

CL   = Comparison Level

CL_{ALT} = Comparison Level for Alternative

-->   = Better Than

<--   = Worse Than

does not measure up to what the individual sees others experiencing in their relationships. However, the outcomes from that relationship are still greater than what could be expected from other alternative relationships that are available. In such an instance, the individual is predicted to stay with a bad relationship rather than opt for what is defined as an even more negative alternative. Finally, type 4 relationships are both unhappy and unstable. They measure up neither to the standard established by the comparison level nor to the available alternatives. One would not expect such relationships to last very long.

This cost-reward framework implies that the decision to divorce will be made only after it is determined that the alternative to sustaining a marital relationship is either more rewarding or less costly than would be the decision to remain with the relationship. It assumes the ability on the part of the individual actor to compare the outcomes of his or her own marital relationship with some internal standard as well as with other options that are available or that are made available in the actor's environment. The reward-cost framework also recognizes changes that may take place in a relationship over time. The termination of an intimate relationship with another may often happen only after drastic shifts have occurred in reward-cost outcomes. That is, relationships that once may have compared favorably both with the comparison level and with comparison levels for alternatives may now have taken a downward turn to the point that they now fall well below either or both of these standards.

Levinger[7] has used somewhat of a different approach to that adopted by exchange theorists. However, his analysis of the process through which individuals reach the decision to divorce still contains important reward-cost considerations, although Levinger prefers to call them "*attractions*" and "*barriers.*" According to Levinger, inducements to remain in a relationship include the attractiveness of that relationship to the individual actor and the restraints or barriers against breaking up that relationship. Attractions include perceived rewards such as the receipt of love, status, goods, services, support, security, and the physical attributes of one's partner. Attractions might also include joint possessions such as a home, joint accomplishments associated with the bearing and rearing of children, and sexual enjoyment.

Barriers to the dissolution of a relationship, on the other hand, include feelings of obligation to each other, concerns about effects of divorce on the children, fears about group and community reactions, religious prohibitions, abstract moral values, concerns about financial costs associated with divorce, and so on. The implication, again, is that as attractions in a relationship decrease or as barriers to the dissolution of that relationship are eroded, the probability of divorce increases.

Finally, Levinger notes that sources of alternative attraction must also be considered, such as the availability of a preferred alternative sexual partner and opportunities for independent income for the wife. These factors are summarized in Table 30.

A third theoretical perspective that is receiving a good deal of current attention is Becker's economic theory of marriage.[8] Becker proposes that marriages are dissolved when the utility of staying married falls below the utility expected from divorce. Thus, the probability of a marriage ending in divorce is lowered by such factors as an increase in the expected value of some positively evaluated factor such as the earning level of the husband, an increase in the time spent in seeking a spouse (age at marriage), and an increase in marital-specific capital (the birth of children). The probability of divorce increases if changes occur in the expected value of negatively sorted variables (e.g., the wife's earnings increase relative to the husband's), by a larger discrepancy in mate traits (e.g., educational level, IQ, religion, race), and so on.

While Becker's theory is based on important economic principles, its predictions are closely aligned with those that emerge from the cost-reward and attraction-barrier frameworks discussed above. Thus, all three perspectives will be utilized to some extent in the following discussion.

Falling Below the Comparison Level: Marital Satisfaction Compared with Others and with Prior Expectations

Married couples frequently assess the happiness and satisfaction of their own marriages by comparing them with those of other couples they know. If they perceive their own relationships to be better than those of others, they are more likely to be satisfied with those relationships. In this sense, then, their marriage

Table 30
Factors Found to Differentiate between High and Low Cohesive Marriages

Sources of Attraction	Sources of Barrier Strength	Sources of Alternate Attraction

Affectional Rewards:
  esteem for spouse
  desire for companionship
  sexual enjoyment
 	
Socioeconomic rewards:
  husband's income
  home ownership
  husband's education
  husband's occupation
 	
Similarity in social status:
  religion
  education
  age
	Feelings of obligation:
	  to dependent children
	  to marital bond
	
	Moral prescriptions:
	  proscriptive religion
	  joint church attendance
	
	External pressures:
	  primary group affiliation
	  community stigma; rural-
	  urban
	  legal and economic bars
		Affectional rewards:
		  preferred alternate
		  sex partner
		  disjunctive kin
		  affiliations
		
		Economic rewards:
		  wife's opportunity
		  for independent
		  income

measures up on the comparison level scale. There are some inherent dangers in this process that few individuals recognize, however. For example, almost everyone has a tendency to put on their best front when in public and conceal negative aspects in their private relationships. Thus, the comparison level against which some couples compare their own relationship is an artificially created comparison level. They measure themselves against the public mask of others. Each person acknowledges the problems that exist in his or her private life but tends to see only the better side of others. Using Goffman's[9] terms, individual "back regions," with all of their problems, are compared against the carefully contrived "front regions" of other people. It is not very likely that the reality of the former will measure up to the artificiality of the latter.

To whatever extent the above is the case, it is obvious that our sample of divorced respondents felt that their marriages fared very poorly when compared with the marriages of other couples they knew. Each respondent was asked the following question: "Compared with other couples you have known, how would you rate the degree of overall satisfaction that you have felt with your marriage?" Responses to this question are summarized in Table 31.

Almost three-fifths of the respondents felt that their marriage that had been terminated through divorce had been somewhat or much less satisfying than were the marriages of other couples they knew. Thus, in terms of the comparison level concepts discussed above, these would have been "unhappy" marriages. However, the remainder of the table affirms the point made earlier that even "happy" marriages are not necessarily stable marriages. A total of 15 percent of the respondents defined their marriage as having been more satisfying than

Table 31

Satisfaction with Former Marriage Compared with Perceived Satisfaction of Other Couples

Satisfaction Compared with Others	Males		Females		Total	
	N	%	N	%	N	%
Much less satisfied	61	30	119	42	180	37
Somewhat less satisfied	39	19	65	23	104	21
About the same	61	30	66	23	127	26
Somewhat more satisfied	23	11	26	9	49	10
Much more satisfied	18	9	8	3	26	5
Totals	(202)	(99)	(284)	(100)	(486)	(99)

were the marriages of other couples they knew. On this comparison level scale, then, these would have been defined as relatively "happy" marriages. However, they apparently did not measure up in terms of the comparison level for alternatives, though this interpretation cannot be accepted uncritically. For example, one partner may have been quite satisfied with his or her marriage and may have felt that the marriage was significantly better than were the marriages of other couples with which he or she was familiar. The spouse in this relationship, on the other hand, may have been quite unhappy, and may have been the one that initiated the divorce. One should keep in mind the psychological need on the part of the respondent to justify the termination of the marriage to an outside party (in this case, the researcher). The overall effect of this need for justification is virtually impossible to determine. In general, however, it seems that these marriages were quite unsatisfactory when compared with the experiences of others.

The differences between male and female respondents on this question are considerable. Women divorcees are significantly more likely than males to report their former marriage as less satisfying (65 percent of the females compared with 49 percent of the males reported their marriage as much or somewhat less satisfying). On the other hand, males respond much more favorably to that former relationship.

Comparison levels are developed not only by observing the relationships of others but also by determining whether or not a relationship is what we expected it to be when we entered into it. To see how the marriages of our respondents had fared on this second criteria, each individual was asked the following question: "Compared with your expectations of marriage before you were married, how did the marriage turn out?" The results on this question are summarized in Table 32.

Table 32
Satisfaction with Former Marriage Compared with Expectations prior to Entering the Marriage

Satisfaction Compared with Prior Expectations	Males		Females		Total	
	N	%	N	%	N	%
Much worse than expected	85	41	166	57	251	51
Somewhat worse than expected	68	33	77	27	145	29
About as expected	41	20	32	11	73	15
Somewhat better than expected	7	3	12	4	19	4
Much better than expected	4	2	3	1	7	1
Totals	(205)	(99)	(290)	(100)	(495)	(100)

Over half of all respondents stated that their marriage had been *much worse* than they had expected it to be. Again, women were much more likely than men to evaluate their former marriage in the most negative terms (57 percent of the female respondents compared with 41 percent of the males chose the most negative alternative).

Of course, most persons do not enter into a marital relationship assuming that it will not work. The fact that the first marriages of all of these people failed would be reason enough to assume that they had not measured up to the expectations held about them by those entering the relationship. However, the overwhelming failure of the marriages to measure up to this "prior expectations" comparison level is interesting. For a very small minority (5 percent), the marriage that had been terminated was rated as better than it had been expected to be. One can only assume that these individuals entered the marriage initially with very low expectations or that the divorce had been initiated by a spouse toward whom they still felt positive affection.

Problems in Marriage

Many of the problems that the exchange theorists like Thibaut and Kelly[10] would refer to as costs in a relationship can be identified by asking individuals to define the major conflicts that arose between them. The divorce literature is filled with hypotheses concerning the nature and types of problems that are likely to lead to divorce. In our survey, each respondent was asked to identify the major reasons why he or she felt that the marriage had failed. Respondents could list as many reasons as they desired but were asked to rank each reason listed in terms of its overall importance. Table 33 provides a summary of these responses. The first column lists all of those reasons identified by the respondents

Table 33
Major Reasons Why Marriage Failed

	Listed First	(Order)	Total Number of Times Listed	(Order)
Infidelity	168	(1)	255	(1)
No Longer Loved Each Other	103	(2)	188	(2)
Emotional Problems	53	(3)	185	(3)
Financial Problems	30	(4)	135	(4)
Physical Abuse	29	(5)	72	(8)
Alcohol	25	(6)	47	(9)
Sexual Problems	22	(7)	115	(5)
Problems with In-Laws	16	(8)	81	(6)
Neglect of Children	11	(9)	74	(7)
Communication Problems	10	(10)	18	(11)
Married Too Young	9	(11)	14	(12)
Job Conflicts	7	(12)	20	(10)
Other	7		19	

as the most important reasons for marital failure by rank order. The second column then lists the total number of times that each of the reasons was listed by the respondents.

A total of 490 of the 500 ever-divorced respondents listed one or more reasons why they felt that their marriage had failed and of these 490, 168 listed infidelity on the part of spouse as the most important reason. Our findings of the importance of extra-marital involvements in precipitating divorce is supported by several other research studies. For example, Hayes, Stinnett, and DeFrain[11] found that for over half of the subjects in their study of men and women who had divorced during middle age, involvement of one of the partners with another person was defined as the precipitating event. Most often, it was the husband who became involved with another woman and was unable or unwilling to terminate the relationship. These researchers report very different experiences for men and women in terms of frequency and type of extra-marital involvement. For example, three-fourths of the men and one-fourth of the women indicated that they had been involved in an extra-marital affair. For men, the first occasion was usually early in marriage without the awareness of the wife. However, serious emotional involvements usually did not occur until the middle years and these affairs resulted in some important personality and behavioral changes. These changes were consequential in precipitating the divorce action. Women typically became involved in an affair as a means of affirming themselves as women, but these involvements tended not to be the major factors that led to the decision to divorce. With our respondents, however, the differences between males and females were not significant.

The second most frequently mentioned cause for marital failure was simply "loss of love" for each other. A total of 103 respondents stated that the major reason for marital dissolution was that they and their spouse no longer loved each other. This item ranked second for both males and females. The two factors of infidelity and loss of love account for fully 55 percent of the first-listed reasons for marriage failure. Other frequently listed reasons were emotional problems, financial problems, and physical abuse.

Turning to the question of the total number of times each reason was listed, the order of the first four items does not change. These four most important reasons, then, include: (1) infidelity, (2) loss of love for each other, (3) emotional problems, and (4) financial problems. In terms of overall ranking, sexual problems came in fifth, though this was listed as the most important reason for marital failure by only 4 percent of the respondents.

Each of these factors can be viewed as costs in a marriage. As such, they can cause the satisfaction that one feels with that relationship to fall below either or both the comparison level or the comparison level for alternatives. When infidelity enters into a relationship, the costs for the injured party may far outweigh the rewards that have otherwise been associated with the marriage. In the overall balance, the individual may feel that he or she is no longer interested in maintaining the relationship. The same holds true for the other factors as well. For example, one of the primary attractions associated with a marriage is the emotional feelings of love that one feels for a spouse. When that love is gone, reasons for continuing the relationship are diminished.

Barriers to Divorce

Even though problems develop in a marriage, there are still strong forces toward keeping that relationship intact. As noted earlier, Levinger refers to these forces as barriers. "Barriers lessen the effect of temporary fluctuations in interpersonal attraction; even if attraction becomes negative, barriers act to continue the relationship."[12] Levinger identifies a number of different types of barriers to divorce, including: (1) material barriers such as the expenses associated with filing a divorce application, paying legal fees, maintaining two places of residence, and so on; (2) symbolic barriers, including feelings of obligation to keep a relationship together even when there are obvious and major problems with that relationship, religious constraints, pressures from primary groups, and pressures that result from fears of community disapproval; and (3) affectional barriers that are linked primarily to concerns about what the divorce will mean for dependent children.

We have noted that many of the traditional barriers to obtaining a divorce have eroded over the past few years. Most states have greatly liberalized their divorce laws and many have moved toward establishing no-fault standards. The traditional legal hassles associated with marital dissolution may therefore be less of a major consideration in many instances, though, as we shall note, issues pertaining to legal costs, child custody, and property division are still important. Equally important have been the changes in public attitudes and perceptions relating to divorce. In the past, to have been divorced meant that one had to bear a major social stigma. In fact, divorce not only brought shame and discredit to the individual parties involved but also to their extended families.[13] Divorce no longer bears this degree of stigma and much of the public accepts it as a rather normal, everyday occurrence.

While these traditional barriers are no longer as imposing as they once were, there remain some hurdles that must be overcome as the individual makes the decision to end an unsatisfactory relationship. To determine the relative importance of these, each respondent in the study was asked to identify what they considered the major barriers that had to be overcome as they reached the decision to obtain a divorce. Table 34 summarizes the responses to this question.

According to our respondents, the single most pressing concern that they faced in making their decisions was financial. As would be anticipated, this was primarily a problem for women. Female respondents were three to five times more likely than male respondents to identify financial concerns as a major barrier to obtaining a divorce. For the women, particularly those with young children, a major fear was that of how they would be able to support themselves and their families without a husband. One can assume on the basis of the frequency with which this factor was mentioned that there are probably a great many wives that put up with unsatisfactory marriages because the alternatives associated with having to provide for themselves and their children are even less satisfactory. For the husbands in the sample who mentioned financial concerns as a major barrier in their decision to divorce, one can assume that these related to worries about alimony and child support and the difficulties associated with having to provide for two families should they decide to marry again at a later time. In addition, both sexes were probably expressing concern about the financial strain associated with having to obtain legal counsel in seeking the divorce.

While financial concerns were the most frequently mentioned, other important barriers were also noted by many of the respondents. A total of 102 persons mentioned concerns about what it would mean for their children. Interestingly, males were twice as likely as females to identify children as a barrier in obtaining a divorce. As we shall see, much of this seems to be associated with fears of loss of custody.

Table 34
Perceived Barriers to Obtaining Divorce

Barrier	Males N	Males %	Females N	Females %	Total N	Total %
			Frequency of Mention			
No Financial Support	20	10	133	36	153	27
Children	54	27	48	13	102	18
Personal Religious Beliefs	27	14	73	20	100	18
Difficulty of Divorce Laws	34	17	30	8	64	11
Parents	23	12	32	9	55	10
Friends	17	9	17	5	34	6
Negative Counsel from Religious Leaders	6	3	14	4	20	4
Fear of Unknown	3	2	11	3	14	2
Spouse Didn't Want Divorce	2	1	6	2	8	1
Neighbors	1	-	3	1	4	1
Other	10	5	6	2	16	3
Totals	(197)	(99)	(373)	(100)	(570)	(101)

When children are born to a union between husband and wife, it now means that decisions the two make no longer affect only themselves but also the children. It has been known for years that many couples stay together not because of their feelings for each other but because of their concerns about what a separation would mean for their children. There is much debate in the literature as to whether or not this is a positive choice, with many experts now arguing that children are actually better off in the long run if their parents terminate a bad relationship than if they maintain that relationship for the sake of the children.[14] At any rate, many of the divorced in our study had to overcome major concerns about what their decision would mean for their children before they were willing to go ahead with the action.

Religious constraints to divorce, like legal and attitudinal constraints, are probably less significant today than they have been in the past. Most religious organizations now recognize divorce as a means for terminating an unsatisfactory relationship. This has not always been the case. In addition, there is less religious stigma associated with divorce than has been true in the past. Nevertheless, a great many people have internalized beliefs which say that divorce is bad and indicative of failure or even personal sinfulness on their part. Largely as a consequence of this, personal religious beliefs came in third in the list of most frequently mentioned barriers that had to be overcome in making the decision to go ahead with the divorce. Religious beliefs were more likely to be listed as a barrier by women than by men.

Religious barriers to divorce were also mentioned by an additional 20 of the respondents, though in a somewhat different context. These individuals indicated that they had to overcome concerns about negative counsel received from their religious leaders. Apparently in these cases, the person himself or herself did not have serious personal religious reservations about obtaining the divorce but was counseled against the action by a religious leader.

While it has been noted that significant changes in many states in recent years have led to the liberalization of divorce laws, the fourth most frequently mentioned barrier to divorce was the difficulty of divorce laws. It is not possible for us to say whether these legal barriers were real or perceived barriers for the respondents. If one is unaware that the divorce laws in one's state have been liberalized, then one may perceive legal constraints as being a greater barrier than they really are. On the other hand, some states do have much tougher divorce laws than do others and for some, the realization of this may cause the individual to think that in a comparative sense, the difficulty of their state's divorce laws constitute a very real barrier to obtaining a divorce. A total of 64 of the respondents identified this as a barrier to be overcome in reaching their decision. Males were twice as likely as females to define this as an important barrier.

The one other factor that received frequent mention as a barrier to divorce—mentioned by 55 of the respondents—was concern about one's parents. In some instances, parents may have actively opposed the decision. In others, the person may have been hesitant because of the embarrassment they felt their decision would cause for their family. Again, this is probably not as significant a factor as it has been in the past, if only because less stigma is now attached to divorce. However, for some of the respondents it was a pressing concern.

The Decision to Divorce: Overcoming Barriers

Because we are dealing with a sample of divorced persons, it is obvious that each of the individuals involved successfully overcame barriers before divorce could be obtained. According to the social exchange framework discussed above, this implies that being "unmarried" was perceived as being less costly or more rewarding than being married. Most of the subjects rightly perceived that there would be important costs associated with their decision. However, *not to* pursue the divorce was seen as even more costly. Using Thibaut and Kelly's[15] terms, the comparison level for alternatives was higher than present outcomes. Or, as

Levinger[16] has stated it, "even if internal attractions are low and barriers offer minimal restraint, a relationship will not be terminated unless an alternative seems more attractive." The alternative need not be another man or another woman. In many instances, it can be singlehood or simply escape from a bad relationship. Of course, this argument only applies to the degree that the respondent actually had control over the divorce decision. If the divorce was initiated by the other spouse, then it is less valid.

These alternatives can be viewed as factors that facilitate or ease the divorce decision. However, other factors such as social support from family and friends might also ease the decision to divorce even though they cannot be considered as alternatives to the marital state. To identify circumstances that helped individuals overcome the barriers noted earlier, including available alternatives, each respondent was asked to identify factors that influenced them in actually seeking a divorce. Table 35 summarizes responses to this question.

The numbers in Table 35 suggest that the single most important factor involved in the decision to go ahead with the divorce despite the stress and trauma associated with such an action was individual personal unhappiness. Female respondents listed this as the most important factor, while for males it was tied for second. The previous table (Table 34) suggests that most of the respondents quite clearly recognized that important costs would be associated with their decision but when the costs associated with staying with the relationship became so high that they outweighed the costs associated with leaving, they left. It is important to recognize, too, that feelings of personal unhappiness are often of a comparative nature. That is, individuals compare their own relationships with those of other couples around them or their own past experience and, as a consequence of such comparisons, feel relatively deprived or satisfied. As has been noted earlier, most of our sample of divorced persons perceived their former marriages to be less satisfying than were the marriages of other couples they knew. Thus, not only were they unhappy but they also perceived that many others with whom they could compare their relationships were much happier with their marriages. This feeling of relative deprivation probably made their situations even more unbearable.

The second most frequently mentioned factor which influenced the decision to divorce was closely related to feelings of personal unhappiness. A total of 58 of the respondents (12 percent of both males and females) simply stated that their decision was most influenced by their desire to get out of a bad situation. Again, in terms of a cost-reward analysis, getting out of a bad relationship was less costly than the alternative of staying with it. Conversely, rewards associated with that decision outweighed the concomitant costs.

It was noted above that the most frequent barrier to seeking a divorce among our respondents was financial concerns. The removal of these financial constraints was ranked as the third most important factor in influencing the respondent to obtain the divorce. A total of 50 of the respondents reported that the opportunities

Table 35
Factors Influencing Decision to Divorce

Factor	Males N	Males %	Females N	Females %	Total N	Total %
			Frequency of Mention			
Personal Unhappiness	18	11	59	19	77	16
Own Desires to Get Out of Bad Situation	19	12	39	12	58	12
Opportunities for Alternative Financial Support	11	7	39	12	50	11
Became Involved with Someone Else	19	12	23	7	42	9
Ease of Divorce Laws	18	11	21	7	39	8
Children's Desires	4	3	32	10	36	8
Parents' Desires	14	9	19	6	33	7
Spouse Made the Decision	18	11	14	4	32	7
Never Loved Each Other	8	5	15	5	23	5
Approval of Religious Leader	2	1	16	5	18	4
Children Grew Up and Left Home	9	6	8	3	17	4
Divorced Friends	10	6	5	2	15	3
Desertion	5	3	8	3	13	3
Non-Divorced Friends	3	2	5	2	8	2
Other	2	1	10	3	12	3
Totals	(160)	(100)	(313)	(100)	(473)	(102)

for alternative financial support was the major factor which influenced their decision. As would be expected, this was more important for women than men. In many instances financial alternatives for women probably included obtaining a job. In fact, some commentators have argued that increased financial independence created by a larger number of women entering the labor force is a prime factor that has contributed to high divorce rates in recent years. Westoff,[17] for example, notes that the opening up of the job market gives women greater opportunity and independence than they have had before. The effect is that a woman who might have hung on to a marriage in the past is now much more willing to leave a relationship that isn't working or a marriage that falls short of some ideal. Scanzoni [18] also notes that as women obtain additional options (often as a result of educational and economic achievements) they can afford to become tougher bargainers in the marriage relationship. Greater access to a wide range of rewards alternative to those supplied by their husbands increases the probability of choosing the option of divorce if they are dissatisfied with the nature of the relationship they have in their marriage.

A fairly large number of the members of our sample reported that the key factor in their decision to divorce was advice received from someone else. Thirty-six reported that it was their children's desire that they divorce (more important for women than men), 33 said that their parents advised in favor of the divorce (more important for men), 15 reported that friends who had obtained divorces counseled them to do likewise, 8 received similar advice from non-divorced friends, and 12 reported that some other person (such as a co-worker, a legal adviser, etc.) influenced them in making the decision. It is apparent from these responses that many persons who choose to divorce rely quite heavily on advice received from others. If we combine all of the factors in Table 35 that involve receiving advice from someone else to complete the divorce process, we find that of the 376 persons who listed specific persons or events that played a major role in their decision, 152 of these and 40 percent made reference to advice or influence from someone else.

The advice received from children may be somewhat surprising but is consistent with clinical findings reported by Rosen. Rosen found that 73 out of 92 children included in her clinical study of the effects of divorce stated in the strongest terms that they would not have chosen to have their parents stay together in conflict. She further reports that "it emerged clearly from what these children said that it was the tensions and hostilities in the marriage rather than the divorce per se which had disturbed them the most."[19] Some sample quotes:

"I remember horrible strife and conflict; a nightmare that would have killed me had it not ended."

"The marriage was the trauma, not the divorce."

"Staying together would be the worst thing they could have done; the quarrels would be so upsetting."

One other factor from Table 35 that probably deserves some special mention is the fact that 39 respondents reported that the key factor in influencing them to finally go ahead with the decision to divorce was the ease of the divorce laws. It will be remembered that a much larger number reported that the difficulty of divorce laws was a prime barrier that they had to overcome in their reaching the decision they did. Thus, it appears that the degree of liberality of a state's divorce laws can be seen both as a help and a hindrance in couples making the decision they do to terminate their marriage. However, it is probably a relatively safe conclusion that when a marriage gets bad enough, one or the other or both of the individuals involved are likely to begin to consider other alternatives, whatever the constraints that are imposed by the law.[20]

In summary, the data in Table 35 imply that the decision to divorce was more influenced by respondent's consideration of the *costs* of the present relationship than by alternatives available to them. Thus, personal unhappiness was perceived was perceived as more important than the availability of alternative financial support or involvement with some other person. Present costs, then, seem more important than alternative rewards.

Family and Friends: Explicit and Implicit Approval of Divorce

Often before the person makes the final decision to terminate what has been defined as a bad marriage, there is some assessment of the degree to which significant others, such as parents and friends, would concur with and support that decision. Miller[21] has noted that "friends are often consulted when one or both partners are considering a divorce. They can shift the balance toward decision to divorce or continuation of the marriage." Miller also notes that the reaction of friends often determines the form the divorce takes and the behavior of the divorcees after it is finalized. Since divorce involves a great deal of trauma and stress and since very few individuals are able to cope with that alone, they frequently look to others who are important to them for guidance and, once the decision has been made, for support of that decision. Two types of approval can be noted. Explicit approval is given when family and friends make it known to the individual that they agree that they should go ahead with the decision to obtain a divorce. In fact, in many instances that decision may only be made after such explicit approval has been granted. In a sense, this involves the other party saying that what the individual is doing, though difficult, is right and given the same circumstances, the other party would probably make the same decision.

Implicit approval may be considered as more behavioral. For example, have parents and friends themselves gone through a divorce? While such individuals may not come right out and say that they approve of such an action, the fact that they have experienced a divorce in their own lives says to the person that they deem divorce an acceptable alternative to a bad relationship.

As can be seen from the figures in Table 36, a clear majority of our respondents felt that close friends and family gave explicit approval to their decision to obtain a divorce. When asked to indicate what percentage of their friends and family approved of their decision, 41 percent of the respondents overall said that "all of them" did. However, females are much more likely to feel they had support from family and friends than were males. Two-thirds of the female respondents said that at least 75 percent of family and friends supported their decision. This was true of 47 percent of males. On the other hand, 12 percent of both sexes reported that none of their close friends and family supported their decision. Given the difficulty associated with divorce in the best of circumstances, it is hard to imagine how it would be if one received no social support for the decision from those whose opinions would mean most. While such instances are uncommon, one can only assume that such divorces are especially traumatic.

Table 36
Percent of Family and Close Friends Who Approved of Divorce

	Males		Females		Total	
	N	%	N	%	N	%
None of them	28	15	28	10	56	12
Less than 25%	26	13	18	6	44	9
25-50%	27	14	24	9	51	11
50-75%	22	11	23	8	45	10
More than 75% but not all	27	14	58	21	85	18
All of them	63	33	130	46	193	41
Totals	(193)	(100)	(281)	(100)	(474)	(101)

What percent of our divorced sample have close friends and family members who are also divorced? When talking about social support for divorce this also becomes a primary question because the fact that others have chosen this alternative offers, at least to some extent, a stamp of approval for one's own action. Table 37 reveals that 83 percent of the sample report that they have some close friends who have gotten divorces.[22] The most common response is for the subject to report that "a few" of their close friends are divorced (79 percent). While just 13 percent report that "most" or "all" of their close friends are divorced, the fact is that a large majority of the respondents have been or are acquainted with divorce through the experience of friends. Male and female responses were virtually identical on this question.

While there is some evidence in the literature that divorce tends to run in families in the sense that parents who divorce are more likely to have children who will divorce, our respondents were more likely to have divorced friends than divorced family members. Twenty-four percent report that their parents have been divorced and almost the same number (25 percent) report that spouse's parents have been divorced.

On the other hand, almost half of the respondents report that one or more of their own brothers or sisters have obtained a divorce and somewhat fewer (41 percent) report that one or more of their ex-spouse's brothers or sisters have obtained a divorce. A majority in both instances have brothers and sisters with stable marriages but many have experienced divorce within the context of their families. Sixteen percent reported that two or more of their own brothers and sisters have divorced and 14 percent report this to be the case for the ex-spouse's brothers and sisters.

Although most of the respondents admit that they were influenced in their

Table 37
Percent of Close Friends Who Are Divorced

| | Males | | Females | | Total | |
	N	%	N	%	N	%
None	38	19	48	17	86	18
A Few	141	69	204	71	345	70
Most of Them	25	12	33	11	58	12
All of them	--	--	3	1	3	1
Totals	(204)	(100)	(288)	(100)	(492)	(101)

Table 38
Percentage of Respondents Whose Own or Former Spouse's Parents Were Divorced

| | Parents Divorced | | | | | | | Spouse's Parents Divorced | | | | | |
| | Males | | Females | | Total | | | Males | | Females | | Total | |
	N	%	N	%	N	%		N	%	N	%	N	%
Yes	48	23	69	24	117	24	Yes	49	25	71	25	120	25
No	157	47	222	76	379	76	No	151	75	217	75	368	75
	(205)	(100)	(291)	(100)	(496)	(100)		(200)	(100)	(288)	(100)	(488)	(100)

decision to obtain a divorce by either the explicit or implicit approval of others, very few of them feel that their own actions have caused someone else to make the decision to terminate their own marriage. For example, when asked if their own divorce had encouraged anyone else to divorce, 87 percent responded that to their knowledge, this was not the case. Nine percent felt that their own action may have had a little influence on the decision of others, 2 percent reported that they felt their decision had had somewhat of an influence, and just 1 percent (five of the respondents) said that their own action had had a great deal of influence in encouraging someone else to obtain a divorce.

In summary, to a great extent those in our study who are divorced say their action received a stamp of approval from family members and others close to them. Many others have witnessed divorce among parents, siblings, or close friends. Very few of our respondents stood alone without approval from significant others or without knowing something of the experience of others with

Table 39
Divorce Experience of Own and Spouse's Brothers and Sisters

Number of Own Brothers and Sisters Divorced	Males N	%	Females N	%	Total N	%
0	105	53	152	55	257	54
1	65	33	80	29	145	31
2	18	9	29	10	47	10
3	8	4	9	3	17	4
4	1	1	7	3	8	2
5	-	-	1	-	1	-
Totals	(197)	(100)	(278)	(100)	(475)	(101)

Number of Spouse's Brothers and Sisters Divorced	Males N	%	Females N	%	Total N	%
0	118	64	153	58	271	61
1	49	26	71	27	120	27
2	12	6	26	10	38	9
3	4	2	7	3	11	2
4	2	1	2	1	4	1
5	-	-	3	5	3	1
Totals	(185)	(99)	(262)	(100)	(467)	(101)

whom they were somewhat close. No doubt this feeling of understanding and support from significant others plays an important role in reaching the decision.

Initiating Divorce Action: Wife's Primary Role

The literature suggests than when the decision is finally reached that a divorce is to be sought, it is more likely to be the female rather than the male who initiates the procedure.[23] This notion is strongly supported by our data. Table 41 summarizes our findings.

The difference in perceptions of male and female respondents to the question of who initiated the divorce procedure is notable: 49 percent of the males said that they took the first step while 51 percent say the action was started by their wives. On the other hand, fully 81 percent of the female respondents reported that they were the ones who started the procedure while only 19 percent attributed the initiation of the divorce action to their husbands. While there is an important difference in these perceptions, both sexes do agree that the wife is the more probable initiator of the divorce action. This suggests that the wife in divorce situations is more likely to be designated (by self or others) as the "injured party" and the one most likely to seek some redress through legal action. (It should be recognized that states with no-fault divorce laws no longer require the labeling of one or the other partner as the "injured party.")

Final Effort to Save the Marriage: Effects of Marital Counseling

In many deteriorating marriages, there are points at which some form of counseling or other professional aid might be critical in helping to put the marriage back on more even ground. More and more individuals, particularly among the middle and upper classes, are seeking such professional help in improving the quality of their relationships. While the admission that professional help is needed is still difficult for most people, it does not carry the negative stigma that it once did. In addition, such help is more readily available now than it has been at any other time and while the potential financial costs entailed may act as a barrier for some couples, the low or no-cost services provided by many public and church-related agencies now puts marriage and family counseling within the reach of practically anyone who is willing to seek it.

Even when counseling is obtained, however, it may not resolve the problems involved. There are many reasons, for example, the marital relationship may have been so damaged before a couple seeks outside help that little can be done to resolve their problems. In other cases, one of the pair may accept counseling reluctantly and only at the insistence of the other partner or outside person or agency. This individual may harbor such negative feelings about what is happening that he or she may actually overtly sabotage what the counselor is trying to accomplish. In other cases, neither of the partners may be willing to pay the

Table 40
Has Own Divorce Encouraged Anyone Else to Divorce

	Males N	Males %	Females N	Females %	Total N	Total %
Not to My Knowledge	180	88	250	87	430	87
Perhaps a Little	17	8	29	10	46	9
Yes, Somewhat	4	2	7	2	11	2
Quite a Bit	2	1	-	-	2	-
A Great Deal	2	1	3	1	5	1
Totals	(205)	(100)	(289)	(100)	(494)	(99)

Table 41
Who Initiates Divorce Action

Initiators of Divorce Action	Males N	Males %	Females N	Females %	Total N	Total %
Self	98	49	223	81	321	56
Spouse	103	51	53	19	256	44
Totals	(201)	(100)	(276)	(100)	(577)	(100)

price that the professional feels would be required to make some improvement in the relationship. Counseling may be started but then terminated before observable progress has been made.

Despite these considerations, we decided to determine the proportion of our sample of divorced persons who had some form of professional marriage counseling and their evaluations of the effectiveness of this counseling in aiding them in resolving their problems. It must be recognized, of course, that we are dealing with a biased sample from the perspective of the marriage counselor, in that we are dealing exclusively with what could be referred to as cases of failure. Adequate comparisons would require including samples of still-married persons who have also received counseling in order to assess the role that counseling may have played in helping them to improve their marriage.

A total of 491 of the subjects responded to the question of marital counseling and of this number, 127 reported that they had received professional help of some type. Eighty percent, or 101 of these 127 persons who reported having received counseling reported that it did not help. The remaining 26 observed that the help came primarily in the form of easing the divorce process rather than making the marriage better. For those who had received counseling, then, the evaluation of its effectiveness was overwhelmingly negative.

Almost as many persons as had received counseling reported that while they had not received professional help, it was their feeling that such help may have saved their marriage or otherwise improved their relationship with their spouse. However, a much larger number of the sample (51 percent of the total) reported that they had received no counseling and that it would have made *no* difference anyway. Again, while these figures give a rather negative impression of the utility of marriage counseling in improving the quality of deteriorating marriages, it must be recognized that we are dealing with only one side of the picture. There may be a great number of strong marriages that have become such through the aid of professional counseling. None of these would be tapped by our data because we are dealing, by definition, with cases of failure.

Summary

This chapter has dealt with the very complex question of how individuals reach the decision to divorce. While we do not assume that all important factors of that decision have received sufficient attention, nevertheless some of the most critical were identified and discussed. Some considerations of this decision are, by their very nature, intrinsically conflicting. For example, perceptions of what is best for children can move one both toward and away from a decision to seek the termination of a relationship. Our analysis at least gives some idea of the factors that people evaluate and weigh in making this critical choice.

We have stressed that even when marriages have gone bad, it is almost never easy for the individuals involved to make the decision to terminate marriages through divorce. Breaking close ties with others with whom we have shared strong emotional and other attachments is always a painful experience both within and outside the marital bond. It is especially difficult within the marital relationship because of the range of possessions and activities that married couples have usually shared.

When the decision to terminate a marriage is made, it is often only after a careful consideration of reward-cost outcomes. When the costs of maintaining a relationship become too high, even "good" marriages can terminate. Conversely, when the costs of terminating a relationship are higher than those associated with maintaining it, even "bad" marriages can continue for long periods of time. Using concepts developed by Thibaut and Kelly,[24] it has been suggested that perceived happiness and satisfaction with a marriage are assessed by comparing the outcomes associated with that marriage with a standard or comparison level developed by each individual based on prior experience and observed experience of others. Stability or permanence of the marriage, however, is more likely to be based on the extent to which that relationship measures up to what could be obtained from any of a number of other alternatives. ''Good'' marriages end when more attractive alternatives appear on the scene. ''Bad'' marriages often endure because the alternatives available to the individuals involved are less attractive than what exists in the marriage. This consideration of costs and rewards has been referred to in other contexts[25] as an assessment of barriers and attractions associated with a given relationship. Both of these perspectives, as well as several others, are useful in considering the decision to seek a divorce.

The most frequent problem identified in the marriages of our respondents as leading to marital failure was infidelity or unfaithfulness on the part of one's spouse. About one-third of the divorced members of the sample reported that their spouse had been unfaithful. Next most important in the list of major problems was an expression of loss of love. Other frequently listed problems were financial difficulties, emotional problems, and physical abuse. Since all of these are important costs associated with the effort to maintain a relationship, they can be considered crucial in adversely affecting the reward-cost balance that is often rather precarious in most marriage situations.

Even though the costs of trying to maintain a marriage may mount, there remain barriers operating to inhibit a decision in favor of divorce. Among our respondents, the most important barriers included financial concerns, impacts of divorce on children, and implications for personal religious beliefs. Financial concerns were especially evident among female respondents who are most likely to feel the economic pinch associated with a divorce. Religious constraints may be less binding today than a few years ago but were still important considerations for a significant segment of the sample.

All of the respondents were, of course, successful in overcoming these barriers. Primary reasons included their high degree of personal unhappiness and the strong desire to end what had become a very difficult relationship. The availability of alternatives was also a feature noted by many of the respondents. For example, opportunities for alternative financial support was especially important for female respondents and involvement with someone else as an alternative source of emotional and sexual gratification was a major factor for some members of both sexes.

Because of the trauma and stress usually associated with the decision to divorce, support for that decision by close friends and family members was usually meaningful to respondents. Friends and family members often shifted the decision either in favor of or in opposition to seeking a divorce. The overwhelming majority of the respondents reported that they had been supported in their decision by a significant proportion of family and close friends. Many of the respondents could also be perceived as receiving implicit approval for their action from the fact that members of their own families as well as close friends had, themselves, already gone through the experience of obtaining a divorce. Whatever the role of these sources of social support in the divorce decision, it is usually the female who initiates the divorce action. Both sexes agreed that this was the case, though females were much more likely than males to attribute the role of initiator to the wife.

Once the marriages of our respondents had deteriorated to the point that one or both spouses were considering divorce action, professional counseling was of little help in righting the situation. While many respondents had received professional counseling, the overwhelming majority of these reported that counseling was of little help in improving their marriage. Among those who had not received such professional assistance, a majority were of the opinion that it would not have helped anyway. Apparently we are dealing with situations in which costs associated with maintaining a relationship are so high that the likelihood of saving the relationship is slim.

Perhaps the most important observation to make here is that the increased availability of alternative sources of financial support as well as companionship and gratification, especially for women, will be critical in understanding future divorce trends. There is no question that the position of women has changed dramatically and this has had an impact on marriage and marital stability. As the educational level of women continues to increase, as more and more make their way in the world of employment, as more choose to delay marriage or delay or even forego having children, women's bargaining power increases and their ability to leave an unhappy or unsatisfying relationship is greater.[26] The data are clear in indicating that women who have the potential for economic independence are more likely to leave a marriage than are women with none. In the past, the costs of leaving a marriage for women may have been higher than the rewards—even when the marriage was not a good one—now the benefits are seen as outweighing the costs.

NOTES

1. Jessie Bernard, "No News, But New Ideas," in Paul Bohannan (ed.), *Divorce and After* (Garden City, N.Y.: Doubleday, 1970), p. 3.

2. Gerald Lenthall, "Marital Satisfaction and Marital Stability," *Journal of Marriage and Family Counseling* (October 1977): 25.

3. Mary W. Hicks and M. Platt, "Marital Happiness and Stability: A Review of the Research in the Sixties," *Journal of Marriage and the Family* 32 (1970): 553-74.

4. J. W. Thibaut and H. H. Kelly, *The Social Psychology of Groups* (New York: John Wiley, 1959).

5. George C. Homans, "Social Behavior as Exchange," *American Journal of Sociology* 63 (1958): 597-606; *Social Behavior: Its Elementary Forms* (New York: Harcourt Brace Jovanovich, 1974).

6. Thibaut and Kelly, *The Social Psychology of Groups*.

7. George Levinger, "Marital Cohesiveness and Dissolution: An Integrative Review," *Journal of Marriage and the Family* (1965): 19-28; "A Social Psychological Perspective on Marital Dissolution," *Journal of Social Issues* (no. 1, 1976): 21-47.

8. Gary Becker, "A Theory of Marriage: Part I," *Journal of Political Economy* 81

(July/August 1973): 813-46; "A Theory of Marriage: Part II," *Journal of Political Economy* 82 (March/April 1974): Sll-S26; *The Economic Approach to Human Behavior* (Chicago: University of Chicago Press, 1976); Gary Becker, Elisabeth Landes, and Robert Michael, "An Economic Analysis of Marital Instability," *Journal of Political Economy* 85 (December): 1141-87; Joan Huber and Glenna Spitze, "Considering Divorce: An Expansion of Becker's Theory of Marital Instability," *American Journal of Sociology* 86 (1980): 75-89.

9. Erving Goffman, *The Presentation of Self in Everyday Life* (Garden City, N.Y.: Doubleday and Co., 1959).

10. Thibaut and Kelly, *The Social Psychology of Groups*.

11. Maggie P. Hayes, Nick Stinnett, and John DeFrain, "Learning About Marriage from the Divorced," *Journal of Divorce* 4 (Fall 1980): 23-29.

12. Levinger, "A Social Psychological Perspective on Marital Dissolution," p. 26.

13. Arthur J. Norton and Paul C. Glick, "Marital Instability in America: Past, Present, and Future," pp. 6-19 in George Levinger and Oliver C. Moles (eds.), *Divorce and Separation: Context, Causes, and Consequences* (New York: Basic Books, 1979).

14. Rhona Rosen, "Children of Divorce: What They Feel About Access and Other Aspects of the Divorce Experience," *Journal of Clinical Child Psychology* (Summer 1977): 24-27; Deborah A. Luepnitz, "Which Aspects of Divorce Affect Children?" *Family Coordinator* (January 1979): 79-85.

15. Thibaut and Kelly, *The Social Psychology of Groups*.

16. Levinger, "A Social Psychological Perspective on Marital Dissolution," p. 40.

17. Leslie Aldridge Westoff, *The Second Time Around: Remarriage in America* (New York: Viking Press, 1977).

18. John Scanzoni, "A Historical Perspective on Husband-Wife Bargaining Power and Marital Dissolution," pp. 20-36 in George Levinger and Oliver C. Moles (eds.), *Divorce and Separation: Context, Causes, and Consequences*.

19. Rosen, "Children of Divorce," p. 24.

20. For a well-developed discussion of this point, see M. Rheinstein, *Marriage Stability, Divorce, and the Law* (Chicago: University of Chicago Press, 1972).

21. Arthur A. Miller, "Reactions of Friends to Divorce," in Paul Bohannan (ed.), *Divorce and After* (Garden City, N.Y.: Doubleday, 1970), p. 74.

22. It should be noted that the time referent on this question is particularly ambiguous. That is, close friends sometimes change with the passage of time and the number of *current* close friends who have divorced may or may not be a good measure of the number who were divorced when the decision to terminate a marriage was made by the respondent.

23. For an excellent discussion of this in a historical context, see Scanzoni, "Historical Perspective on Husband-Wife Bargaining Power and Marital Dissolution"; see also Antonette M. Zeiss, Robert A. Zeiss, and Stephen M. Johnson, "Sex Differences in Initiation of and Adjustment to Divorce," *Journal of Divorce* 4 (Winter 1980): 21-33.

24. Thibaut and Kelly, *The Social Psychology of Groups*.

25. See Levinger, "Marital Cohesiveness and Dissolution"; "A Social Psychological Perspective on Marital Dissolution."

26. Scanzoni, "Historical Perspective on Husband-Wife Bargaining Power and Marital Dissolution."

Chapter 5

Reactions to Divorce
and Adjustments After

Introduction

Chapter four reviewed the major factors that figured in the decision made by our respondents to terminate their marriages. Specific attention was given to the types of problems most influential in leading a husband and wife to choose divorce over the option of continuing to try and make a life together. We also reviewed the major barriers to divorce, such as the presence of children and individual religious beliefs. In this chapter we turn to the period following that fateful choice. How do the partners involved react to the divorce experience? What are its personal costs for them? What happens during the actual divorce process in such areas as personal contact and living arrangements? What kinds of settlements are made and how do the people involved react to those settlements? And, most importantly, how do individuals who have gone through a divorce begin to put their lives together again and are they able to do that successfully?

As noted earlier, each year for almost two decades, divorce has affected an increasing number of Americans. We are fast moving toward the time when having a direct experience with divorce (either one's own, or that of one's parents or offspring) will be the norm. This means that an ever-increasing number of individuals are having to deal with the problems of reestablishing order and continuity to a life that has been disrupted (often severely) by a divorce. However, high-quality research dealing with how persons who experience divorce adjust to that experience is still relatively rare. Rose and Price-Bonham [1] have argued that since Goode's [2] study of divorced women in Detroit, research has been concerned only tangentially with the problem of adjustment to divorce.

Clearly, adequate additional research dealing with the comparative ease or difficulty of adjustment of the male divorcee relative to the female divorcee is lacking. For example, Weiss[3] notes that "as yet there have been no survey studies comparable to Goode's in which men as well as women were interviewed." While Goode[4] argues that the experience of women in divorce may not be particularly different from those of men, data specifically comparing the two are sorely needed (see also Weiss).[5] Because of the paucity of prior work comparing the experience of men and women in divorce, such comparisons will receive special attention in this chapter.

Divorce as Stress-Inducing

When two people have been intimately involved in a marital relationship for a period of time, the dissolution of that relationship usually entails some degree of pain and stress. The literature includes numerous reports which suggest that the newly divorced are likely to suffer at least some amount of personal disorganization, anxiety, unhappiness, loneliness, low work efficiency, increased drinking, and other problem behaviors.[6]

Much of the literature was recently summarized by Bloom, White, and Asher[7] who note the major impacts of marital disruption in several specific areas listed below.

Psychopathology. "Of all the social variables relating to the distribution of psychopathology in the population, none has been more consistently found to be so crucial for the population than marital status. Persons who are divorced or separated have been repeatedly found to be over-represented among psychiatric patients, while persons who are married and living with their spouses have been found to be under-represented. . . . Admission rates into psychiatric facilities are lowest among the married, intermediate among widowed and never-married adults, and highest among the divorced and separated."[8] These authors note further that the ratio of admissions for divorced and separated persons to those for married persons into inpatient facilities varies from 7 to 1 to 22 to 1 for males and from 3 to 1 to 8 to 1 for females.

Motor Vehicle Accidents. Statistics on automobile fatalities and accident rates indicate that the divorced are far more vulnerable than are the married or single persons. For example, Bloom, White, and Asher cite research that indicates that automobile fatality rates average about three times as high among the divorced as among the married and the accident rate of persons undergoing divorce doubles during the period between six months before and six months after the divorce date.

Divorce Morbidity. There is a long tradition of research that suggests that life stress is strongly linked with a variety of physical illnesses. Marital disruption generally ranks as one of the most serious life stress events; therefore, one would anticipate a relationship between marital disruption and a variety of other problems. One of the most clearly established links is that between divorce and drinking-related problems. Bloom, White, and Asher point to several studies indicating that alcoholism is more prevalent among the divorced than among the married. They also cite Carter and Glick's[9] conclusion that "a relatively large proportion of people who have serious trouble with their health are likely to have serious trouble in becoming married, maintaining a viable marriage, or becoming remarried."

Suicide, Homicide, and Disease Mortality. Bloom, White, and Asher summarize the literature concerning suicide, homicide, and illness by noting that several "sources of data serve to link marital disruption to deaths from suicide, homicide, and from specific diseases. The maritally disrupted are consistently found to be over-represented among all three groups."[10]

Few couples get married without believing that they love or hold otherwise positive attractions toward one another. The literature on stress strongly suggests that the fact that love has dimmed or that attraction has faded does not mean that termination of the relationship may be considered lightly or is without great difficulty and heartache for one or both of the partners. We should note that the amount of stress experienced may rise when there are children and the estranged couple realize that their decision affects the lives of others as well.

As a measure of the amount of stress associated with divorce experienced by the respondents in the Intermountain Divorce Study, each was asked to characterize that experience. The responses to this question are summarized in Table 42.

Looking at the total sample first, almost a quarter of all respondents characterized their divorce experience as traumatic, even a "nightmare." Most of the others reported some degree of stress but not at the level of this first quarter. Thirty percent stated that the experience had been stressful but could have been worse, and an additional 10 percent said that the experience was more stressful than it should have been but was bearable. One-fifth reported the experience to be unsettling in that normal patterns of interaction and behavior were disrupted but felt that it was actually easier than they had anticipated. For a minority (17 percent) the experience was reported as relatively painless. Apparently in the latter cases, the couple had little or no difficulty in reaching an agreement on what was to be done, both agreed on the nature of the settlement, and other lives were little affected by the decision. However, such cases are rare and in most instances, people are hurt and lives are changed and disrupted.

It should be noted that there is some debate in the literature on the question of comparative stress of divorce for women and men. For example, Bernard[11] argues that the psychological costs are greatest for men. Our findings tend to contradict this point for several reasons. Perhaps the most important was recently identified by Glenn.[12] He notes, "Men may more often than women have strong sources of self-esteem other than their performance in their family roles. Whereas some aspects of man's life may be relatively unaffected by a divorce, it is unlikely that any important aspect of a woman's life will not change." In other words, the woman's self-identity is more likely to be closely intertwined with home and family. Since divorce impacts most heavily on these very things, it

Table 42

Characterization of Experience in Seeking and Obtaining Divorce

Characterization	Males N	Males %	Females N	Females %	Total N	Total %
Traumatic Experience, a Nightmare	31	16	79	27	110	23
Stressful but Could Have Been Worse	58	30	89	31	147	30
More Stressful Than Should Have Been, but Bearable	21	11	28	10	49	10
Unsettling, but Easier Than Anticipated	45	23	54	19	99	20
Relatively Painless	40	21	40	14	80	17
Totals	(195)	(101)	(290)	(101)	(485)	(99)

is understandable that her world is likely to be more shattered than is true for the male.

This idea is supported by recent qualitative research by Wise.[13] Her study dealt with divorced women who were all long-married, members of middle- and upper-middle-class families with children still living at home. Wise notes that all of these women were functioning well enough, at least overtly. They all maintained well-run homes and took good care of themselves and their children. They were not part of a clinical population and did not define themselves as being in need of psychological intervention. Nevertheless, she states: "I found that all these women, one to four years postseparation, were experiencing considerable psychological distress: depression, anger, feelings of vulnerability, low self-esteem, preoccupation with loss, fears of loneliness and aging, awareness of loss of status, fears about financial security and lack of support systems, feelings of being incomplete without a husband, difficulties coping with parenting pressure, and reconciliation fantasies."

A second factor (which will receive more attention later in this chapter) is that the impact of divorce on women is frequently greatest in the financial area. This can result in severe financial strains and, often, poverty—conditions found to be associated with poor divorce adjustment.[14]

It is clear that the divorcing person is faced with a number of important losses. These include not just loss of spouse but, in many instances, economic loss, loss of friends, loss of regular contact with children, and loss of place in the community. The specific losses differ from situation to situation. As we shall see, the father who loses custody of his children is likely to respond quite differently than the divorced male who had no children; both may have quite different experiences than does the woman who gains custody of children in the divorce proceedings. In other words, the traumas of divorce come from a number of sources but the combined effect of these, at least for our respondents, creates a more difficult overall experience for women than for men.

Numerous factors were identified by our respondents as contributing to the trauma associated with their own divorce. A few identified the legal process itself by noting bad experiences with lawyers or courts. Others made reference to the pain and anguish felt by the children or to the financial strain. The most common factor identified as making the divorce so traumatic and stressful, however, was simply a feeling of personal failure. Almost one-third of all respondents made reference to this one item. It was noted in chapter four that one of the primary barriers that individuals must overcome in deciding to seek a divorce is the feeling of obligation to keep a relationship intact even when it is not a good relationship. Most persons have internalized the belief that marriages are not temporary relationships and that upon entering them, we are making a commitment to their permanence. Thus, despite increasingly liberal attitudes toward divorce, its occurrence in one's life is still seen as an admission of failure and this feeling of having failed appears to be the key factor in causing trauma and stress for the divorced person.

Periods of Greatest Stress

While much has been said and written about the trauma of divorce, and while it is generally accepted that going through a divorce is extremely difficult *no matter how bad the marriage was*, for most of our respondents the price paid in terminating the marriage appears to have been worth it. This conclusion is reached from an assessment of responses to questions which asked the respondents to evaluate the relative difficulty for them of different periods of time both before and after the divorce. First, they were asked which of the following periods was most difficult for them and then which of the periods was best for them and their children: (1) before the decision to divorce; (2) after deciding to divorce but before the final decree; (3) the period just after the divorce; or (4) now. Table 43 summarizes responses to these questions.

According to our sample of respondents, the period before the decision to divorce was the most difficult one. This was a period of increasing conflict between the spouses and a time when increasing consideration was being given to choosing divorce as an alternative to a bad relationship. Fully 55 percent of all the respondents identified this as the most difficult time for them, with females somewhat more likely than males to make this choice.

For a majority, then, once the decision was made to go ahead with the divorce things got better. However, for others, more difficult times were still ahead.

Table 43
Characterization of Worst and Best Periods in Obtaining Divorce

Time Period	Most Difficult Time						Best Time for Self and Children					
	Males		Females		Total		Males		Females		Total	
	N	%	N	%	N	%	N	%	N	%	N	%
Before Decision to Divorce	99	50	169	58	268	55	42	22	20	7	62	13
After Deciding but Before the Final Decree	49	25	57	20	106	22	9	5	17	6	26	6
The Period Just After	47	23	56	19	103	21	25	13	40	15	65	14
Now	5	2	8	3	13	3	117	61	194	72	311	67
Totals	(200)	(100)	(290)	(100)	(490)	(101)	(193)	(101)	(271)	(100)	(484)	(100)

Twenty-two percent of all respondents said that the most difficult time occurred after they decided to obtain a divorce but before the final decree was granted. Apparently this was a time of loneliness, self-doubt, and fear about the future and what it would hold. Another 21 percent defined the most difficult period as time immediately following the divorce.

Once one has made it through the decision, the final decree, and the period immediately following, things apparently get much better. Only three percent of the sample identified the present as the most difficult time.

Turning to the other side of the picture, when respondents were asked to specify which period was *best* for them *and their children*, two-thirds chose the present period. However, for the other third of the sample, some earlier time period was defined as better. Thirteen percent felt that the time prior to the decision to divorce had been best. For many of these, the divorce may have been initiated by a spouse toward whom they still felt a good deal of affection. For others, difficulties associated with facing the world or raising children alone may be more stressful than living in an unhappy marriage. Husbands were *three times* as likely as wives to rate the pre-divorce period as better for themselves and their children. Part of this is a function of the fact that wives are more likely to gain custody of children when the divorce is granted. Because of this, they are more likely to be able to maintain a continuing positive relationship with the children. For 6 and 14 percent, respectively, the best times were between decision to divorce and final decree and the period immediately following divorce.

The long-term success of adjustment to divorce indicated by our respondents is generally supported by other research. For example, Hayes, Stinnett, and DeFrain [15] report that three-fourths of the respondents in their study of men and women who divorced in middle age responded in a positive way to the question, "How do you feel at the present time about the divorce?" Two-fifths of their respondents indicated that they should have initiated the divorce sooner and another one-third reported that they were much happier now. Similarly, during in-depth interviews with a sample of divorcees living in the Boston area, Brown, Feldbergh, Fox, and Kohen [16] found that a significant majority of the women studied felt that things were "easier now" for them than when they were with their husbands prior to their divorce. On the basis of their evidence, these authors argue that despite the problems faced by their respondents, the experience of having to head a family on their own was often better than what they had experienced during their marriages.

Both Goode [17] and Weiss [18] reported that the time of final separation was the point of highest trauma for their respondents. Chiriboga and Cutler [19] also found the time of final separation to be a high stress point but they also note the period immediately before the divorce decision as another major time of stress. Their respondents, like ours, referred most frequently to the present as a time of relief. Perhaps this means, as Brandwein et al. [20] suggest, that divorce needs to be viewed as a short-term crisis situation and not a long-term disruption.

Changes in Lifestyle and Modes of Adjustment

The individual disorganization created by divorce results at least in part from the fact that traditional patterns of life that have often been established through many years of living together are now disrupted. The lives of most individuals prior to divorce have come to exhibit a significant degree of pattern and consistency. Individuals generally are comfortable with this because it allows them to know what they can anticipate from others and what others can expect from them. While many persons talk about the boredom that they feel with the "routine" of their lives, they feel very uncomfortable when that routine is destroyed.

For the person who goes through a divorce, an entire life is often turned topsy-turvy; intimate bonds with another individual are broken; relationships with children are changed; friendship patterns are disrupted; different living arrangements must be established; employment must often be obtained; and so on. In the following sections, we briefly review some of the major changes that occurred in the lives of our sample and the adjustments that they made to these changes.

Changes in Living Arrangements

The decision to obtain a divorce has some obvious implications for living arrangements between the persons involved. On the one hand the divorce has not yet been granted and they are still legally bound together. However, on the other hand, the fact that the relationship has become so untenable that they have decided to terminate it argues against their wanting to maintain past living arrangements. To determine what types of arrangements are established during this interim period, each respondent was asked to specify what they did after one of the partners filed for divorce but before the final decree was granted. Table 44 summarizes the responses to this question.

Looking first at the overall sample, in only 3 percent of the cases in which one of the two had filed for divorce did the estranged couple continue to live together. Two percent said they continued to live together as before and 1 percent reported that while they continued to live in the same house, they maintained separate rooms.

The far more common procedure was for one or both of the spouses to move out of what had been their common residence. Thirty-two percent reported that after the divorce filing, the spouse moved out and another 32 percent reported that they, themselves, moved out. A total of 27 percent reported that both spouses moved out, which may reflect an inability to agree who should retain the home or apartment, difficulties associated with maintaining an expensive home for one of the partners and a separate apartment for the other, and so on. At any rate, the instances in which the estranged couple shared living arrangements while waiting for the divorce to be finalized were extremely rare.

Table 44
Living Arrangements after Filing for Divorce

	Males		Females		Total	
	N	%	N	%	N	%
Continued as Before	4	2	7	2	11	2
Lived in Same House but Separate Rooms	5	2	2	1	7	1
Spouse Moved Out	53	26	102	36	155	32
Respondent Moved Out	89	44	67	24	156	32
Both Moved Out	47	23	84	29	131	27
Other	4	2	23	8	27	6
Totals	(202)	(99)	(285)	(100)	(487)	(100)

Important differences between male and female responses are evident in the data. Males are more likely to report that they moved out (44 percent to 24 percent) while females are more likely to report that the spouse moved out (36 percent to 26 percent). The most common pattern from the reports of both sexes, then, is that following the filing for divorce, the husband seeks some other living arrangement.

In addition to making adjustments in terms of living arrangements between spouses, there is also the question of what happens to children during the interim. Each respondent was asked if the children stayed with anyone else during this time. Twenty percent reported that there were no children involved, 72 percent answered negatively, and just 8 percent responded in the affirmative. In most cases, then, children remained with one of the spouses (usually mother) during the period before the final divorce decree. When children were placed with someone else, it was almost always with a member of one of the couple's immediate family, such as the parents of the mother.

Common Possessions in Divorce Settlement

When two people live together in a legally established relationship, they tend to accumulate possessions that are usually viewed as joint property. Even when a highly structured sex-role division of labor exists between the spouses, items purchased from the earnings of one are treated as the property of both because the contribution of the other spouse, though different, is still essential to the relationship. When that legally established relationship is terminated through the

Table 45
Property Settlements

	Males		Females		Total	
	N	%	N	%	N	%
None	46	24	102	39	148	33
Most to Me	8	4	28	11	36	8
50-50 Split	78	41	105	40	183	40
Most to Spouse	32	17	18	7	50	11
All to Spouse	28	15	9	3	37	8
Totals	(192)	(101)	(262)	(100)	(464)	(100)

process of divorce, the problem of how to divide common possessions is often a most trying one. Our respondents were each asked to describe the type of property settlement that was made when they were divorced from their spouse. Table 45 summarizes responses to this question.

Exactly one-third of the respondents reported that no property settlements were made when the divorce was finalized. For some of these individuals, informal agreements may have been reached before the marriage was formally terminated. Others may have attempted to reach some sort of agreement at a later point. However, for this important segment of the sample, no formal property settlement was reported. Women were significantly more likely than men to report no property settlement (39 percent compared with 24 percent).

Among those who did reach some formal property settlement, the most common by far was for the estranged couple to divide their common holdings on something approximating a 50-50 basis. Two-fifths of the sample reported that their property was divided in the form of an equal split (41 percent of the male respondents and 40 percent of the females). Only 8 percent reported that most of the property went to themselves in the settlement (11 percent of the females and 4 percent of the males), while a larger number (19 percent) reported that most or all of the property went to their spouse in the settlement. Males were three times as likely to say that most or all property went to the spouse.

Whatever the arrangement, a majority of the sample tended to express satisfaction with it. When asked to report their feelings about the arrangement, 70 percent said they either felt good or very good. This was true of almost equal percentages of male and female respondents. However, about a fifth of those responding were very negative about the settlement and reported that they felt ''terrible'' about the arrangement. Another 6 percent were somewhat less neg-

Table 46
Feelings About Property Settlements

	Males		Females		Total	
	N	%	N	%	N	%
Very Good	5	3	10	5	15	4
Good	116	66	147	67	263	66
Frustrated	12	7	10	5	22	6
Terrible	43	24	39	18	82	21
Just Glad to Get Out	1	1	13	6	14	4
Totals	(177)	(101)	(219)	(101)	(396)	(101)

ative but reported that they were frustrated with the settlement. A smaller number (4 percent of the sample) simply stated that they were so glad to get out of the marriage that they had not cared what arrangements were made.

Effect of Divorce on Social Participation

As has been implied above, the process of obtaining a divorce has a generally disruptive effect on the social lives of the individuals involved. Not only are intimate ties with others, such as a former spouse and children, broken or modified but friendship patterns and social interaction networks are often changed significantly. For example, the newly divorced person may discover that the friends with whom they had previously spent much of their time were actually more the friends of their former spouse than of themselves. Such networks are soon changed by the divorce action. Even when this is not the case, the divorcee may find that most of the social activities that friends and others engage in are couple-oriented and that they have now become the "extra" person—which is usually uncomfortable and often embarrassing. As a consequence, the divorced person may fall back upon ties with immediate family members to a greater extent than before the divorce.

To assess changes in social participation and contact resulting from divorce, several questions were asked each respondent. Table 47 summarizes reports of changes reported in levels of participation in organizations and clubs as a result of the divorce. The data reveal that the most common pattern was *not* one of withdrawal and self-imposed isolation following the divorce. While 19 percent of the respondents reported less participation in organizations and clubs, almost twice as many (37 percent) reported an increase in such participation. The most

Table 47
Impact of Divorce on Participation in Organizations and Clubs

	Males N	Males %	Females N	Females %	Total N	Total %
More participation	70	34	114	40	184	37
No change	102	50	112	39	214	44
Less participation	32	16	62	21	94	19
Totals	(204)	(100)	(288)	(100)	(494)	(100)

common response, however, was that there had been no appreciable change in level of social participation as a consequence of the divorce action (44 percent of the respondents).

There are some interesting differences in the pattern of male and female responses on this issue. Females are more likely than males to report both higher participation (40 percent compared with 34 percent) and lower participation (21 percent compared with 16 percent). Males, on the other hand, are more likely to report no change in participation level. This finding contradicts some of the literature on the effect of divorce on social participation. For example, it has been argued that men are more likely to engage in increased social activity than are women to meet basic companionship and ego needs. [21] Men are also less likely to be tied down at home with child custody. Perhaps additional light can be shed on this question if future research gives more attention to the nature and types of social participation of the sexes following divorce.
to the nature and types of social participation of the sexes following divorce.

Apparently the family does become a more important source of social support following a divorce than it was before. At least the amount of contact increases. Tables 48 and 49 report the amount of contact with one's own and spouse's relatives prior to the divorce and then the change in amount of contact following the divorce.

As can be seen from the data, respondents report considerable contact both with their own and with spouse's relatives prior to the divorce. Fifty-eight percent report considerable personal contact with their own relatives and only slightly fewer (54 percent) report a high level of contact with spouse's relatives. It is interesting that females report more contact with both their relatives and spouse's relatives prior to the divorce than do the males.

As would be expected, the divorce changes these patterns rather dramatically. Contact with one's own relatives increases somewhat while that with spouse's relatives drops significantly. This pattern is somewhat stronger for females than males. Almost a third of the subjects report increased contact with their own

Table 48
Contact with Own and Spouse's Relatives Before Divorce

	Own Relatives						Spouse's Relatives					
	Males		Females		Total		Males		Females		Total	
	N	%	N	%	N	%	N	%	N	%	N	%
Little or No Contact of Any Kind	31	15	18	6	49	10	51	25	58	20	109	22
Some By Mail or Phone But Not Personal	67	33	93	32	160	32	43	21	76	26	119	24
Considerable Contact	50	24	57	20	107	22	58	28	67	23	125	25
Frequent Contact, More Than Monthly	58	28	123	42	181	36	54	26	90	31	144	29
Totals	(206)(100)		(291)(100)		(497)(100)		(206)(100)		(291)(100)		(497)(100)	

Table 49

Change in Contact with Own and Spouse's Relatives following Divorce

	Own Relatives						Spouse's Relatives					
	Males		Females		Total		Males		Females		Total	
	N	%	N	%	N	%	N	%	N	%	N	%
More	50	25	108	38	158	32	5	2	11	4	16	3
Same	121	60	150	52	271	55	29	14	50	17	79	16
Less	31	15	30	10	61	12	170	83	226	79	390	81
Totals	(202)	(100)	(288)	(100)	(490)	(99)	(204)	(99)	(287)	(100)	(491)	(100)

Table 50
Contact with Former Spouse

	Males N	Males %	Females N	Females %	Total N	Total %
Little or No Contact of Any Kind	142	70	206	73	348	71
Some by Mail or Phone but Not Personal	36	18	51	18	87	18
Considerable Contact	10	5	10	4	20	4
Frequent Contact, More Than Monthly	16	8	17	6	33	7
Totals	(204)	(100)	(284)	(101)	(488)	(100)

family while most of the remainder said the level remained largely constant. On the other hand, fully 81 percent report decreased contact with spouse's relatives. For the smaller numbers for whom contact remains stable or even increases, in-laws may continue to play a supportive role and/or both may be residents of smaller communities where it is virtually impossible to avoid frequent contact.

Once the divorce is obtained, the amount of contact one maintains with the former spouse decreases significantly. Over seven out of ten of the respondents report that they have little or no contact with the former spouse and an additional 18 percent report some contact by mail or phone but nothing personal. Only 11 percent report contact on a continual basis. It can only be assumed that much of the continued contact involved such issues as dealing with children, working out financial and property questions that may not have been totally resolved in the divorce settlement, and so on. Unfortunately, no specific information on the nature of the contact was obtained.

For only a small percentage of our sample, however, does there remain ambivalence created by continued contact between divorced spouses. Other studies have found rather considerable contact of different types to occur between individuals who have terminated their formal relationship. For example, Weiss [22] reports that it is not particularly unusual for a couple to fight with one another through their lawyers and even to testify against one another in the courts, yet to see one another in the evening as friends or as lovers. He also, however, clearly defines the ambivalence that this creates:

Couples who establish post marital relationships in which their discrepant feelings are allocated to separate settings sometimes try to keep the positive aspects of their relationship secret from all but their most intimate friends. Having told their family and their lawyers how much they have suffered at each other's hands, a husband and wife can hardly admit that they now look forward to evenings together. As a result, some couples may temporarily adopt a bizarre variation of the marital practice of hiding fights from public view; now they may be estranged in public but affectionate in private.

Income and Divorce

The effect of income on divorce and the effect of divorce on income can be viewed from a number of different angles. For example, it has been argued in the literature for some time that there is a direct link between social class and marital stability.[23] Thus, the higher one's income, the more one would anticipate a stable marriage. However, the effect of income on the propensity to divorce can also be treated in a comparative sense. That is, actual level of income may be less important than is the degree to which that level of income compares to that of one's close friends and associates. [24] Marital tensions related to finances instead of absolute deprivation in a country such as the United States.

Other studies have suggested that another possibly important linkage exists between income and marital instability. These studies imply that significant changes in income level, whether upward or downward, have a negative impact on marital stability—that is, marriages in which there occurs a major shift *in either direction* in level of income are more likely to be ended by divorce.[25]

Data collected from our sample of divorced persons are primarily comparative in nature. That is, each respondent was asked to compare his or her income with that of closest friends and associates both before and after the divorce. Responses to these questions are summarized in Table 51.

Before-divorce income levels of the respondents tend to be very close to those of nearest friends and associates. Fifty-seven percent report that their incomes were about the same while 22 percent report that their incomes were lower and an equal number report higher incomes. Female respondents were more likely than male respondents to report lower pre-divorce incomes but even here, 7 out of 10 report similar or higher incomes. It does not, therefore, seem very likely that feelings of relative deprivation, resulting from the fact that close friends and associates were financially better off, were major factors in influencing the decision to seek a divorce. Financial strains may have been a source of conflict in many marriages but this apparently was not based strictly on comparisons between own and other's income. The major problems may arise for the 11 percent (16 percent of the female respondents and 3 percent of the males) who report that their before-divorce incomes were "much lower" than was the case for closest friends and associates.

As would be anticipated, the effect of *divorce on income* appears to be a more significant one. Almost one-third of the subjects report their incomes following divorce to be "much lower" than that of closest friends and associates. This is about three times the number who reported much lower pre-divorce incomes. An additional 16 percent state that their post-divorce incomes were somewhat

Table 51
Income Compared with Closest Friends and Associates

| | Before Divorce | | | | | | After Divorce | | | | | |
| | Males | | Females | | Total | | Males | | Females | | Total | |
	N	%	N	%	N	%	N	%	N	%	N	%
Much lower	7	3	45	16	52	11	14	7	137	48	151	31
Somewhat lower	13	6	40	14	53	11	25	12	52	18	77	16
About the same	122	60	153	54	275	57	114	57	76	27	190	39
Somewhat higher	49	24	44	15	93	19	35	17	17	6	52	11
Much higher	11	5	3	1	14	3	13	6	2	1	15	3
Totals	(202)(100)		(285)(100)		(487)(101)		(201) (99)		(284)(100)		(485)(100)	

lower than those of closest friends and associates. Only 14 percent of the sample report higher post-divorce incomes.

This important impact on income levels occurs *primarily* for the females in the sample. Pre-divorce reports are usually based on husband's or combined husband-wife's income. If there are initially two breadwinners in the home, it natural that the income level of both will decline when there is only one bread-winner left. However, the more dramatic decline often occurs in traditional households where wives have filled the child-care and housekeeper roles and husbands have been the breadwinners. Following the divorce, the only immediate source of income for the wife is often the (frequently small) alimony and child support payments that come from the former spouse. Almost half (48 percent) of all female respondents report their post-divorce income to be *much lower* than that of friends and relatives. Virtually none of them report *much higher* income, though almost one quarter of the males do so report.[26]

The overall immediate impact for women following divorce, then, is *downward* economic mobility. The relationship is stronger here than for any other variable included in the analysis. Prior research seriously challenges the assumption that child support payments considerably increase the income of divorced females. For example, Everly,[27] in a review of child support and/or alimony payments in Onondaga County, New York, for a 12-month period in 1975 and 1976, found that over half of the females with child custody were not awarded any child support or alimony. For those who were awarded child support, the median annual amount was $1,560. And, even if a woman is awarded such payments by the court, this is no guarantee that they will be received. Everly reports a national survey of divorced women which reveals that even among those awarded payments from their former husbands, only 46 percent collect on a regular basis.

These findings suggest that while the divorce experience for males and females differs in many important respects, the most significant difference occurs in impacts on income level. For women, this usually means immediate and dramatic downward economic mobility. For men, the change is much less important and more of them, in fact, experience upward economic mobility than experience downward mobility. We noted earlier in this chapter that women were more likely than men to define the divorce experience as stressful and traumatic. It appears from our findings on post-divorce income that much of this is directly attributable to financial problems.

Summary

Because of the ever-higher divorce rates in this country, an increasing number of men and women are faced with the challenge of adjusting to the changes wrought in their lives through the disruption of their marriages. This chapter reviewed the reactions of our respondents to their divorce experience and the adjustments in their personal lives that have been necessitated by the divorce.

Almost without exception, people who go through a divorce experience some degree of personal disorganization, including higher levels of anxiety, fear, and loneliness. For most respondents, their divorce did cause some personal stress and trauma. However, for women in the sample, the divorce was more personally disruptive than was the case for men. The latter were more likely to characterize the experience as relatively painless. For both sexes, the key trauma-inducing factor was feelings of personal failure. Even though we are much more accepting of divorce than we were a few years ago, most persons who go through a divorce experience still define it as an indication of personal failure on their part.

Despite the personal stress associated with divorce, most respondents demonstrated a clear recovery and were quite convinced that the price they had to pay in terminating a bad marriage was worth it. The period before the decision to divorce was specified as the most difficult period, though others associated a good deal of stress with the time between the decision to divorce and the final decree and the time immediately after the divorce had become final. Overwhelmingly, the present was defined as the best period compared with these other times. The only exception to this occurred when males were asked to identify the best time for them and their children. In this instance, they identified the period prior to the divorce as best. The fact that the wife and mother is more likely to gain child custody could well account for this finding.

Almost immediately upon reaching the decision to obtain a divorce, one or both of the estranged couple moves out of their common residence. Only very rarely do the two continue living together after one or the other party has filed for divorce. However, if there are children, the children are likely to remain with one or the other spouse (usually mother) during this period.

Establishing an acceptable property settlement is often one of the most difficult tasks for divorcing couples. One-third of the subjects in our study reported that no property settlement at all was made when their divorce was finalized. Among those who did reach some settlement, the most common procedure was for the couple to divide their common holdings on about an equal basis. If more of the property went to one or the other spouse, the wife seemed to come out on the better end of the deal. Perhaps as a consequence of this, females in the study were more likely than males to express satisfaction with the arrangements that were made.

Because of the disrupting effect of divorce on the social lives of the couple, one would anticipate important changes in the nature and types of social participation and social interaction in which they engage. When asked to indicate the changes that occurred in their social activities, the pattern was not one of withdrawal and self-imposed isolation. Both sexes were more likely to indicate increased participation in clubs and organizations than decreased participation. Females, significantly more often than males, reported increases in their interaction with family members. Somewhat surprisingly, our respondents report relatively little continuing contact with the former spouse following the divorce. However, ''contacts'' through one's attorney may not have been included in the self-reports.

While before-divorce incomes of our respondents compared quite favorably with those of their closest friends and associates, after-divorce incomes tended to be rather lower. This was particularly true for females who often were left only with rather meager alimony and child support payments. The immediate impact of divorce for women was usually downward economic mobility.

Our findings indicate that the divorce experiences of males and of females are not the same. The self-reported experiences and paths of adjustment to divorce were quite different for males and females in our sample. While some of these differences clearly favored the male, others lessened the negative consequences of divorce for women.

Notes

1. Vicki L. Rose and Sharon Price-Bonham, "Divorce Adjustment: A Woman's Problem?" *Family Coordinator* 22 (July 1973): 291-97

2. William J. Goode, *Women in Divorce* (New York: Free Press, 1956).

3. Robert S. Weiss, "The Emotional Impact of Marital Separation," *Journal of Social Issues* 32 (no. 1, 1976): 135.

4. Goode, *Women in Divorce*.

5. Robert S. Weiss, *Marital Separation* (New York: Basic Books, 1975).

6. Gerald Curin, Joseph Veroff, and Sheila Feld, *Americans View Their Mental Health* (New York: Basic Books, 1960); Rose and Price-Bonham, "Divorce Adjustment"; Weiss, "The Emotional Impact of Marital Separation"; Morton M. Hunt and B. Hunt, *The Divorce Experience* (New York: McGraw-Hill, 1977); E. M. Hetherington, M. Cox, and R. Cox, "The Aftermath of Divorce," pp. 149-76 in J. H. Stevens, Jr., and Marilyn Mathews (eds.), *Mother-Child, Father-Child Relations* (Washington, D.C.: National Association for Education of Young Children, 1978); Robert S. Weiss, "The Emotional Impact of Marital Separation," pp. 201-10 in George Levinger and Oliver C. Moles (eds.), *Divorce and Separation: Context, Causes and Consequences* (New York: Basic Books, 1979).

7. Bernard L. Bloom, Stephen W. White, and Shirley J. Asher, "Marital Disruption as a Stressful Life Event," pp. 184-200 in George Levinger and Oliver C. Moles (eds.), *Divorce and Separation: Context, Causes, and Consequences*.

8. Bloom, White, and Asher, "Marital Disruption as Stressful," p. 185.

9. Hugh Carter and Paul C. Glick, *Marriage and Divorce: A Social and Economic Study* (Cambridge, Mass.: Harvard University Press, 1976).

10. Bloom, White, Asher, "Marital Disruption as Stressful," p.190.

11. Jessie Bernard, "Foreword," pp. ix-xv in George Levinger and Oliver C. Moles (eds.), *Divorce and Separation: Context, Causes, and Consequences*.

12. Norval D. Glenn, "The Well-Being of Persons Remarried after Divorce," *Journal of Family Issues* 2 (March 1981): 63-64.

13. Myra J. Wise, "The Aftermath of Divorce," *American Journal of Psychoanalysis* 40 (no. 2, 1980): 151.

14. Sharon Price-Bonham and Jack O. Balswick, "The Noninstitutions: Divorce, Desertion, and Remarriage," *Journal of Marriage and the Family* 42 (November 1980): 959-72.

15. Maggie P. Hayes, Nick Stinnett, and John DeFrain, "Learning About Marriage from the Divorced," *Journal of Divorce* 4 (Fall 1980): 23-29.

16. Carol A. Brown, R. Feldbergh, E.M. Fox, and J. Kohen, "Divorce: Chance of a New Lifetime," *Journal of Social Issues* (no. 1, 1976): 119-33.

17. Goode, *Women in Divorce*.

18. Robert S. Weiss, *Marital Separation*.

19. David A. Chiriboga and Loraine Cutler, "Stress Responses Among Divorcing Men and Women," *Journal of Divorce* 12 (Winter 1978): 95-106.

20. R. A. Brandwein, C. A. Brown, and E. M. Fox, "Women and Children Lost: The Social Situation of Divorced Mothers and Their Families," *Journal of Marriage and the Family* 36 (August 1974): 498-514.

21. Hetherington, Cox, and Cox, "The Aftermath of Divorce."

22. Weiss, "The Emotional Impact of Marital Separation," p. 144.

23. Arthur J. Norton and Paul C. Glick, "Marital Instability in America: Past, Present, and Future," pp. 6-19 in George Levinger and Oliver C. Moles (eds.), *Divorce and Separation: Context, Causes, and Consequences*: George Levinger, "A Social Psychological Perspective on Marital Dissolution," pp. 37-60 in Levinger and Moles (eds.), *Divorce and Separation: Context, Causes, and Consequences*; Frank Furstenberg, Jr., "Premarital Pregnancy and Marital Instability," pp. 83-98 in Levinger and Moles (eds.), *Divorce and Separation: Context, Causes, and Consequences*.

24. Letha Scanzoni and John Scanzoni, *Men, Women, and Change: A Sociology of Marriage and the Family* (New York: McGraw-Hill Book Co., 1976).

25. Andrew Cherlin, "Work Life and Marital Dissolution," pp. 151-66 in Levinger and Moles (eds.), *Divorce and Separation: Context, Causes, and Consequences*.

26. It should be noted that a decrease in income has been found in the literature to be associated with poorer post-divorce adjustment, though overall the problem is greater for women than for men. See Graham B. Spanier and Margie E. Lachman, "Factors Associated with Adjustment to Marital Separation," *Sociological Factors* 13 (October 1980): 369-81; see Antonette M. Zeiss, Robert A. Zeiss, and Stephen M. Johnson, "Sex Differences in Initiation of and Adjustment to Divorce," *Journal of Divorce* 4 (Winter 1980): 21-33.

27. Kathleen Everly, "New Directions in Divorce Research," *Journal of Clinical Child Psychology* 6 (Summer, 1977): 7-10.

Chapter 6

Remarriage

Introduction

Previous chapters have examined recent trends in divorce in the United States and in the Rocky Mountain region. Comparisons have been made between divorced and non-divorced persons and the major reasons for divorce, as well as adjustments to the divorce experience, have been analyzed. Implications for the family to increasing divorce rates have also been considered. We turn now to a discussion of divorced persons who remarry, including a comparison between first and later marriages.

Whatever one prefers to believe that divorce statistics indicate, the fact remains that most persons who obtain a divorce will remarry. Or, as Leslie Westoff[1] has put it, "Old-fashioned, once-in-a-lifetime, till-death-do-us-part marriage may be going on the rocks these days, but remarriage has been booming." It is estimated that four out of every five divorced persons will eventually marry again. This includes three-fourths of the divorced women and five-sixths of the divorced men.[2] These figures have led some analysts to argue that the married state is definitely a preferred state, though that need not be limited to the original union. Spanier and Glick[3] conclude that "one is impressed with the great propensity to remarry in the United States. Apparently, the typical American whose first marriage ends before middle age is sufficiently attracted to marriage to be willing to enter into a second marriage relatively soon after the failure of the first marriage." Norton and Glick[4] cite Institute of Social Research data which show that married people generally indicate a higher level of life satisfaction than do single people, and Hunt's[5] data suggest that many of those who have divorced do not see themselves as successful until they remarry.

While very extensive research has been conducted on the topic of marital happiness and success of first marriages, comparatively little has dealt with the success of the remarriage of persons who have been divorced. Glenn and Weaver[6] note that evidence on the topic tends to be fragmentary and dated. The absence of a history of high-quality research on remarriage is readily demonstrated by Schlesinger's[7] "Remarriage—An Inventory of Findings," which is filled with contradictory conclusions usually drawn from small and unrepresentative research samples. In fact, Condie[8] suggests that, based on the research literature available, one could reach three conflicting conclusions: (1) remarriages are less happy than first marriages, (2) remarriages are equally as happy as first marriages, and (3) remarriages are happier than first marriages.

In support of the first argument, statistics consistently report that remarriages are slightly more likely to be terminated by divorce than are first marriages.[9] Cherlin[10] argues that there are important problems in remarriages that cannot exist in first marriages. These problems, he feels, are created by a more complex family structure (ex-spouses, ex-in-laws, children from one or potentially both of the former marriages, and so on). Furthermore, there is less direction for handling these complex relationships and the potential problems that grow out of them. Basically, each family is left to devise its own solutions and the work of establishing rules in complex relationships increases the potential for conflict and, in turn, the potential for a divorce. It has also been argued that the experience of once having gone through a divorce makes it easier to do it again if the second (or third or later) marriage doesn't work.

However, Halliday[11] argues that divorce rates are not very reliable indicators of the success of second marriages. He points out that divorce is "a particularly poor indicator of disunity in first marriages, principally because it places undue emphasis on one indicator of marital quality." Halliday feels that a significant proportion of the population does not have recourse to divorce as a means of solving a problem of marital discord in a first marriage because of religious and other restraints on divorce. Many of these restraints, however, are removed for the remarried, leading to the probability that a higher percentage of "bad" marriages will be terminated. The greater propensity to divorce among the remarried, then, may not mean poorer quality marriages.

Despite the lack of research attention given to remarriage, some important problems facing those who remarry are now beginning to be discussed. One of these has to do with the very nature of the structure of remarriage that was noted above. It is coming to be generally recognized that the structure of remarriages poses adaptation problems for the partners for which earlier socialization in the nuclear family provides an inadequate role model.[12] Some of the major differences in structure between first marriages and marriages following divorce include the following factors. While the boundaries of the nuclear family are usually well defined (husband, wife, and children), this is frequently not true of remarriages. For example, ex-spouses are more or less involved and more or less important, new roles become evident (such as step-parent, step-child), and so on. In the second place, the source of economic subsistence changes. In the typical nuclear family, the family usually depends upon the earnings of the father or both parents. In the reconstituted family, other actors may be important. For example, a former spouse may be providing child support payments or the husband in the new marriage may have financial obligations to a former wife and children. Finally, while the psychic boundaries of the nuclear family serve to focus authority and affection inward, in the reconstituted family both of these may be focused outward at least to some extent. For example, children may withhold affection from a new step-parent and direct it to the biological parent who is living elsewhere.

Bohannan[13] also emphasized the difficulties associated with the absence of clearly defined and socially accepted role relationships in the reconstituted family. He notes: "Stepparents are not 'real' and the culture so far provides no norms to suggest how they are different." Ambiguity of status is similarly identified by Price-Bonham and Balswick[14] as contributing to adjustment difficulties for those who remarry. This is particularly important when the remarriage includes children from a marriage, but ambiguity of status can also affect those remarriages for which there are no children. This same point is reinforced by Westoff [15] when she notes that "the family can no longer be thought of as a neat, encap-sulated entity, simple and easily definable.... We have been taught to think of family as the biological family (parents and children related by blood ties). Well, that's not *the* family any longer. That's only *one* kind of family."

Walker and Messinger [16] summarize these important differences as follows:

The modern remarriage family lacks several of the boundary-maintaining conditions available to the first marriage family. It lacks the common household residence of natural parents and children and, likewise, the common household locus of parental authority and often of economic subsistence. In the remarriage family with children from a previous marriage, parental authority as well as economic subsistence may be shared with the former spouse of one or both adult partners. Similarly, the likelihood of filial affection being concentrated within the remarriage household is minimal. The affections and loy-alties of children in a remarriage family are often divided, even torn, between two parental households. Furthermore, the remarriage family lacks much of the shared family expe-rience, the symbols and the rituals that help to maintain the psychic boundaries of the first marriage family.

Despite the growing interest in remarriages, there is much that we do not know about them. Westoff[17] has noted that "remarriage has always been sketchily dealt with. If the victims of divorce can be shown the tricks of how to grow strong and rebuild their lives, most writers then leave them drifting off into the sunset in this newfound state. What really happens to them afterward has never been properly pursued."

Support for this argument is most evident in the literature dealing with the correlates of marital success and happiness. While literally hundreds of studies have been done on the correlates of success and happiness in first marriages, remarriages have received only passing attention. This chapter is developed to help fill this serious gap in the literature by examining some of the most important correlates and determinants of marital happiness of remarried persons. While the previous three chapters have focused primarily on the 500 members of the Intermountain Divorce Study who had been divorced, our attention here will be given to the 369 of these 500 who had remarried at the time of the study.

Assessing Marital Happiness

One of the primary concerns in this chapter is to assess the degree of marital satisfaction expressed by the remarried portion of our larger sample. Three different indicators of marital satisfaction—all of which have a comparative component—were used in the questionnaire. First of all, each of the respondents was asked to compare his or her present marriage with the former marriage that had ended in divorce. A five-point response ranged from "much better" to "much worse." Second, each of the remarried persons was asked to rate the degree of overall satisfaction they felt with their current marriage compared with that of other couples they knew. Again, a five-point response was used, ranging from "much more satisfied" to "much less satisfied." Finally, the respondents were asked to compare their present marriage with the expectations they had had for that marriage prior to its occurrence. Responses ranged from "much better than I expected" to "much worse than I expected." Perceptions were also obtained on these latter two questions for the earlier marriage or the one that had ended in divorce.

These measures of marital satisfaction are somewhat atypical. They are strictly comparative, in the sense that respondents were asked to evaluate their current marriage in comparison with some other standard—their own earlier marriage, the marriages of others, or their own prior expectations. Thus, one must use some caution in interpreting the results. For example, some of the respondents may rate their present marriage as "much better" than the prior marriage even though the present marriage is still not a happy or satisfying relationship. Such instances probably would be rare but may occur to some extent in the data. A primary reason for a general feeling of confidence in the indicators is that responses to the question comparing present and prior marriages are highly consistent with the other two comparison questions. For example, the fact that large majorities of the respondents felt that their current marriage surpasses in quality both the marriages of other couples used for comparison purposes and the expectations held for that marriage prior to entering into it causes us to feel that the question comparing current and prior marriages is a reliable indicator of overall marital satisfaction.

Several independent variables were used in order that their adequacy as predictors of marital satisfaction among the remarried might be tested. In large part, these were selected from the literature on satisfaction of first marriages. Specifically, we examined the effect of children (either from the present or from prior unions), religious indicators, social class, length of time married, and age at marriage. Presence of children was ascertained by asking three questions: (1) whether the couple had any children from their present marriage, (2) whether the respondent had any children from a prior marriage, and (3) whether the respondent's spouse had any children from a prior marriage. Three religious indicators were also used. These included (1) religious identification of respondent and spouse (i.e., Catholic, Protestant, etc.), (2) religious activity of respondent and spouse (i.e., frequency of attendance at religious services), and (3) religious homogeneity (that is, are Protestants married to Protestants, Jews to Jews, etc.). Social class was treated by dividing the occupations used in the Duncan index into blue-collar and white-collar categories. Age at the time of remarriage was obtained for the spouse only. Primarily for comparison purposes, problems associated both with the former marriage and with the remarriage will also be noted.

Comparative Happiness of Remarriages

Early evidence summarized by Glenn and Weaver[18] suggests that people who have divorced and then remarried tend to be about as satisfied with their marriages as are people in first marriages. Their own data from three national surveys conducted in 1973, 1974, and 1975 support this contention; they found no substantial difference in the reported marital happiness of remarried and never-divorced respondents.

In a more recent paper that also utilizes national survey data, Glenn[19] concludes that marital failure typically has no profound long-term effects on the happiness of divorced people who remarry. In other words, the never-divorced and the ever-divorced who have remarried are about equally likely to express satisfaction with the marriages and to express overall satisfaction with their lives. He concludes: "The findings are consistent with the view that the high American divorce rate is not so much a symptom of pathology in the institution of marriage as it is a reflection of rather effective mechanisms for replacing poor marriages with better ones." On the other hand, Glenn found that the happiness of divorced persons who have not remarried is far below that for either first or remarriages.

The evidence is even more clear in indicating that remarried persons consider their new marriages more satisfactory than the one ending in divorce. Our data support this contention. As noted above, three specific questions were asked each of the respondents to assess this issue. First, each person was asked to compare their marriage that ended in divorce with that of other couples they had known and to compare that marriage with the expectations they had held regarding it prior to the marriage. Second, those persons who had remarried were asked to compare their present married life with their former married life. Third, the remarried were asked to compare their present marital satisfaction with that of other couples they knew and with the expectations they had for the marriage prior to entering it.

Looking at the second question first, fully 88 percent of the remarried in the sample stated that their present marriage was "much better" than the former marriage that had ended in divorce. An additional 7 percent said that the present marriage was a little better. While these figures support trends noted by others in the literature, the percentage who were willing to say that the present marriage is better (95 percent of the total) is very high. However, it must be cautioned that many of those whose second marriages were also "bad" may have already terminated these marriages with a second or third divorce. Thus, our remarried group probably includes largely those who are satisfied with their new marriage to the extent that they would not hesitate to rate it significantly better than a previous marriage that had ended in failure. It is also interesting to note that a clear majority of the respondents felt that the experience they gained in the earlier marriage helped them in adjusting to the present marriage. Sixty-five percent felt that the earlier experience made present adjustments easier, 26 percent felt that it made no difference, and only 9 percent felt that the prior experience made adjustment to the present relationship more difficult.

Table 52 summarizes responses to questions asking all respondents to rate the marriage that had ended in divorce with marriages of others they knew, and similarly asking the remarried to rate their current marriage with those of others with whom they were familiar.

As would probably be expected, the respondents rated their marriage that had ended in divorce as much less satisfying than they perceived the marriages of others around them. For example, 37 percent stated that the marriage that had ended in divorce was much less satisfying than were the marriages of other couples they had known, and an additional 21 percent said the marriage was somewhat less satisfying (see chapter four for a more complete discussion of these findings). On the other hand, three-fifths of the remarried respondents said they were much more satisfied with their current marriages than were other couples they knew. While there has to be a certain amount of dissonance reduction reflected in these responses, they also indicate an expression of a high level of satisfaction with the remarried state.

Table 53 examines responses to the question of the extent to which one's marriage measured up to expectations that were held about it prior to its occurrence. The same general trends are evident in these data. Concerning the marriage that ended in divorce, over half of the respondents stated that the marriage had been much worse than they had expected, and an additional 29 percent felt that it had been somewhat worse than they had expected (see chapter four). Of course, most people do not enter into a marital relationship assuming that it will not work. The fact that the first marriages of all of these people failed would be reason enough to assume that they had not measured up to the expectations held about them by those entering the relationship. For a very small minority (5 percent), the marriage that had been terminated was rated as better than it had been expected to be. One can only assume that these individuals entered the marriage initially with very low expectations, or that the divorce had been initiated by a spouse toward whom they still felt positive affection.

The remarried persons, on the other hand, rated their current marriages as better than they had dared anticipate them to be. A total of 44 percent said their marriages were "much better" than they had expected them to be, and an additional 23 percent said they were somewhat better. Only 10 percent of the

Table 52
Satisfaction with Present and Former Marriage Compared with Perceived Happiness of Other Couples

Satisfaction Compared With Others	Present Marriage[a]		Divorced Marriage[b]	
	N	%	N	%
Much Less Satisfied	11	(3)	180	(37)
Somewhat Less Satisfied	10	(3)	104	(21)
About the Same	40	(11)	127	(26)
Somewhat More Satisfied	82	(23)	49	(10)
Much More Satisfied	211	(60)	26	(5)

a. Question: Compared with couples you have known, how would you rate the degree of overall satisfaction thay you feel with your current marraige?

b. Question: Compared with other couples you have known, how would you rate the degree of overall satisfaction that you _felt_ with your marriage?

Table 53
Satisfaction with Present and Former Marriage Compared with Expectations prior to Entering the Marriage

Satisfaction Compared With Prior Expectations	Present Marriage[a]		Divorced Marriage[b]	
	N	%	N	%
Much Worse Than Expected	11	(3)	251	(51)
Somewhat Worese Than Expected	24	(7)	145	(29)
About as Expected	81	(23)	73	(15)
Somewhat Better Than Expected	83	(23)	19	(4)
Much Better than Expected	155	(44)	7	(1)

a. Question: Compared with your expectations of marriage _before_ your present marriage, how is your marriage turning out?

b. Question: Compared with your expectations of marriage _before_ you were married, how did your marriage turn out?

remarried were experiencing marriages that were worse than they had expected them to be. Again, the responses probably reflect an important degree of dissonance reduction, but they also suggest that the remarried are, comparatively, a happily married group.

Problems in Former and Present Marriages

The divorce literature is filled with hypotheses concerning the nature and types of problems between spouses that are likely to lead to divorce. In our survey, each respondent was asked to identify the major reason why they felt that their marriage had failed. Respondents could list as many reasons as they desired but were asked to rank each reason listed. Chapter four provides a detailed discussion of these responses.

As discussed in chapter four, a total of 490 of the 500 ever-divorced respondents listed one or more reasons why they felt that their marriage had failed, and of these 490, 168 listed infidelity on the part of spouse as the most important reason. Thus, for over a third of the subjects, this was perceived as the number one reason for the divorce. An additional 103 subjects stated that the major reason for marital dissolution was that they and their spouse no longer loved each other. These two factors accounted for fully 55 percent of the first listed reasons for marriage failure. Other frequently listed reasons were emotional problems, financial problems, and physical abuse.

Turning to the question of the total number of times each reason was listed, the order of the first four items does not change. These four most important reasons, then, included: (1) infidelity, (2) loss of love for each other, (3) emotional problems, and (4) financial problems. In terms of overall ranking, sexual problems comes in fifth, though this was listed as the most important reason for marital failure by only 4 percent of the respondents.

We have already noted that the types of problems that develop between spouses in remarriages are likely to vary somewhat since remarriages usually present a very different structure, primarily because they involve a number of actors that were not present in the first marriage (such as ex-spouses, children from former marriages, and so on). The literature typically identifies two major problems that emerge in remarriage: children and money. Messinger[20] reports that the two dominant problems in the remarriages that he studied were problems associated with children from former marriages and monetary difficulties. Price-Bonham and Balswick,[21] in summarizing prior research, note that the major adjustment problems in reconstituted families—that is, in those remarriages that include at least one child from one of the spouses' former marriage—occur in the areas of children, finances, and ambiguity of roles.

Spanier and Glick[22] report that children are important in another regard when considering remarriage following divorce. Using national survey data, they found that the greater the number of children, the greater the handicap women have in remarrying again. The presence of children is assumed to introduce strong economic and social constraints for the woman who seeks to remarry. However, Koo and Suchindran[23] argue that the presence of children is only important as it interacts with the age of the woman. While for women divorcing before age 25, having no children increased their chances of remarriage over that of women with children, for women ending their marriage at age 35 or older, being childless actually decreased their remarriage prospects. There was no effect for women divorcing in the age range of 25 to 34. Further, these authors concluded that beyond the effect of the absence of children for the youngest and oldest ages, in none of the age-at-divorce groups did the number of children affect the likelihood of remarriage.

Responses from those members of our sample who have remarried are at least partly consistent with prior research. These responses also clearly indicate that the major problem that remarried respondents are experiencing in their current marriages are quite different from those that occurred in the marriage that failed. When asked to rank the major problems they are experiencing in their new marriages, financial difficulties is the overwhelming number one choice (see Table 54). A total of 37 percent of those who listed problems included financial problems as their number one concern. It will be remembered that this was listed as a distant fourth in the list of major problems in the marriage that had been terminated. In part, the increasing financial difficulties could result from attempts to combine two separate households; that is, each spouse in the remarriage may have brought children to the union from a previous marriage. For husbands, particularly, problems may also result from helping to support a previous family through alimony and child-care payments. Slightly over half of the respondents (51 percent) indicated that their current spouse had children from an earlier marriage (though this does not mean that the children were living with the currently married partners). Financial problems also ranked first in the list of total problems mentioned.

It is also interesting to note that sexual problems take on relative greater significance among the remarried. While sexual problems were ranked seventh among the first-listed problems in those marriages terminated by divorce, they were ranked third among the remarried. Again, this may be a function of two individuals bringing to their union rather different backgrounds and expectations that have developed, at least in part, from intimate relationships with another partner in an earlier marriage. Infidelity, listed first among the divorced as a reason for their marriage failure, was an insignificant problem among the re-married in that it was mentioned by only five persons as the most important problem in their current union and by seven persons overall. Similarly, while loss of love for each other was listed as the second most important reason for failure of the first marriage, only five of the remarried listed this as a problem in their current marriage.

Significantly, the existence of a former spouse seems to make little difference in terms of contributing to the problems of current remarriages, at least as these are reflected in arguments between the spouses. Each respondent was asked the

Table 54
Major Problems Identified in Current Marriage

	Listed First (N)	(Order)	Total Number of Times Listed	(Order)
Financial Problems	55	(1)	74	(1)
Emotional Problems	21	(2)	49	(2)
Sexual Problems	17	(3)	30	(3)
Spouse's Former Marriage	17	(3)	25	(4)
Problems with In-Laws	9	(5)	25	(4)
Conflict Over Children	9	(5)	15	(6)
Neglect of Children	7	(7)	10	(7)
No Longer Love Each Other	5	(8)	10	(7)
Infidelity	5	(8)	7	(9)
Own Former Marriage	1	(10)	4	(10)
Physical Abuse	1	(10)	3	(11)
(N = 369)				

frequency with which they and their present spouse argued about their former marriage or spouse. A total of 77 percent reported that they never had such arguments and an additional 12 percent reported that this seldom occurred. Fewer than 2 percent reported frequent disagreements over such prior relationships. It should be emphasized, however, that the absence of arguments about a former spouse or a former marriage is not proof that ex-spouses do not contribute to problems among the remarried. Many of the problems that do emerge in the areas of finances and children emerge *because* there is a former spouse to which the partners in the remarriage must relate.

Correlates of Marital Satisfaction

Data presented to this point clearly suggest a high level of marital satisfaction among the remarried, at least as measured by the three indicators used in this study: (1) comparing present and former marriages; (2) comparing present marriage with other marriages with which the respondent was familiar; and (3) comparing present marriage with expectations held prior to the marriage. The literature on marital satisfaction among first marriages suggests a number of factors that affect the degree of happiness that couples attribute to their marriages.

These include such factors as the presence of children, similarity of religious identification and activity, social class position, age at marriage, and length of time married. We will briefly review each of these factors in terms of their influence on the marital happiness of the remarried.

Table 55 presents a summary of Pearson correlations between the three measures of marital satisfaction and the various independent variables used in the study. These will be treated by category in the following discussion.

Presence of children. There is much debate in the literature concerning whether the birth of children strengthens a marriage relationship or makes it less satisfying to the partners involved. Our data on remarriage reflect a rather mixed impact of children on the satisfaction the partners express with that relationship. In response to the question comparing the respondent's present marriage with their former marriage, 91 percent of those who have children from the *present union* said the marriage was much better. However, only a somewhat smaller percentage of those without children from the present marriage (86 percent) also rated it much better. The difference between these two figures is not statistically significant but is indicative of the trend noted in the zero-order correlations: those with children from the present marriage tend to rate it comparatively better but the statistical relationship tends to be very weak.

Somewhat surprisingly, a stronger relationship is noted between comparative satisfaction with the marriage and the fact that the respondent had had children from a former marriage. One possible explanation for this finding is that the individual respondent's own feelings of life satisfaction and happiness are strengthened by the fact that they have close relationships with their offspring—even though these offspring may not be from their current marriage. Thus, they see themselves as comparatively more happy than they would be without such relationships. The matter tends to be somewhat different, however, when the children come from the spouse's former marriage. Looking just at some percentage figures first, when the respondent's spouse had children from a previous marriage, 86 percent rated their present marriage as much better than the one which ended in divorce. However, this figure climbed slightly to 90 percent when the spouse did not have children from a previous marriage. Again, these figures can only be viewed as trends because the difference between the two percentages is not significant and the Pearson correlation for these variables shows no relationship at all. An overall conclusion seems to be that contrary to what we sometimes read, the presence of children does not make a remarriage worse. Their effect, though small, is in a positive direction. This argument does not discount the importance of step-parent/step-child adjustment problems. However, it does suggest that the rewards of parenting can sometimes outweigh those difficulties.

Religion. The religious identification and level of activity of the respondent have relatively little impact on their expression of comparative satisfaction with their current marriage. The highest bivariate correlations (.12 in both cases) are between respondent's religious identification and happiness of current marriage

Table 55

Pearson Correlations between Three Measures of Satisfaction with Remarriage and Selected Independent Variables

Independent Variables	Happiness of Current Marriage Compared with Prior Marriage	Happiness of Current Marriage Compared with Perceived Happiness of Other Couples	Happiness of Current Marriage Compared with Expectations Prior to the Marriage
Children from Present Marriage	.11[a]	.01	.09[a]
Respondent has Children from Former Marriage	.22[c]	.17[b]	.11[a]
Spouse has Children from Former Marriage	.00	.07	.05
Respondent's Religion	.01	.12[a]	.04
Spouse's Religion	.08	.08	.18[c]
Respondent Religious Attendance	.05	-.01	.12[a]
Spouse Religious Attendance	.11[a]	.07	.12[a]
Religious Dummy Variables			
Mormon	.08	.18[c]	.21[c]
Catholic	.12[a]	.12[a]	.17[b]
Protestant	.05	-.04	-.10[a]
Jewish	.03	.07	.09[a]
Respondent Occupation	.12[a]	.02	.03
Spouse Occupation	-.12[a]	-.12[a]	-.02
Spouse Age at Marriage	-.06	.06	.07
Length of Time Married	.11[a]	.13[b]	.17[b]
MULTIPLE R	.42[c]	.48[c]	.47[c]
MULTIPLE R^2	.17[b]	.23[c]	.22[c]

a = r significant at .05 level

b = r significant at .01 level

c = r significant at .001 level

compared with perceived happiness of others, and respondent's religious activity and happiness of current marriage compared with expectations prior to marriage.

Similarly, religious identification and activity of spouse, by themselves, have relatively little influence on the degree of satisfaction expressed by our respondents with their present marriage. For example, among the remarried, the following percentages by major religious category indicate that their current marriage was much better than their earlier marriage: Catholics, 83 percent; Protestant, 90 percent; Jewish, 91 percent; Other, 95 percent; No religion, 81 percent. These data suggest that Protestants, Jews, and those with affiliation with less well-known religious groups express greater satisfaction while Catholics and those with no religion express somewhat less satisfaction. However, there are no major differences among these figures, and, on the whole, they indicate a high level of satisfaction with one's present marriage whatever the religious faith (or lack thereof) of one's spouse. Religious identification of spouse does have a somewhat greater impact on expressions of current marital happiness compared with expectations prior to the marriage. In this case, those married to Jews and other religious groups such as Mormons expressed more satisfaction.

When we examine the religious activity of one's spouse, the following percentages reported their current marriage to be much better than their prior marriage: regular attenders, 93 percent; frequent attenders, 89 percent; occasional attenders, 91 percent; attenders only on special occasions, 84 percent; nonattenders, 82 percent. While there are no major differences among these figures, they do indicate an interesting trend that is generally consistent with the existing literature. That is, respondents who are married to regular church attenders tend to express greater satisfaction with their present marriages than do respondents married to spouses who never attend religious services. This is supported by the trend noted in each of the correlations reported in Table 55.

The final attempt to measure the effect of religion on marital satisfaction was to examine the effect of religious congruence in a dummy variable analysis format. In this case, if a Mormon was married to a Mormon, he or she was assigned a value of one. A Mormon married to a person of any other religious faith was assigned a value of zero. A Catholic married to a Catholic was assigned a value of one, and so on. The results are rather mixed. It appears from the data that if Mormons are married to Mormons and Catholics are married to Catholics, they are likely to report higher levels of comparative marital satisfaction in their remarriage. However, the relationships for Protestants and Jews tend to be less strong, and in two instances, are even reversed. That is, Protestants married to other Protestants report lower levels of comparative satisfaction.

Occupation. Though the findings tend to be somewhat inconsistent, the literature generally reports that persons in white-collar occupations express a higher level of marital satisfaction than do persons in blue-collar occupations. Our findings for remarried persons support this trend (though the correlations are generally very small) if we consider only the occupation of the respondent. The opposite is the case when spouse's occupation is used. In this instance, persons who are married to blue-collar individuals report slightly greater satisfaction on the particular indicators used in this study than do persons married to persons with white-collar occupations.

Age at marriage and length of time married. There has now accumulated rather extensive evidence that age at marriage is strongly related with probability of marital success (see the detailed discussion of this issue in chapter three). Teenage marriages have been found to be twice as likely to end in divorce as marriages that occur when couples are in their twenties.[24] We would anticipate that this would be a less critical factor in remarriages because, by definition, they will occur at a higher average age than is the case for first marriages. This assumption is generally supported by the bivariate correlations reported in Table 55. In each instance, the correlation between spouse's age at marriage and comparative marital satisfaction is small, and, in one instance, the relationship is actually reversed, suggesting that the younger remarriages may be as happy or more so than those which occur at a later age. Again, however, there would be some support for this in the literature in that persons who marry for the first time after the age of 30, like those who marry in their teens, tend to have less stable marriages than those who marry in their twenties. The literature on remarriages also suggest that, particularly for women, the younger they are when they divorce the more attractive they are as remarriage partners.[25]

On the other hand, length of marriage is always positively related to perceived marital happiness. The correlations in this instance are not large but are consistent. This would be anticipated since the "bad" marriages would, in many instances, already have been terminated by divorce.

The multiple correlations combining the effects of the 15 independent variables on the reported level of marital happiness are .42, .48, and .47. The amount of explained variation (R^2) is never higher than 23 percent. This would suggest that many of the correlates of marital satisfaction among the first married are not particularly effective in explaining marital satisfaction among those who have divorced and then remarried.

Summary

As the divorce rate continues to climb, the number of people living in second, third, or even later marriages will also continue to increase, even though the remarriage rate is now slightly lower than it was a few years ago. As a consequence, more of the attention that has been devoted to understanding marital satisfaction and happiness among first marriages now should be focused on understanding these same outcomes among the remarried.

By definition, remarriages occur among older and more experienced individuals, a fact that might cause one to argue that they should be better than first marriages. However, the individuals involved also bring with them other problems that must be confronted, such as children from former marriages of one or both of the spouses. All things considered, do remarriages tend to be more or happy than first marriages, and what are the important correlates of happiness among the remarried?

On the one hand, data presented above suggested that in several senses, remarriages are happy marriages. Our respondents rated them as much better than their previous marriages that had ended in divorce (certainly not an unexpected finding). They also tended to rate them as better than the marriages of others they knew and as better than they had anticipated them to be prior to their occurrence. These latter two findings were contrary to the case for the prior marriage which was rated as worse than the marriages of others and not as good as expectations held for the marriage prior to entering into it.

However, as Westoff[26] has noted, "Love may be lovier, the marriage may be better, but couples are still vulnerable to the problems of living with another person, the unbelievable complexities of trying to make two families into one, as well as the problems inherent in the institution of marriage itself." Marriage is indeed not a foolproof relationship, either the first time or the second time. However, our data reveal that comparatively, those who are remarried do quite well and are able to develop relationships that are rewarding and satisfying. And, particularly when we compare the remarried with singles or with divorced persons who do not remarry, the overall life satisfaction of the remarried is much higher.

On the other hand, none of the variables often noted to be useful predictors of marital satisfaction among the first-married were strongly related to the three indicators of marital satisfaction among the remarried. The effect of children, either from the present relationship or from a former marriage, was positively related but not strongly so to the indicators of satisfaction. Religious activity and congruence were also positively, but weakly, related to the measures of satisfaction. Occupation as an indicator of social class had mixed effects and length of marriage was a consistent—though again, not strong—predictor of the dependent variable.

It seems that research models developed to increase our knowledge and understanding of marital satisfaction among the remarried need to consider other factors that have not been included in the models used to predict satisfaction among the first-married. Because of the increasing number of persons affected, the topic deserves more attention in the future.

NOTES

1. Leslie Aldridge Westoff, *The Second Time Around: Remarriage in America* (New York: Viking Press, 1977), pp. 2-3.

2. Arthur J. Norton and Paul C. Glick, "Marital Instability: Past, Present, and Future," *Journal of Social Issues* 32 (no. 1, 1976): 5-20.

3. Graham B. Spanier and Paul C. Glick, "Paths to Remarriage," *Journal of Divorce* 3 (Spring 1980): 287.

4. Norton and Glick, "Marital Instability," p. 18.

5. Morton Hunt, *The World of the Formerly Married* (New York: Fawcett World Library, 1966), p. 285.

6. Norval D. Glenn and Charles N. Weaver, "The Marital Happiness of Remarried Divorced Persons," *Journal of Marriage and the Family* 39 (May 1977): 331.

7. Benjamin Schlesinger, "Remarriage—An Inventory of Findings," *Family Coordinator* (October 1968): 248-50.

8. Spencer J. Condie, "Role Bargains and Role Profits of First Married and Subsequently Married Couples," unpublished manuscript, Department of Sociology, Brigham Young University, 1978.

9. Paul C. Glick, "Remarriage: Some Recent Changes and Variations," *Journal of Family Issues* 1 (December 1980): 455-78.

10. Andrew Cherlin, "Remarriage as an Incomplete Institution," *American Journal of Sociology* 84 (November 1978): 634-50; "Religion and Remarriage-Reply," *American Journal of Sociology* 86 (no. 3, 1980): 636-40.

11. Terrence C. Halliday, "Remarriage: The More Complete Institution?" *American Journal of Sociology* 86 (no. 3, 1980): 630-35.

12. Kenneth N. Walker and Lillian Messinger, "Remarriage After Divorce: Dissolution and Reconstruction of Family Boundaries," *Family Process* 18 (June 1979): 185-92.

13. Paul Bohannan, "Divorce Chains, Households of Remarriage, and Multiple Divorcers," in Paul Bohannan (ed.), *Divorce and After* (New York: Doubleday, 1970), p. 119.

14. Sharon Price-Bonham and Jack O. Balswick, "The Noninstitutions: Divorce, Desertion, and Remarriage," *Journal of Marriage and the Family* 42 (November 1980): 959-72.

15. Westoff, *The Second Time Around*, p. 3.

16. Walker and Messinger, "Remarriage After Divorce," p. 186.

17. Westoff, *The Second Time Around*, p. 4.

18. Glenn and Weaver, "The Marital Happiness of Remarried Divorced Persons."

19. Norval D. Glenn, "The Well-Being of Persons Remarried After Divorce," *Journal of Family Issues* 2 (March 1981): 70.

20. L. Messinger, "Remarriage Between Divorced People with Children from Previous Marriages: A Proposal for Preparation for Remarriage," *Journal of Marriage and Family Counseling* 2 (no. 2, 1976): 193-99.

21. Price-Bonham and Balswick, "The Noninstitutions."

22. Spanier and Glick, "Paths to Remarriage," pp. 283-98.

23. Helen P. Koo and C. M. Suchindran, "Effects of Children on Women's Remarriage Prospects," *Journal of Family Issues* 1 (December 1980): 497-515.

24. Paul C. Glick and Arthur J. Norton, "Marrying, Divorcing, and Living Together in the U.S. Today," *Population Bulletin* 32 (October 1977): 1-41.

25. James A. Sweet, "Differentials in Remarriage Probabilities," working paper 73-29, (Madison, Wisc.: Center for Demography and Ecology, 1973); Douglas T. Gurak and Gillian Dean, "The Remarriage Market: Factors Influencing the Selection of Second Husbands," *Journal of Divorce* 3 (Winter 1979): 161-73.

26. Westoff, *The Second Time Around*, p. 5.

Chapter 7

Concluding Thoughts on Replication, Regional Specification, and Future Research

Viewing our work in the context of the existing literature on divorce, we identify at least four ways that it extends or amplifies the prior research. These major contributions are in replication and extension, quantification, regional specification, and methodological innovation.

Replication and Extension

Most of the findings described in preceding chapters parallel the findings of previous investigators. However, the research that produced these earlier findings, as noted in chapter one, derives mainly from studies conducted in the metropolitan areas of California or the Midwest, and typically involves relatively small samples drawn from court records, from the membership of special interest organizations, or from the caseloads of social service agencies. The replication of some of these findings, using data collected at a different time, in a different region, with different sampling techniques and different data-collection instruments, greatly enhances their credibility. Where our findings and previous research point to similar conclusions, we have the benefit of "triangulation" in the best sense of the word:

The most persuasive evidence comes through a triangulation of measurement processes. If a proposition can survive the onslaught of a series of imperfect measures, with all their irrelevant error, confidence should be placed in it. . . . It is only when we naively place faith in a single measure that the massive problems of social research vitiate the validity of our comparisons.[1]

Among the findings of previous researchers that seem to deserve greater credence as a result of the findings of the Intermountain Divorce Study are these:

- Age at marriage and marital stability are positively associated, with the probabilities that a marriage will end in divorce particularly high for persons who marry before age 20.
- To a limited extent, divorce tends to "run in families." That is, the probabilities that one's marriage will end in divorce increases if one's parents were divorced. Also, divorce seems to run in families of orientation, in that brothers or sisters of our respondents were described as having high rates of divorce.
- The wife is the formal initiator of the divorce action in most cases.
- Following the filing for a divorce, it is typical for the husband to move out of the common residence; in about one-fourth of the cases, both spouses abandoned the former common residence.
- Children usually stay with the mother during the period of separation and the divorce process.
- The process of divorce and adjustment to it is more stressful for women than for men.
- Religiosity and marital stability are positively related. Persons married in civil ceremonies are more prone to divorce than those married in religious ceremonies, and church attenders are less likely to divorce than non-attenders.
- Educational attainment and marital stability are positively related.
- The marital satisfaction of remarried persons is at least as high as that in intact first marriages, and when the indicator of satisfaction refers to the gap between the present situation and expectations prior to marriage, the remarried show significantly higher rates of satisfaction than persons in intact first marriages. Moreover, the link between marital happiness and marital stability is neither direct nor predictable; "unhappy" marriages persist and some "happy" marriages end in divorce.
- Divorce is painful, even for partners hopelessly mismatched.

Many of the findings which parallel earlier work extend that work by adding elements or perspectives or by providing quantitative parameters or gender controls. Among the findings which we think qualify as extensions as well as replications of prior work are the various gender comparisons made possible by our sizable sample of divorced men. For example, the perceived barriers to divorce differ by gender; divorced women cited financial concerns as the most important obstacle to their divorce, followed by personal religious beliefs which discouraged divorce, and concern about the effects of divorce on their children. Worry about financial concerns is much more a perceived barrier to divorce for women than for men. Divorced men cited concern for their children first, followed by perceptions about the legal ramifications of getting divorced, personal religious beliefs, and concern about parental reactions.

The factors ultimately influencing the decision to divorce also differ by gender. For women, escaping a situation of personal unhappiness and the awareness of opportunities for alternative financial support are paramount, while for men being involved with someone else ranks as high as personal unhappiness or desire to escape a bad situation as a factor prompting the decision to divorce.

Among both men and women, the approval of close friends and relatives is often a critical factor in the decision to divorce. Over half of the respondents said that most of their family and close friends approved of the decision to divorce. Advice received from relatives and friends is frequently a deciding factor, and especially for women, their children's desires to escape a situation of conflict and hostility may be a decisive element.

The most frequently mentioned "causes" for marital failure as seen by divorced persons were infidelity, loss of love for each other, emotional problems, and financial problems, in that order. Persons who had divorced generally viewed their former marriages as less satisfying than were the marriages of other couples they knew prior to their divorce. Compared to divorced men, divorced women were more negative about the levels of satisfaction and the degree to which their former marriages had matched their expectations.

About two-thirds of the respondents identified the present, typically some years after the divorce, as the best time for them and their children. For most divorced persons, the period just before the decision to divorce was finally made was seen as the worst time; for about one in four, the period between that decision and the final decree was the worst time. The period immediately following the divorce was also very difficult. The most frequently mentioned stress of divorce was a feeling of personal failure. However, in life-stage perspective, divorce seemed to be a short-term crisis; most divorced people, looking back, defined their present situation as happier than it would have been had they not divorced.

The most common property settlement following divorce was a 50-50 split, but this occurred in only about 40 percent of the cases. The next most common situation was an "informal" property split. There were gender differences in the perceptions of being "taken," in the sense that all of the common property ended up going to one spouse or the other, with one man in six reporting that his spouse got everything, but only 3 percent of women reporting this situation. Men were twice as likely as the women to say that most of the property went to their ex-spouse, but divorced women were significantly more likely to say there had been no formal property settlement. Most respondents expressed satisfaction with the way the property settlement had been carried out, whatever the mechanics of the split had been.

Contact with relatives following a divorce either increases or is maintained at about the same level as before the divorce. Only one respondent in eight said that the divorce had had the effect of decreasing their contact with their own relatives, and gender differences in contact with kindred were small. Divorced women were more likely than men to report increased contact with their own relatives (38 versus 25 percent, respectively). As might be expected, what declines is contact with one's former in-laws. In about 80 percent of the cases both men and women said that after the divorce, there was a marked decline in contact with former in-laws.

About 70 percent of formerly married persons reported little or no contact with the former spouse, and about 20 percent said there had been some mail or telephone contact but not personal contact. Only about 10 percent of the formerly married said they had considerable or frequent contact with former spouses, and there are no gender differences in frequency of contact.

Women are more likely than men to say that prior to divorce their family incomes were lower than those of their closest friends and associates, but for most divorced persons, reports of former (pre-divorce) family income placed it on a par with that of friends and associates. However, when these same divorced persons compared their post-divorce financial situation to that of friends and associates, over half of the divorced women said their situation was worse (and 48 percent said their incomes were "much lower") while most men reported comparable or higher incomes than before the divorce. Women seem to pay a heavy economic price for their freedom from former husbands. That is, the financial burden of divorce falls much more heavily on women than on men. Only 7 percent of the divorced women report higher incomes following divorce, compared to almost one-fourth of the men. Divorced women are apt to experience immediate and fairly dramatic downward economic mobility.

Most married respondents described their present marriage as better than the former marriage, and 83 percent said their present marriage was more satisfying than that of other couples they knew. Also, two-thirds rated their present re-marriage as more satisfying than they had expected it to be. Major problems identified in current remarriages were financial (mentioned by 37 percent of those who listed problems), problems in sexual adjustment, emotional problems, prob-lems related to the spouse's former marriage, in-law problems, and conflict over children.

Despite these problems, in the Intermountain Divorce Study remarriages were characterized as highly satisfying and generally successful. The presence of children did not seem to strain the marriage unduly. The rewards of parenting seemed to outweigh the costs, even when the children were step-children, or when one's own children were in custody of a former spouse.

In remarriages as in first marriages, there was a positive correlation between religiosity as measured in a variety of ways and marital satisfaction. At least among Mormons and Catholics, same-faith remarriages seemed to be happier than religious intermarriages.

Quantification

The contributions of the Intermountain Divorce Study to the quantification of the divorce process are related to its role in replication. We have singled out some findings for special mention because so much of the divorce literature is qualitative in nature, and so much is localized, as in major monographs focused on divorced people in such cities as Philadelphia, Detroit, San Francisco, or Boston, or in books that refer to "representative samples" or use data apparently collected from persons in all walks of life and every region of the United States, but do not provide much numerical documentation for their generalization. Also, because divorce research has concentrated on recently divorced persons and on women, there is some benefit to having data on the problems and processes of divorce as viewed by both men and women, and to recording the perceptions of those divorced for many years as well as the more recently divorced segment of the ever-divorced population.

The potential contribution of the Intermountain Divorce Study to future studies of divorce is enhanced by the sizable samples (4,606 completed instruments on the Phase I screening survey, 500 completed in the Phase II process of divorce survey) which make it possible to establish fairly reliable benchmarks for correlates of marital stability. Much of the quantitative detail about demographic correlates of divorce appears in Appendix B, and for many items it is possible to make comparisons by individual state. The overrepresentation of men in responses to the initial screening instrument (but not to the Phase II instrument on the process of divorce) enables us to generalize with more assurance about the characteristics of divorced and married men in the eight-state area than was previously possible.

The contributions of the Intermountain Divorce Study to understanding the quantitative parameters of the divorce experience among western families are easily illustrated. For instance, consider the divorce rate. The periodic vital statistics reports from the National Center for Health Statistics reveal divorce rates for the late 1970s in the vicinity of 5 per 1,000 population per year. In the year ending June 1980, for example, the divorce rate nationally was 5.2 per 1,000 population.[2] Such figures for divorces in a given year take on added meaning when placed in the context of cumulative divorce experience. Our Phase I survey revealed that 1,265 of the 4,606 respondents said that they, their spouse, or both had been divorced at some previous time. Thus, a minimal estimate of the prevalence of one or more divorced persons in the households of the intermountain west is 27 percent. When we controlled for marital status and estimated the percentage divorced among the ever-married populations (see Appendix B, Table 60), we found that between 14.5 percent and 26.9 percent of all ever-married persons in the region had been divorced at least once. In other words, between one-fourth and one-sixth of all persons in the eight-state area who had ever been married had also been divorced.

Other useful quantitative benchmarks available from the Intermountain Divorce Survey have to do with the relationship between religion and divorce. This relatively neglected topic is illuminated by the data on religious preference and divorce among 3,990 married couples obtained as part of the Phase I survey. Analysis by denominational preference of husband and wife reveals marked differences between same-faith and interfaith marriages in the probability that one or both partners have experienced a divorce. The probabilities that a person in a same-faith marriage has ever been divorced range between 6 percent and 14 percent (for Catholic-Catholic and Protestant-Protestant marriages, respectively), while in interfaith marriages the probabilities that one of the partners has been divorced are much higher, ranging from 17 to 40 percent, with both the type of religious combination (Catholic-Protestant, Catholic-No Preference, Mormon-Protestant, etc.) and differences in which spouse prefers which denomination having substantial impact on the total experience of divorce among interfaith couples.[3]

Consider another example. Research on divorce often focuses only on the recently divorced or those whose present marital status is divorced. Yet our regional surveys reveal that the presently divorced segment of the ever-divorced population is always a minority of the ever-divorced, and that the size of the fraction of the ever-divorced represented in the presently divorced differs sharply by gender. Most persons in the Phase I screening survey who identified themselves as remarried were remarried following divorce rather than following widowhood. In the entire region, the presently divorced represented only one-third of the combined remarried and presently divorced population, but among men only 23 percent of the combined remarried and presently divorced population were presently divorced, compared to 47 percent for the women (see Appendix B, Table 58).

Our regional figures are generally congruent with U.S. Census statistics on the percentages of ever-married persons who have been divorced; compare (Appendix B, Table 60) the 1976 rates for individual states in the Intermountain Divorce Study (from 14 percent in Utah to 27 percent in Nevada, with a median of 18 percent) with those from the 1970 U.S. Census (15 percent in Utah to 32 percent in Nevada, with a median of 17 percent).

The gender differentials in the consequences of divorce take on added meaning when the scale of the economic gap between divorced men and women is documented numerically. It is one thing to say that women suffer an economic disadvantage following divorce. The extent of the disadvantage, however, is thrown into sharp relief by results showing that while only 30 percent of divorced women said their income prior to divorce was lower than that of their closest friends and associates, 66 percent of these same women said their post-divorce income was lower than that of the same comparison group. The percentage of divorced women estimating their incomes as roughly equivalent to that of their closest friends was only 27 percent, less than half the comparable figure for divorced men (57 percent).

Finally, in contrast to a growing body of literature, largely qualitative, that suggests or recommends that divorced couples continue to be "friends," or share a parenting role amicably in the emerging family form that ties parents to stepchildren or to their own children now being reared by a remarried former spouse, is the sobering reality among divorced people in the intermountain West that about 90 percent of divorced persons have no personal contact with their former spouse, and 70 percent of both divorced men and women claim "little or no contact of any kind."

Our comparisons of marriage and divorce statistics in the eight western states, and particularly the detailed comparisons among Nevada, Idaho, and Utah, often reveal striking differences from national rates. If nothing else, the sharp differences should make us cautious about applying national statistics or trends to individual cities or regions. The comparative state-by-state analyses in chapter two reveal drastic variations from state to state in refined divorce rates, age-specific divorce rates, and crude divorce rates. In fact, whatever the indicator, the western states manifested major differences among themselves, and frequently differed substantially from U.S. rates. Remarriage rates also showed sharp interstate differences, and so did many of the other indicators often cited as correlates of divorce and remarriage, such as fertility rates, economic trends, and the ethnic and religious composition of the population.

Regional Specification

The accounts of the divorce process summarized in this book are those of residents in the eight-state region known as the mountain states. Not all of the people who answered our queries lived in the mountain states when they obtained their divorces, but all resided there in 1976-1977 at the time of the two surveys. Their descriptions of the events leading up to their divorces and the adjustments which followed represent the experiences and definitions of the ever-divorced population in these eight states as they recalled them as prompted by the items in our questionnaires.

Early in chapter two we demonstrated that in its marriage and divorce rates the mountain states region differed markedly from the United States as a whole. For more than a century the divorce rates in the mountain states have been much higher than the national rates. Along with the Pacific Coast states, the mountain states have historically been areas where the divorce laws were "liberal," and hence the constraints holding "unhappy" marriages together in these states presumably have been weaker than in states with stricter statutes. Consequently, we do not expect the characteristics and problems of the divorced populations in other states necessarily to match those of the people we have studied.

Not only in their history, but in the ratio of metropolitan to urban and urban to rural population, in demographic and religious composition of the population, in the industrial/agricultural base and in cultural background and values of the people, the mountain states differ from other regions of the nation. We are uncertain about whether the results of research on divorced persons living in Detroit or Philadelphia apply to people in other cities or regions, and similarly the degree to which our findings can be generalized beyond the borders of the mountain states is an empirical question. However, we can affirm that the patterns and processes analyzed in the preceding chapters are those described to us by the divorced people in the mountain states, and that they have a generality far beyond that of most sample surveys of the divorced.

We have tried to place the survey data in appropriate historical context and to provide appropriate, detailed trend analysis for selected "atypical" states within the region. Against this historical and statistical backdrop we have told how people whose marriages failed came to the decision to divorce, the stages in the divorce process, and the personal and social adjustments to divorce as remembered by our respondents, many of whom had remarried by the time they encountered our questionnaires. Appendix B summarizes many of the demographic characteristics of the sample by individual state as well as for the region as a whole. Researchers in other settings may wish to compare the characteristics of their samples with those presented in Appendix B as part of the process of estimating the degree of congruence between the experiences of the divorced population of the mountain states and that of residents in other areas.

In our view, the Intermountain Divorce Study has permitted us to generalize about selected aspects of divorce as they apply to an entire region, rather than merely to selected populations of individual cities or clients of certain organizations or agencies. The extent to which the characteristics and patterns we have discovered in the mountain states fit those of people in other places or times remains to be demonstrated in future research.

Methodological Innovation

The use of screening questions or even screening questionnaires as part of a multi-stage survey is not a new procedure. However, as we reviewed the divorce literature, it appeared that the technique had rarely been used to study divorce, particularly to study divorce in an entire region. None of the landmark divorce studies are regional studies in the true sense of the word. The work of the Hunts[4] perhaps comes closest; their findings are described as characteristic of all sections of the nation and of the major segments of the population, but their sampling procedures were admittedly loose and the populations represented are not specified with any degree of precision.

What was innovative about the Intermountain Divorce Study was not the two-stage technique itself, but rather its use in a multi-state study of divorce. We discussed previously the liabilities of the questionnaire method for studying divorce. Many researchers, and most authors of the "landmark studies" have opted for in-depth questioning and therefore been limited to methods of interview, case history, or content analysis of diaries and personal research logs. Other divorce studies are more superficial by design, and abandon attempts to know the details of individual experience in any qualitative sense in exchange for more superficial data on a limited set of behavioral and attitudinal indicators. Studies of the former kind have produced a great deal of fascinating information of questionable generality. Studies of the latter kind, among which we number our own surveys, produce more superficial information, but at the same time their findings may be generalized with some confidence to much larger populations. Both kinds of research are necessary if we are to understand social processes as complex as marriage and divorce.

Suggestions for Future Research

A traditional way to conclude a research monograph is to identify topics of study which need additional work, or to refer to perplexing, inconsistent, or contradictory findings which deserve attention. Here we shall first recall some of our findings which are not entirely consistent with previous research on divorce, in the hope that future researchers may resolve some of the inconsistencies or specify the conditions under which different, and hence no longer inconsistent, outcomes may occur. Finally, we shall list some aspects of the divorce process which seem to us to have been ignored or at least only partially illuminated by other researchers as well as the present investigators.

Some students of divorce, notably Carter and Glick,[5] have reported that persons who marry late—at age 30 or later—are more apt to divorce than are those who marry in their twenties. We found no evidence of this pattern among our respondents. More intensive study of the characteristics of persons who marry late, and of the linkage between those characteristics and marital stability, clearly is needed. Moreover, if present national trends continue, we may expect the percentage of married people who married after age 30 to increase.

We found no evidence that non-whites in the mountain states have higher divorce rates than the whites. However, our findings in this matter are very tentative, based on relatively small subsamples of non-whites. Furthermore, the confidence that may be placed in our findings on divorce among non-whites is further eroded by the knowledge that persons who return mail questionnaires are apt to be a biased segment of the non-white population, presumably better educated and with higher incomes than non-whites generally. Therefore, our suggestion for future research is merely that more work be done on marriage and divorce among non-white populations in contexts where they comprise a smaller minority of the population than is the case in many of the metropolitan areas where the extant research on divorce has usually been conducted.

Our finding that most of the respondents reported no change in their level of social participation, or even reported increases in organizational activity following divorce, is not entirely inconsistent with prior research. The factors that determine whether one who is in the process of divorce or is recently divorced will try to maintain or increase affiliative ties need to be explored in much greater detail than they have been. We hypothesize that the variables related to a divorcing person's decision to maintain, increase, or decrease social involvement—in formal organizations as well as with kindred—vary greatly by cultural context, rural-urban setting, family background, social class, and perceived opportunity for meaningful affiliation. Among the pressing research questions are: What kinds of organizations do the recently divorced drop out of, and which do they seek out? What segment of the divorced population associates with groups such as Parents Without Partners, and how do they differ from people who shun such self-help organizations but maintain or create other kinds of organizational ties?

The finding that the variables that predict marital satisfaction in intact first marriages do not accurately predict satisfaction in remarriages is not original to this study. What is apparent from our findings as well as earlier studies of remarriage, however, is that the variables that are related to satisfaction in remarriage have not been identified and defined with sufficient clarity to adequately account for the observed variance in marital satisfaction among the remarried. Much more research on remarriage is needed, not only because it continues to be an underworked field of investigation, but also because an increasing percentage of married couples include at least one partner who has been married before.

We are not experts on marriage counseling and have not explored the research literature on the "success" of marriage counseling. Our impression from a limited exposure to that literature is that sound evaluations of the effectiveness of marital counseling are quite rare. The consensus among our respondents was that where marital counseling was sought and obtained, it did not help to "save the marriage." The majority of our respondents had not received any professional counseling during the process of their divorce, and they generally were of the opinion that even if professional counseling had been received, it would have made no difference in the final outcome as far as their divorce was concerned. It is our impression that multi-state surveys of married couples might identify couples whose marriages had been sufficiently troubled that marital counseling was obtained, and that the type and effectiveness of that counseling might be evaluated by the persons who received it, including those whose marriages remained intact as well as those who eventually divorced.

Finally, we think that the interplay between religiosity in its various dimensions and marital stability needs to be studied. The research literature on religion and divorce is not large, and mostly consists of reports of the relationship between denominational preference or religious homogamy and the probabilities of divorce. Our limited analyses suggest that among interfaith marriages there are quite substantial differences in divorce rates, depending upon the specific gender-denominational configuration represented in the marriage, as well as upon the extent of religious activity of the marriage partners. Religiosity is a complex variable, including the dimensions of personal devotionalism, public ritual observance, type and intensity of belief, and quality of personal religious experience, and the ways that each of these is related to marital satisfaction or conflict, the combinations that increase or decrease the probabilities of divorce, have scarcely been touched by empirical researchers in either the family or the sociology of religion disciplines.

These topics for future research—the characteristics of late marriages and their relationship to divorce, marital instability among non-whites when they represent very small minorities of the general population, the relationship between organizational affiliation and the characteristics of the divorced person, the correlates of satisfaction and stability in remarriage, the evaluation of the impacts of marital counseling on the quality and longevity of marriage, and the exploration of the effects of the various dimensions of religiosity upon marital stability—are not the only avenues of study that seem promising at present. However, with the possible exception of the study of marital stability among non-white minorities, all of these topics seem appropriate for large-scale survey research of regional or national scope. That they are also fertile fields for the more traditional interview surveys of divorced people in local metropolitan or organizational settings does not diminish our hope that a combination of careful qualitative and intensive small-scale studies with appropriate regional surveys will swiftly fill these gaps in our knowledge.

Notes

1. Eugene J. Webb, Donald T. Campbell, Richard D. Schwartz, and Lee Sechrest, *Unobtrusive Measures: Nonreactive Research in the Social Sciences* (Chicago: Rand McNally & Co., 1966), pp. 3, 34.

2. U.S. Department of Health and Human Services, Public Health Service, National Center for Health Statistics, *Monthly Vital Statistics Report*, Vol. 31, No. 6, September 9, 1982, p.3.

3. Howard M. Bahr, "Religious Intermarriage and Divorce in Utah and the Mountain States," *Journal for the Scientific Study of Religion* 20 (September 1981): 251-61.

4. Morton M. Hunt, *The World of the Formerly Married* (New York: McGraw-Hill, 1966); Morton M. Hunt and Bernice Hunt, *The Divorce Experience* (New York: McGraw-Hill, 1977).

5. Hugh Carter and Paul C. Glick, *Marriage and Divorce: A Social and Economic Study* (Cambridge, Mass.: Harvard University Press, 1976).

Appendix A

Research Methodology

The Intermountain Divorce Study which provides the basis for most of the analysis presented in this book was designed to obtain information about a large representative sample of divorced persons by means of a two-phase research design. Phase I was a screening procedure used to identify individuals who had been divorced from a random sample of households. Phase II was an effort to elicit responses from the divorced persons identified in Phase I. Both phases used a mail survey format.

PHASE I

Sample

The sampling frame for Phase I of the Divorce Study was a compilation of all current telephone directories for the eight intermountain states (Arizona, Colorado, Idaho, Montana, Nevada, New Mexico, Utah, and Wyoming). The number of questionnaires initially sent to each state was determined by the population of that state according to the 1970 Census and ranged from a high of 2,958 in Colorado to a low of 472 in Wyoming. Households were chosen in a random systematic fashion by selecting a random starting point and using a systematic skip interval thereafter. Businesses were deleted, leaving a total sample list of 11,014 households.

Since most entries for families in the telephone directory are listed by the husband's name, the majority of the questionnaires were addressed to Mr. ————. However, where the person listed was obviously a woman, the questionnaire was addressed to Ms. ————.

The Questionnaire

The questionnaire used in this phase of the research was a short, thirty-one item instrument entitled "Family Stability Study." The front page of the questionnaire contained the logo and address of the Eyring Research Institute (a Provo, Utah research organization that assisted with the project) and brief instructions for completing the questions. The items contained in the questionnaire were mainly demographic, but the key questions pertained to past and present marital status of the respondent (and spouse, if ever married). Questions about expectations for and satisfaction with marriage were also included.

Data Collection

Systematic analyses of variations in the methods of mail surveys have shown that at least four key elements affect response rates: apparent importance of the topic to the respondent, frequency and number of contacts, degree of personalization of the contact, and appearance and apparent complexity of the instrument (including considerations of length, amount of white space, and arrangement of the items). The questionnaire itself was concise—only three pages of questions, plus an introductory title page. It was reduced to fit on both sides of a folded 8-and-1/2-by-11-inch sheet of paper. In addition, the format was simple; most questions could be answered by checking a response or writing in a number, such as age or number of brothers and sisters.

Our case for the importance of the study rested on the idea that the family is the basis of society, and that through an individual's participation in such research, it would be possible to better understand the current status of the family and help strengthen it in the future. A final note on the questionnaire again emphasized that the project promised to be "unusually interesting and useful," and that a summary of the initial results could be obtained upon request.

The importance of the role of the respondent in the study was both implicit and explicit. Reference was made to the scientific nature of the sample and "honest, sincere, and frank answers" were encouraged. Personalization of the communications with the respondent also implied a degree of importance—letters were addressed to a particular person rather than "occupant," and stamps were pasted on the envelopes rather than using metered postage. Inside, printed letters were hand-signed in a different color of ink.

With too much obvious personalization, respondents may feel that confidentiality is threatened. Therefore, anonymity was assured in three ways: an assertion that general or regional patterns, not individuals, were of interest; a formal request that the respondent did not put his or her name or other personal identification on the questionnaire; and a note stating that the number stamped on the front of the questionnaire was only an aid in keeping track of who had returned the questionnaire and who had not. Only 45 people took the trouble to blot out or cut out the ID number.

A final condition in this phase that may have affected the response rate was an increase in postal rates about two weeks after the initial mailing. Aware of the impending increase, we solicited the help of the respondents by enclosing a note telling them of the increase and asking that they return their completed questionnaires in the business reply envelope as soon as possible, preferably before the rate increase. Inasmuch as the initial mailing took place in December, a recognition of any inconvenience the timing and the postal increase may have caused was included in a follow-up letter in January.

As mentioned, the initial mailing was sent between December 10 and December 15, 1975. Each potential respondent received a questionnaire, cover letter, postage increase notice, and business reply envelope. About four weeks later, a follow-up mailing on January 16, 1976 was sent to all those who had not responded. It contained a new cover letter, questionnaire, and business reply envelope. The letter again emphasized the importance of the study and explained that the Eyring Research Institute was a private non-profit organization involved in programs to improve the quality of life in American society. Potential respondents were also told that although the letter was addressed to one person, either spouse could complete the questionnaire.

Of the total 11,014 questionnaires originally mailed, 1,245 were not deliverable because the respondent had moved or died. This left 9,769 potential respondents. From these, 152 persons returned a note refusing to participate. After the two mailings, 4,606 completed, usable questionnaires were received, for an overall response rate of 47.1 percent. Returns by state are logged in Table 56. Response rates were highest in Utah (59.2 percent) and lowest in Nevada (39.7 percent).

As the questionnaires came in, returns were catalogued on a master list according to marital status. A total of 1,265 of the 4,606 persons who returned the questionnaire reported that they or their spouse were or had been divorced. Data on the entire sample were coded, keypunched, cleaned, and stored on computer tape.

PHASE II

Sample

Using the master list compiled from Phase I, the sample for Phase II of the Intermountain Divorce Study was composed of the 1,265 persons who indicated either they or their spouse had been or were divorced. When respondents indicated that both they and their spouse had been divorced, questionnaires were sent to both persons.

The Questionnaire

The instrument used in the second phase of the research was a nine-page, sixty-eight item questionnaire, reduced to a 5 1/2-by-8 1/2-inch booklet. It focused on an individual's experiences in divorce and adjustment after divorce. Titled simply "Divorce Study," sponsorship for this phase was identified as the Family Research Center at Brigham Young University.[1] The description and instructions on the title page referred to the Phase I questionnaire which the respondent had received and returned several months earlier. While recognizing that some people would not like to bring up the past, researchers emphasized that there was much information missing in the understanding of divorce, information the respondent could help provide by completing the questionnaire.

The series of questions began with items about the social participation of the divorced person including association in voluntary organizations as well as contact and interaction with relatives, in-laws, and the ex-spouse. Other questions asked about expectations about and satisfaction from the marriage that ended in divorce; reasons for marriage failure; influences toward and barriers to divorce; experiences with the legal system; property settlements; approval of divorce by others; living arrangements during the process of divorce; and the emotional experience of divorce at different times before, during, and after the decree. The last questions were mainly demographic—age at marriage, type of marriage ceremony, number of children, occupation, religion, and other family members who were divorced. For respondents who were remarried, an additional section dealt with present marital satisfaction, problems, and demographic information about the current spouse.

Table 56
Response Rates for Phase I

State	Number Sent	Deceased or Moved	Refused	Returned	Percent Returned
Arizona	2,305	276	43	917	45.2
Colorado	2,958	444	39	1,165	46.3
Idaho	915	84	9	395	47.5
Montana	932	63	13	382	44.0
Nevada	736	83	11	259	39.7
New Mexico	1,312	186	16	479	42.5
Utah	1,384	70	13	778	59.2
Wyoming	472	39	8	206	47.6
No state				25	
TOTAL	11,014	1,245	152	4,606	47.1

Data Collection

The data collection in Phase II followed a similar process to that for Phase I of the Divorce Study with only a few variations. The same attention was paid to the importance of the study and the respondent's place in it. Anonymity issues were also similar, but Phase II questionnaire had no visible ID number as did the Phase I instrument. The questionnaire was longer, although it was still simple and most questions could be answered by circling the appropriate response. Two open-ended questions, one about property settlements and another about factors which made the divorce so traumatic, were included.

The initial mailing of the detailed divorce questionnaire of Phase II occurred in April 1977. Each of the 1,265 potential respondents received in a metered, address-labeled envelope, a cover letter, questionnaire, business reply postcard, and business reply envelope. The cover letter noted that despite interest in divorce, very little was known about the process and problems involved; therefore, the Family Research Center, in conjunction with the Eyring Research Center, was continuing the study on divorce begun several months earlier. The respondent was again reminded of previous participation (as on the cover of the questionnaire) and asked to complete the enclosed questionnaire. Either the addressee or the spouse (whoever had been divorced) were invited to answer the questions. If the researchers had made a mistake and neither had been divorced, respondents were instructed to write "never divorced" on the postcard and return it. Since the questionnaires were not visibly numbered, the numbered postcards were included with the materials to be signed and returned when the questionnaire was completed and sent, so that researchers could mark people off their list who had responded. (A series of four dots on the questionnaires enabled researchers to identify the ID numbers and check the returned questionnaires off the list.)

Three weeks later, about May 6, 1977, a second mailing went out to those who had not yet responded. A different cover letter, another copy of the questionnaire, and a business reply envelope were included in this follow-up. The cover letter stressed the importance of knowledge about divorce for policy-making and educational purposes and emphasized the specific nature of the sampling process and unique contribution of each person.

The two mailings resulted in 265 questionnaires that were not deliverable (usually the prospective respondent had moved or died). An additional 157 persons reported that they had not been divorced. In many of these instances, it appears that the person filling out the initial screening questionnaire [from Phase I] had reported that he or she was married to someone who had been divorced but he/she personally, had not been. Rather than passing the second [Phase II] questionnaire on to the previously divorced spouse, the respondent sent it back with the notation that he or she didn't fulfill the criteria of having been divorced. This reduced the number of possible respondents to 843. Sixty-three of these people indicated a refusal in writing, others simply did not respond. Altogether, 500 completed questionnaires were returned for an overall response rate of 59 percent. Response rates for each state are given in Table 57. The highest rate of return was from Colorado (63.3 percent) and the lowest rate was from Montana (48.4 percent). Eleven questionnaires were returned for which we were unable to verify the respondent's state of residence.

PHASE I AND II COMBINED

In order to obtain a more complete picture of each respondent, we wanted to have a file on each person made up of data from both phases of the Divorce Study. Since we had information on certain demographic items on both questionnaires, these were matched to produce the desired sets of records.

Each Phase II questionnaire had two ID numbers, one corresponding to the Phase I number originally assigned to a respondent, and the second, Phase II number assigned later. Phase I numbers were matched, along with the demographic items. The number of brothers and sisters of the respondent, age at marriage, and whether or not the respondent's parents were divorced were items common to both questionnaires and were used for computer matching. This procedure yielded 356 cases where we had data from the same person at the two different times.

Often the respondent for the Phase I questionnaire was not divorced but had a spouse who had been divorced. Therefore, when the second [Phase II] questionnaire was sent to that household requesting that the divorced person complete it, the spouse of the original respondent answered the questions. In these cases, the Phase I number was the same even though a different person had responded. During the process of matching, such husband-wife pairs were determined by checking the ID number and additional demographic data about the spouse on either questionnaire and comparing it to demographic data on the respondent of the other questionnaire. For example, the respondent's age on Phase I was compared to the spouse's age on Phase II. Allowing for the amount of time between the two phases, if the two ages were similar, the questionnaires were

Table 57
Response Rates for Phase II

State	Number Sent	Deceased or Moved	Refused	Never Divorced	Returned	Percent Returned
Arizona	279	59	16	34	113	60.8
Colorado	293	79	11	37	112	63.3
Idaho	111	9	9	17	44	52.9
Montana	90	16	6	12	30	48.4
Nevada	107	21	5	10	45	59.2
New Mexico	129	41	1	9	41	51.9
Utah	189	28	12	28	77	57.9
Wyoming	64	11	3	10	25	58.1
Washington[a]	2	1	0	0	1	100.0
North Dakota[a]	1	0	0	0	1	100.0
No state					11	
TOTAL	1,265	265	63	157	500	59.0

a. Respondents from these states lived in the Mountain States during the initial sampling in Phase I and were therefore included in the study.

considered to have been completed by husband and wife. Other items used in the matching were age at marriage, number of brothers and sisters, whether or not their parents were divorced and, in some cases, occupation and religion. This type of matching resulted in the identification of 129 husband-wife pairs.

Only 15 of the Phase II respondents could not be matched as the same person or as a spouse of a Phase I person. The 356 questionnaires matched as the same person, plus the 129 husband-wife pairs, plus the 15 unmatched returns account for all 500 completed Phase II questionnaires.

PHASE I QUESTIONNAIRE

Will you please answer the following questions for yourself and for your spouse (if married) as the questions apply? Please circle the correct answer or fill in the blank. If single, just answer questions which apply.

1. What is the present marital status of <u>yourself</u> and your <u>spouse</u>?

		Yourself	Spouse
1	First marriage, presently living together	_____	_____
2	Remarriage	_____	_____
3	Single, never lived as a couple	_____	_____
4	Divorced, not now living as a couple	_____	_____
5	Widowed, not now living as a couple	_____	_____
6	Permanently separated but not divorced	_____	_____
7	Living together as husband and wife but not married	_____	_____

2. Counting your present marriage, how many times have you been married? _____

3. What type of marriage did you and your present spouse have?

    1 Civil   4 Temple
    2 Church   5 Civil followed by Church, Synagogue, or Temple
    3 Synagogue   6 Other

4. Who performed the marriage ceremony?

    1 Civil Authority
    2 Religious Authority
    3 Other (specify _____)

5. What is your sex? 1 Male   2 Female

6. How many brothers and sisters did <u>you</u> have in all? _____

7. How many of them were older than yourself? _____

8. How many brothers and sisters did your <u>spouse</u> have in all? _____

9. How many of them were older than he or she? _____

10. Which do you consider <u>yourself</u>?

    1 White   4 American Indian
    2 Black   5 Chicano or Mexican American
    3 Asian American   6 Other (specify _____)

11. What does your <u>spouse</u> consider him or herself?

    1 White   4 American Indian
    2 Black   5 Chicano or Mexican American
    3 Asian American   6 Other (specify _____)

12. What is <u>your</u> present age? _____

13. What is your <u>spouse</u>'s present age? _____

14. What is <u>your</u> religious preference?

    1 Catholic   4 Mormon
    2 Protestant   5 Other than these
       (specify _____)   6 No preference
    3 Jewish

15. What is your spouse's religious preference?

    1 Catholic   4 Mormon
    2 Protestant   5 Other than these
    3 Jewish   6 No preference

16. How often do you attend religious services?

    1 Regular attendance (weekly)
    2 Frequent attendance (at least monthly)
    3 Occasionally (several times a year)
    4 Only on special occasions (once or twice a year)
    5 Not at all

17. How often does your spouse attend religious services?

    1 Regular attendance (weekly)
    2 Frequent attendance (at least monthly)
    3 Occasionally (several times a year)
    4 Only on special occasions (once or twice a year)
    5 Not at all

18. Sources of income for past year (please circle an answer in each column)

	Husband's Earnings	Wife's Earnings	Other Income
None	1	1	1
$1 - 1,999	2	2	2
2,000 - 3,999	3	3	3
4,000 - 5,999	4	4	4
6,000 - 7,999	5	5	5
8,000 - 9,999	6	6	6
10,000 -11,999	7	7	7
12,000 -14,999	8	8	8
15,000 -19,999	9	9	9
20,000 -29,999	10	10	10
30,000+	11	11	11

19. Which of the following best describes your present employment? (If you have more than one job, select the category which best describes your primary job.)

    1 Unemployment   7 Craftsman or Foreman   13 Professional
    2 Student   8 Clerical Worker   14 Farm Owner, Renter, Manager
    3 Housewife   9 Sales Worker   15 Farm Laborer
    4 Retired   10 Official   16 Service Worker
    5 Laborer   11 Proprietor/Manager
    6 Skilled Laborer   12 Semiprofessional

20. Which of the following best describes your spouse's present employment?

    1 Unemployment   7 Craftsman or Foreman   13 Professional
    2 Student   8 Clerical Worker   14 Farm Owner, Renter, Manager
    3 Housewife   9 Sales Worker   15 Farm Laborer
    4 Retired   10 Official   16 Service Worker
    5 Laborer   11 Proprietor/Manager
    6 Skilled Laborer   12 Semiprofessional

21. How much schooling did you complete?

    1 grade school only   4 some college
    2 some high school   5 college graduate (4 year degree)
    3 high school graduate   6 graduate degree

22. How much schooling did your spouse complete?

    1 grade school only   4 some college
    2 some high school   5 college graduate (4 year degree)
    3 high school graduate   6 graduate degree

3. How many children do you have? _____

4. How old were you when you were first married? _____

5. How old was your spouse when he or she was first married? _____

6. If divorced, how old were you at the time of divorce? _____ Your spouse? _____
   (If divorced more than one time, report 1st divorce.)

7. If divorced, in what state were you living when divorced? _____

8. Compared with other couples you know, how satisfied would you rate your
   current marriage? (last marriage if widowed)

1	Much less satisfied	4	Somewhat more satisfied
2	Somewhat less satisfied	5	Much more satisfied
3	About the same	6	Never married

9. Compared with your expectations of marriage before you were married, how has
   your current (last if widowed) turned out?

1	Much worse than I expected	4	Somewhat better than expected
2	Somewhat worse than I expected	5	Much better than expected
3	About as I expected	6	Never married

10. Were your parents ever divorced? Yes   No

11. Were your spouse's parents ever divorced? Yes   No

That is all of the questions. Thank you very much for your participation in
what we believe will be an unusually interesting and useful project.

If you would like a summary of the initial results, please write or type your
name and address on a separate sheet of paper and send it to us, either along with
your questionnaire or separately. Thanks, again.

PHASE II QUESTIONNAIRE

DIVORCE STUDY
Family Research Center
Brigham Young University

One of the most serious gaps in knowledge of the modern family is about divorce. It is amazing how little is known about the problems people face in divorce and how they try to solve them and readjust their lives.

In recognition of this need, the Family Research Center is sponsoring the final stage of a study of people's experience in divorce. You probably received and returned a questionnaire several months ago about family life in which you indicated that you had been divorced. We recognize that some people do not want to bring up the past and that others think that their problems are unique to them. However, there seems to be enough common experiences that perhaps some useful first steps toward a better understanding of divorce could be made if we knew a few simple facts about the process of divorce.

The enclosed questionnaire has been designed to obtain some of the missing information so that a better understanding can be developed of why people divorce and how they adjust to the divorce.

We respectfully ask that you please fill the questionnaire out to the best of your ability and return it in the enclosed business reply envelope. Please be sure not to put your name on the questionnaire. We have provided a card with an identification number on it so that we can check people off the mailing list as their questionnaire is returned. Your responses will never be associated with your name in any way; we are interested in the general patterns that come from combining answers from the entire sample, not in any one person's responses.

We think that you will find answering the questions a simple process; most can be answered by circling a number or filling in a blank. Feel free, however, to write any additional comments or explanations you care to on any questions.

Thank you very much for this important service. Only through such surveys can we finally begin to understand the totality of people's experience in divorce. Please answer and return this week.

If you have been divorced more than once, please answer questions for first marriage.

1. HOW LONG HAS IT BEEN SINCE YOUR DIVORCE WAS FINAL? _____

2. WHICH OF THESE PERIODS WOULD YOU SAY WAS MOST DIFFICULT FOR YOU?

    1 Before decision to divorce   3 The period just after the divorce
    2 After deciding to divorce but   4 Now
       before final decree

3. WHICH OF THESE PERIODS WOULD YOU SAY WAS BEST FOR YOU AND YOUR CHILDREN?

    1 Before decision to divorce   3 The period just after the divorce
    2 After deciding to divorce   4 Now
       but before final decree

4. HAS YOUR PARTICIPATION IN ORGANIZATIONS AND CLUBS CHANGED SINCE YOUR DIVORCE?

    1 More participation   2 Same participation   3 Less participation

24. WHICH OF THE FOLLOWING DO YOU SEE AS THINGS THAT INFLUENCED YOU TO ACTUALLY SEEK A DIVORCE? (circle as many as apply)

1 Parent's desires
2 Children's desires
3 Divorced friends
4 Ease of divorce laws
5 Opportunity for alternative financial support
6 Non-divorced friends
7 Children grew up and left home
8 Approval of religious leader
9 Other (specify _____)

25. ALL THINGS CONSIDERED, HOW WOULD YOU CHARACTERIZE YOUR EXPERIENCE IN SEEKING A DIVORCE?

1 A traumatic experience, a nightmare
2 A very stressful experience, but might have been worse
3 More stressful than it should have been, but bearable
4 Somewhat unsettling, but easier than I anticipated
5 Relatively painless

26. IF MORE TRAUMATIC OR STRESSFUL THAN YOU THINK IT SHOULD HAVE BEEN:

a. What factors do you think made your divorce so traumatic and stressful?
_____

b. How might things have gone easier for you? _____
_____

27. WHAT KIND OF PROPERTY SETTLEMENTS WERE MADE, IF ANY? _____
_____

28. HOW DID YOU FEEL ABOUT THESE ARRANGEMENTS? _____

29. COMPARED TO THE TIME DURING THE PERIOD OF FINAL SEPARATION FROM FORMER SPOUSE, HOW ARE THINGS NOW?

1 Better   2 About the same   3 Worse

30. COMPARED TO THE TIME IMMEDIATELY AFTER THE DIVORCE, HOW ARE THINGS NOW?

1 Better   2 About the same   3 Worse

31. NUMBER OF BROTHERS AND SISTERS (Please include half-brothers and half-sisters, if any, as well as any brothers or sisters who may no longer be living)

_____ Yourself   _____ Ex-spouse

32. DID YOUR MOTHER WORK OUTSIDE THE HOME WHILE YOU WERE GROWING UP?

1 No
2 Yes, part-time or occasionally
3 Yes, full-time, most of the time you were growing up

33. YOUR AGE AT FIRST MARRIAGE _____

34. AGE OF EX-SPOUSE AT FIRST MARRIAGE _____

35. TYPE OF MARRIAGE WHICH ENDED IN DIVORCE.

1 Civil
2 Church
3 Synagogue
4 Tempple
5 Civil followed by Church, Synagogue, or Temple
6 Other

36. DO YOU HAVE ANY CHILDREN FROM THE FORMER MARRIAGE?

1 No   2 Yes (If yes, how many? _____)

37. DID YOUR SPOUSE HAVE CHILDREN FROM A PREVIOUS MARRIAGE?

    1 No   2 Yes (If yes, how many? _____)

38. HOW DID YOUR INCOME BEFORE THE DIVORCE COMPARE WITH THAT OF YOUR CLOSEST
    FRIENDS AND ASSOCIATES? (circle one)

    1 Much lower than theirs   4 Somewhat higher than theirs
    2 Somewhat lower than theirs   5 A great deal higher than theirs
    3 About the same

39. HOW DID YOUR FAMILY INCOME SOON AFTER THE DIVORCE COMPARE WITH THAT OF YOUR
    CLOSEST FRIENDS AND ASSOCIATES?

    1 Much lower than theirs   4 Somewhat higher than theirs
    2 Somewhat lower than theirs   5 A great deal higher than theirs
    3 About the same

40. ARE YOU PRESENTLY EMPLOYED?

    1 No   2 Yes (If yes, what kind of work do you do?
                                          _____)

41. DID YOU WORK BEFORE YOUR DIVORCE?

    1 No   2 Yes (If yes, what kind of work did you do?
                                          _____)

42. YOUR RELIGIOUS PREFERENCE AT THE TIME OF YOUR DIVORCE.

    1 Catholic   4 Mormon
    2 Protestant   5 Other than these (please specify)
    3 Jewish   6 No preference

43. RELIGIOUS PREFERENCE OF YOUR EX-SPOUSE AT THE TIME OF DIVORCE.

    1 Catholic   4 Mormon
    2 Protestant   5 Other than these (please specify)
    3 Jewish   6 No preference

44. WERE YOUR PARENTS EVER DIVORCED?

    1 No   2 Yes

45. WERE YOU EX-SPOUSE'S PARENTS EVER DIVORCED?

    1 No   2 Yes

46. NUMBER OF YOUR BROTHERS AND SISTERS WHO WERE DIVORCED, IF ANY. _____

47. NUMBER OF YOUR EX-SPOUSE'S BROTHERS AND SISTERS WHO WERE DIVORCED, IF ANY. _____

48. WHAT IS (WAS YOUR FATHER'S MAIN OCCUPATION? (Please specify title of job
    and type of industry.) _____

49. WHAT WAS YOUR EX-SPOUSE'S MAIN OCCUPATION? _____

50. HOW OFTEN DID YOU GO RELIGIOUS SERVICES BEFORE YOUR DIVORCE? (circle one)

    1 Regular attendance (weekly)
    2 Frequent attendance (at least monthly)
    3 Occasionally (several times a year)
    4 Only on special occasions (once or twice a year)
    5 Not at all

51. HOW OFTEN DID YOUR FORMER SPOUSE GO TO RELIGIOUS SERVICES BEFORE YOUR DIVORCE?

     1 Regular attendance (weekly)
     2 Frequent attendance (at least monthly)
     3 Occasionally (several times a year)
     4 Only on special occasions (once or twice a year)
     5 Not at all

- -

     If you have remarried, please answer the rest of the questions. If you have
not remarried, you have finished the questionnaire. Thank you very much.

- -

52. IN GENERAL, HOW DOES YOUR PRESENT MARRIED LIFE COMPARE TO YOUR FORMER
     MARRIED LIFE?

     1 Much better   4 A little worse
     2 A little better   5 Much worse
     3 About the same

53. DO YOU FEEL THAT THE EXPERIENCES YOU HAD IN YOUR FORMER MARRIAGE MAKE
     IT HARDER OR EASIER TO GET ALONG IN YOUR PRESENT MARRIAGE?

     1 Harder   2 Easier   3 No effect

54. WHICH OF THE FOLLOWING (IF ANY) WOULD YOU DEFINE AS MAJOR PROBLEMS IN YOUR
     CURRENT MARRIAGE? (Please select as many as apply; place a 1 by the most
     important reason, a 2 by the next most important reason, and so on.)

_____ No longer love each other   _____ Neglect of children
_____ Physical abuse   _____ Emotional problems
_____ Infidelity (spouse is involved   _____ Problems with in-laws
       with someone else)   _____ Former marriage of spouse
_____ Financial problems   _____ Other (specify _____
_____ Sexual problems   _____)

55. COMPARED WITH OTHER COUPLES YOU HAVE KNOWN, HOW WOULD YOU RATE THE DEGREE OF
     OVERALL SATISFACTION THAT YOU FEEL WITH YOUR CURRENT MARRIAGE? (circle one)

     1 Much less satisfied   4 Somewhat more satisfied
     2 Somewhat less satisfied   5 Much more satisfied
     3 About the same

56. COMPARED WITH YOUR EXPECTATIONS OF MARRIAGE BEFORE YOUR PRESENT MARRIAGE,
     HOW IS YOUR MARRIAGE TURNING OUT?

     1 Much worse than I expected   4 Somewhat better than I expected
     2 Somewhat worse than I expected 5 Much better than I expected
     3 About the same

57. HOW OFTEN WOULD YOU SAY THAT YOU AND YOUR PRESENT SPOUSE ARGUE ABOUT YOUR
     FORMER MARRIAGE OR SPOUSE?

     1 Frequently   4 Seldom
     2 Once in a while   5 Never
     3 We used to, but not now

58. NUMBER OF BROTHERS AND SISTERS YOUR SPOUSE HAS _____

59. HOW LONG HAVE YOU BEEN MARRIED TO THIS SPOUSE? _____

60. AGE OF SPOUSE AT THIS TIME _____

61. TYPE OF MARRIAGE.

    1 Civil   4 Temple
    2 Church   5 Civil followed by Church, Synagogue, or Templ
    3 Synagogue   6 Other

62. DO YOU HAVE CHILDREN FROM THIS MARRIAGE?

    1 No   2 Yes (If yes, how many? _____)

63. DID YOUR SPOUSE HAVE CHILDREN FROM A PREVIOUS MARRIAGE?

    1 No   2 Yes (If yes, how many? _____)

64. IF EMPLOYED, WHAT IS YOUR SPOUSE'S MAIN OCCUPATION? (Please specify job title
    and type of industry.) _____

65. RELIGIOUS PREFERENCE OF SPOUSE.

    1 Catholic   4 Mormon
    2 Protestant   5 Other (please specify)
    3 Jewish   6 No preference

66. SPOUSE'S ATTENDANCE OF RELIGIOUS SERVICES.

    1 Regular attendance (weekly)
    2 Frequent attendance (at least monthly)
    3 Occasionally (several times a year)
    4 Only on special occasions (once or twice a year)
    5 Not at all

67. WERE SPOUSE'S PARENTS DIVORCED?

    1 No   2 Yes

68. IF ANY, NUMBER OF SPOUSE'S BROTHERS AND SISTERS WHO WERE DIVORCED. _____

Notes for Appendix A

1. The entire study was a joint project of the Eyring Research Institute
and the Family Research Center. Phase I carried the ERI logo and name while
Phase II was sent from the Family Research Center.

Demographic Description
of the Sample

The demographic characteristics of respondents discussed here are those reported in Phase I of the overall study described in Appendix A. Although a total of 4,606 questionnaires were returned, the total N for each table is generally lower due to non-response on certain items.

Sex and Race

Men comprised 58.4 percent of those responding to the initial questionnaire; 41.6 percent were women. The racial composition of the sample included a large majority of whites (93.7 percent), though four major ethnic groups were represented. The largest minority group (2.9 percent of all respondents) claimed Chicano or Mexican American heritage, while less than 1 percent identified themselves as black, Asian American, or American Indian. An additional 1.7 percent wrote in some other ethnic identity. New Mexico had the highest proportion of non-whites (18 percent) with 10.3 percent Chicano or Mexican American. Nevada was the only state with more than 1 percent black (1.2 percent). Wyoming had the highest proportion of whites (99 percent) and the fewest minorities; 1 percent were Chicano or Mexican American.

Age

Respondents ranged in age from 16 to 97 years old and the largest percentage were in the 25-29 age group. The median age for the entire sample was 43.7 years, but the median age for each state ranged from 40.1 years in Nevada where respondents were slightly younger to 47.0 years in Arizona where respondents were slightly older than the regional average. The age distribution of the sample was such that most had reached the usual age at first marriage for American men and women. At the same time, most were old enough to have experienced at least one lifetime divorce.

Marital Status

Given the age composition of the sample and the focus of the study on marital experience, comparatively few of the respondents were single; only 5.2 percent had never married or lived together as a couple. Arizona had the most single respondents with 6.4 percent and Idaho had the fewest with 2.6 percent of those responding (see Table 58). The great majority of the respondents were married when they completed the questionnaire; 67.8 percent were in a first marriage presently living with their spouse and an additional ll.8 percent were remarried following a divorce or the death of a spouse. Utah had the highest proportion of those in a first marriage with 72.0 percent and Nevada had the lowest proportion with 59.6 percent presently living with their first spouse. The state picture was reversed for remarriages; Nevada had the most, 17.6 percent, and Utah had the fewest with 9.8 percent of the respondents being remarried.

In all states a higher proportion of men than women reported themselves as married, and in all but Nevada, more men than women reported themselves as remarried.

With the exception of two states, New Mexico and Wyoming, more women than men reported themselves as separated. The study had a total of 31 separated respondents (0.7 percent), but there were so few separated persons in each state that comparisons between states are not meaningful.

As in the separated category, more women than men indicated that they were divorced and no longer living as a couple. In the entire region, 6.0 percent of the sample reported they were currently divorced. The proportion of those currently divorced ranged from a high of 7.8 percent in Nevada to a low of 4.1 percent in Idaho.

The usual pattern of sex differences in the proportion widowed was found among our sample. In all states, more women than men had been widowed—from four times as many women as men in Montana to eighteen times more women than men in Utah.

In addition to those respondents who were never married or were single and had never lived as a couple, there were 1.1 percent of the total who were living together but were not married. In all states but Arizona and Idaho, more women than men indicated that they were living together as husband and wife but were not married. The state with the most respondents in this situation was Nevada where 2.4 percent were living together, and the state with the fewest respondents living together was Utah where 0.7 percent reported this arrangement.

When the marital status composition in each state is considered, Nevada and Utah show the most distinctively different patterns. In comparisons with the other intermountain states, Nevada has the lowest proportion of those in a first marriage and the lowest proportion of widows. This state also has the highest proportion of persons currently separated or divorced, of persons in a remarriage, and of those living together but not married. Utah is on the other end of the scale in most of these marital status distinctions. Utah has the highest percentage of married persons in a first marriage, but the lowest percentage of married persons in a remarriage. Utah also has the lowest percentage of respondents who are separated and the fewest respondents who are living together without marriage.

Comparison with Census on Marital Status

In order to determine if there was bias in the marital status of our respondents, comparisons were made with the 1970 Census in certain categories: percent presently married, percent in a remarriage, and percent ever-divorced. The proportion of respondents in each category were compared with the proportion identified by Census data. The number of cases in each table may differ due to non-response on certain items and different ways of classifying persons or families.

Table 59 shows the percent of respondents currently married and living with their spouse in the same household, including those in a first marriage and those in a remarriage. These respondents are compared with families reporting a married head of the household with spouse present in the 1970 Census. In all cases, the percent married in the divorce study was lower than in the Census, averaging 8.9 percentage points less. However, the relative position of each state compared with the other states was basically the same. There were two exceptions: Wyoming had relatively more married persons and Arizona had relatively fewer.

When proportions of those who were married more than once and currently living with their spouse in a remarriage are compared for our sample and the Census, the results are similar. In most cases there were fewer remarried persons in the sample than in the Census reports. In only one state, New Mexico, did we have a higher percentage of both male and female remarried respondents. There were also higher percentages of remarried males in our sample from Idaho and Wyoming. In the Census figures, more men than women are found in remarriages in all states. This same pattern was observed in our sample in all states except Nevada where there were more women than men who reported themselves as remarried. Differences in all cases were generally small.

A comparison of ever-married divorced persons is given in Table 60. The proportion of ever-divorced persons in the Divorce Study ranged from a low of 14.5 percent in Utah to a high of 26.9 percent in Nevada. In the Census, Utah was lowest with 14.7 percent divorced and Nevada was highest with 31.7 percent ever-divorced. Percentages of ever-divorced persons in the Divorce Study were generally lower than those in the Census population. However, in New Mexico and Wyoming the Divorce Study had a higher proportion of divorced respondents.

Although the Divorce Study usually reported smaller proportions of respondents in all comparisons, the marital composition of our sample seems to be fairly representative of the population reported in the Census. Therefore, any bias would probably be consistent and an underestimate if anything.

Religion

The majority of respondents in the mountain region claimed some religious preference; only 10.9 percent had no preference. For those claiming affiliation, 17.6 percent were Catholic, 45.8 percent were Protestant, and 20.6 chose the Church of Jesus Christ of Latter-Day Saints (Mormon). Jews made up 1.2 percent and the remaining 3.9 percent preferred some other religion than those listed (see Table 61).

There was a great deal of state variation among the religious groups. Catholics made up from four percent of the population in Utah to 26.2 percent in New Mexico, while Colorado, Montana, and Nevada all had over 20 percent of the respondents giving Catholic as a religious preference.

Over half of the respondents in all but three states were of some Protestant faith. Idaho and Nevada were over one-third Protestant, but Utah had only 9.4 percent of its respondents choosing a Protestant religion. On the opposite end of the ranks, Wyoming had the most Protestants with 63.9 percent of all respondents from that state.

Table 58
Marital Status of Respondents, by Sex, for Each Mountain State

	First Marriage		Remarriage		Single		Divorced		Widowed		Separated		Living Together		Total N
	N	%	N	%	N	%	N	%	N	%	N	%	N	%	
Arizona	(571)	64.4	(110)	12.4	(57)	6.4	(67)	7.6	(66)	7.4	(7)	0.8	(8)	0.9	886
Male	(357)	69.6	(75)	14.6	(32)	6.2	(26)	5.1	(13)	2.5	(3)	0.6	(7)	1.4	513
Female	(214)	57.4	(35)	9.4	(25)	6.7	(41)	11.0	(53)	14.2	(4)	1.1	(1)	0.3	373
Colorado	(784)	69.8	(113)	10.1	(71)	6.3	(68)	6.0	(69)	6.1	(7)	0.6	(12)	1.1	1124
Male	(522)	79.0	(67)	10.1	(32)	4.8	(23)	3.5	(9)	1.4	(2)	0.3	(6)	0.9	661
Female	(262)	56.6	(46)	9.9	(39)	8.4	(45)	9.7	(60)	13.0	(5)	1.1	(6)	1.3	463
Idaho	(269)	69.5	(53)	13.7	(10)	2.6	(16)	4.1	(32)	8.3	(2)	0.5	(5)	1.3	387
Male	(171)	72.8	(39)	16.6	(6)	2.6	(8)	3.4	(7)	3.0	(1)	0.4	(3)	1.3	235
Female	(98)	64.5	(14)	9.2	(4)	2.6	(8)	5.3	(25)	16.4	(1)	0.7	(2)	1.3	152
Montana	(261)	70.2	(41)	11.0	(17)	4.6	(17)	4.6	(30)	8.1	(2)	0.5	(4)	1.1	372
Male	(162)	77.9	(24)	11.5	(10)	4.8	(5)	2.4	(7)	3.4	--	--	--	--	208
Female	(99)	60.4	(17)	10.4	(7)	4.3	(12)	7.3	(23)	14.0	(2)	1.2	(4)	2.4	164
Nevada	(152)	59.6	(45)	17.6	(15)	5.9	(20)	7.8	(13)	5.1	(4)	1.6	(6)	2.4	255
Male	(97)	66.9	(24)	16.6	(10)	6.9	(8)	5.5	(2)	1.4	(2)	1.4	(2)	1.4	145
Female	(55)	50.0	(21)	19.1	(5)	4.5	(12)	10.9	(11)	10.0	(2)	1.8	(4)	3.6	110
New Mexico	(301)	64.6	(61)	13.1	(17)	3.6	(27)	5.8	(51)	10.9	(4)	0.9	(5)	1.1	466
Male	(190)	72.2	(36)	13.7	(9)	3.4	(10)	8.8	(14)	5.3	(3)	1.1	(1)	0.4	263
Female	(111)	54.7	(25)	12.3	(8)	3.9	(17)	8.4	(37)	18.2	(1)	0.5	(4)	2.0	203
Utah	(546)	72.0	(74)	9.8	(36)	4.7	(42)	5.5	(53)	7.0	(2)	0.3	(5)	0.7	758
Male	(372)	80.3	(53)	11.4	(14)	3.0	(17)	3.7	(4)	0.9	--	--	(3)	0.6	463
Female	(174)	59.0	(21)	7.0	(22)	7.5	(25)	8.5	(49)	16.6	(2)	0.7	(2)	0.7	295

	First Marriage		Remarriage		Single		Divorced		Widowed		Separated		Living Together		Total N
	N	%	N	%	N	%	N	%	N	%	N	%	N	%	
Wyoming	(133)	65.5	(28)	13.8	(8)	3.9	(13)	6.4	(15)	7.4	(3)	1.5	(3)	1.5	203
Male	(81)	69.2	(19)	16.2	(6)	5.1	(5)	4.3	(3)	2.6	(2)	1.7	(1)	0.9	117
Female	(52)	60.5	(9)	10.5	(2)	2.3	(8)	9.3	(12)	14.0	(1)	1.2	(2)	2.3	86
Mountain Region	(3017)	67.8	(525)	11.8	(231)	5.2	(270)	6.1	(329)	7.4	(31)	0.7	(48)	1.1	4451
Male	(1952)	75.0	(337)	12.9	(119)	4.6	(102)	3.9	(59)	2.3	(13)	0.5	(23)	0.9	2605
Female	(1065)	57.7	(188)	10.2	(112)	6.1	(168)	9.1	(270)	14.6	(18)	1.0	(25)	1.4	1846

Table 59

Comparison of Percent Married Persons, Intermountain Divorce Study 1976 and U.S. Census 1970

	Divorce Study		U.S. Census	
	Base Total [a]	Percent Married	Base Total [b]	Percent Married
Arizona	886	76.8	438,389	87.7
Colorado	1124	79.9	547,165	88.2
Idaho	387	83.2	179,448	90.3
Montana	372	81.2	171,812	89.0
Nevada	255	77.2	124,170	87.2
New Mexico	466	77.7	242,740	85.6
Utah	758	81.8	249,741	90.1
Wyoming	203	79.3	84,703	90.1

a.   Divorce Study--households with respondent currently married (first marriage or remarriage) and living with spouse.

b.   U.S. Census--families with married head, spouse present

Utah had the highest proportion of respondents claiming a single religion; 78.4 percent chose Mormon as a religious preference. The next highest proportion of Mormons was found in Idaho with 34.7 percent. The lowest percentage of Mormons was in Colorado where only 2.2 percent chose Mormon as a religious preference.

Jews made up only a small percentage in any state. The largest proportion of Jewish preferences was in Arizona where 2.5 percent responded with this choice. Less than one percent chose Jewish in Idaho, New Mexico, Utah, and Wyoming, and no one in Montana preferred Jewish as a religious identification.

Those who chose "other" as a religious preference made up from 1.8 percent of the respondents in Montana to 5.5 percent in Colorado. "No preference" was given most often in Nevada (20.1 percent of respondents) and least often in Utah where 6.0 percent said thay had no religious preference.

The majority of respondents in all states chose Protestant or Catholic as a religious preference with the exception of Utah where most chose Mormon. Although Jews were represented in each state except Montana, there were few claiming Jewish as a religious preference and relatively few chose other religions in any of the states. Only about 11 percent had no religious preference at all.

Education

Both men and women are quite well educated in the mountain region. Over eighty percent of the respondents had completed at least a high school education and over half

Table 60
Comparison of Ever-Married/Divorced Persons, U.S. Census 1970 and Intermountain Divorce Study 1976

	Divorce Study		U.S. Census	
	Total Ever-Married	Percent Ever-Divorced	Total Ever-Married	Percent Known Divorced
Arizona	851	19.6	959,246	19.9
Colorado	1081	16.2	1,193,170	17.3
Idaho	380	15.0	391,524	17.8
Montana	361	15.5	373,747	15.8
Nevada	238	26.9	278,506	31.7
New Mexico	457	20.1	514,931	15.9
Utah	736	14.5	531,878	14.7
Wyoming	195	21.0	186,583	17.1

had had some college. In the region as a whole, only 5.9 percent had completed only grade school and an additional 10.6 percent had some high school but not a high school diploma (see Table 62).

When educational attainments are compared by state, Utah has the lowest percentage (12.9 percent) of its respondents who are less than high school graduates. Montana had the most respondents with only a grade school education (8.3 percent) and Idaho had the largest proportion of all without a high school diploma (21.7 percent compared with Utah's 12.9 percent).

The state with the highest proportion of college graduates (including graduate degree holders) is New Mexico where 33.9 percent of all respondents had graduated from college. Colorado followed with 31.1 percent college graduates and graduate degree holders. The lowest percentage of college graduates was found in Wyoming where 21.8 percent of all respondents had a college degree. Overall, Utah, Arizona, and Colorado had the respondents with the most education and respondents from Wyoming, Idaho, and Montana had the least education.

Occupation

Throughout the mountain states over half the women and almost a fourth of the men in our sample were not employed. The male portion of this group includes 17.4 percent retired persons, 2.9 percent unemployed and 2.5 percent students. Women not in the labor force are mainly housewives (35.6 percent), others are retired workers (12.5 percent), unemployed (3.8 percent), or students (2.3 percent). The most evident state-by-state difference is the relatively low proportion of housewives in New Mexico (30.0

Table 61
Religious Preference of Respondents, by State

	Catholic		Protestant		Jewish		Mormon		Other		No Preference		Total N
	N	%	N	%	N	%	N	%	N	%	N	%	
Arizona	164	(18.1)	490	(54.0)	23	(2.5)	77	(8.5)	34	(3.7)	120	(13.2)	908
Colorado	249	(21.6)	675	(58.4)	18	(1.6)	25	(2.2)	63	(5.5)	125	(10.8)	1155
Idaho	51	(12.9)	151	(38.2)	1	(0.3)	137	(34.7)	16	(4.1)	39	(9.9)	395
Montana	97	(25.5)	208	(54.7)	---	-----	24	(6.3)	7	(1.8)	44	(11.6)	380
Nevada	61	(23.6)	90	(34.7)	4	(1.5)	38	(14.7)	14	(5.4)	52	(20.1)	259
New Mexico	125	(26.2)	266	(55.6)	4	(0.8)	11	(2.3)	22	(4.6)	50	(10.5)	478
Utah	31	(4.0)	72	(9.4)	2	(0.3)	602	(78.4)	15	(2.0)	46	(6.0)	768
Wyoming	22	(10.7)	131	(63.9)	1	(0.5)	24	(11.7)	5	(2.8)	22	(10.7)	205
Mountain States	800	(17.6)	2083	(45.8)	53	(1.2)	938	(20.6)	176	(3.9)	498	(10.9)	4548

Religious Preference

Table 62
Years of Schooling Completed by Respondents, by State

	Grade School		Some High School		High School Graduate		Some College		College Graduate		Graduate Degree		Total N
	N	%	N	%	N	%	N	%	N	%	N	%	
Arizona	54	(5.9)	89	(9.8)	216	(23.7)	291	(31.9)	135	(14.8)	126	(13.8)	911
Colorado	71	(6.2)	109	(9.6)	281	(24.6)	326	(28.6)	221	(19.4)	113	(11.7)	1121
Idaho	21	(5.4)	63	(16.3)	99	(25.6)	101	(26.1)	69	(17.8)	34	(8.8)	387
Montana	31	(8.3)	40	(10.7)	99	(26.5)	101	(27.0)	64	(17.1)	39	(10.4)	374
Nevada	12	(4.7)	26	(10.1)	74	(28.8)	78	(30.4)	46	(17.9)	2	(8.2)	238
New Mexico	32	(6.8)	51	(10.9)	107	(22.8)	120	(25.6)	89	(19.0)	70	(14.9)	469
Utah	27	(3.5)	72	(9.4)	201	(26.1)	257	(33.4)	144	(18.7)	68	(8.8)	769
Wyoming	14	(6.9)	24	(11.9)	63	(31.2)	57	(28.2)	30	(14.9)	14	(6.9)	202
Mountain States	262	(5.9)	474	(10.6)	1140	(25.5)	1331	(29.8)	798	(17.8)	466	(10.4)	4471

Table 63
Occupation of Employed Respondents, by Sex

	Arizona		Colorado		Idaho		Montana		Nevada	
	Male	Female	Male	Female	Male	Female	Male	Female	Male	Female
Professional, Semi-professional	49.4%	43.9%	43.7%	44.3%	33.9%	34.4%	42.9%	43.8%	41.7%	27.9%
Official, Proprietor, Manager	13.6	7.5	13.5	5.9	15.1	8.2	10.1	1.4	15.7	13.1
Sales	5.2	8.1	6.8	6.4	4.7	4.9	4.2	11.0	4.6	6.6
Clerical	2.6	25.4	2.8	25.6	1.0	27.9	2.9	26.0	3.7	42.6
Craftsmen, Foremen	14.5	1.7	10.9	0.9	9.4	1.6	6.5	1.4	15.7	--
Skilled Laborer	8.1	4.0	11.3	6.4	15.6	8.2	13.1	4.1	9.3	1.6
Laborer	2.9	5.2	4.4	3.2	3.1	8.2	4.2	5.5	2.8	6.6
Farm Operator, Owner	0.9	1.2	4.2	3.2	14.1	6.6	11.3	4.1	--	--
Farm Worker	--	--	0.6	0.5	2.6	--	1.2	--	--	--
Service Worker	2.9	2.9	1.8	3.7	0.5	--	3.6	2.7	6.5	1.6
Total N	346	173	542	219	192	61	168	73	108	61

194

	New Mexico		Utah		Wyoming	
	Male	Female	Male	Female	Male	Female
Professional, Semi-professional	45.5%	45.9%	40.9%	35.3%	39.6%	34.2%
Official, Proprietor, Manager	12.3	8.7	15.0	5.9	7.3	2.6
Sales	4.7	2.2	4.2	12.6	3.1	5.3
Clerical	1.9	26.1	3.3	29.4	1.0	34.2
Craftsmen, foremen	12.3	2.2	12.3	0.8	19.8	2.6
Skilled Laborer	11.8	4.3	16.2	4.2	7.3	--
Laborer	2.8	3.3	3.3	6.7	7.3	7.9
Farm Operator, Owner	4.7	3.3	2.8	--	8.3	7.9
Farm Worker	0.9	--	0.3	0.8	1.0	--
Service Worker	2.8	1.1	1.7	4.2	5.2	5.3
Total N	211	92	359	119	96	38

percent) and the relatively high proportion in Utah (41.9 percent) and Wyoming (41.2 percent).

Occupational categories for all employed persons are shown in Table 63. By far the largest occupational category represented among our sample is professional and semi-professional. The highest proportions of professionals and semi-professionals were in Arizona where 49.4 percent of the men and 43.9 percent of the women were classified as such. New Mexico was second with almost equal proportions of men and women, 45.5 and 45.9 percent, considered professional or semi-professional. Nevada had the highest proportion of clerical and the second highest proportion of service workers, but no farmers or farm workers. Idaho had the highest proportion of farmers and farm workers as well as the highest proportion of skilled laborers and the second highest proportion of unskilled laborers. Idaho also had the fewest professionals and semi-professionals. Wyoming is noteworthy in that there were relatively more craftsmen aand foreman, laborers, and service workers than in other mountain states.

In states where the educational levels are lower, fewer persons reported professional and semi-professional positions and more persons reported farm and labor occupations, such as Idaho and Wyoming. Correlations are also found in states where respondents have relatively more education. The highest proportions of professionals and semi-professionals are in Arizona and New Mexico where there are relatively more college graduates and persons with graduate degrees.

Occupational differences between men and women are most striking in clerical jobs where there are eleven times as many working women as working men, 28.0 and 2.6 percent respectively. In two other categories, craftsmen and foremen, and skilled labor occupations, a much higher proportion of men than women are found. In the remaining occupational categories, differences are not great between men and women.

Throughout the region, the general occupational pattern includes only a few major state variations. For example, although there is little difference in the regional proportions of men and women in professional and semi-professional occupations, in Nevada there is a distinct difference. Professional and semi-professional men accounted for 41.9 percent of the employed male respondents while 27.9 percent of the employed women were in this category—the largest difference between men and women in any state. The greatest difference between men and women in clerical occupations is in Wyoming where only one man reported his occupation in this category. In Utah, as in most of these states, more women than men reported sales-related occupations and the difference in proportions in Utah is greater than in other mountain states. All states exhibit patterns much like the regional average for other occupational categories.

Income

Data on income were gathered for both husband and wife in all respondent households. Family income was computed by adding these two figures with the amount of other income stated. Exact amounts were not available; therefore, all figures may be considered as falling within a certain range. Totals were figured by combining midpoints of ranges (see Table 64).

In all states, husband's income averaged about twice as high as wife's income. This may be due to the fact that over half of the women in our sample were not employed outside the home. However, about a third of these women still report earnings.

When all wives are considered, most women earn less than $3,000 per year. One-third

Table 64
Income in the Mountain Region

	Husband's Income		Wife's Income		Other Income		Total Family Income[a]	
	N	%	N	%	N	%	N	%
None	84	(2.3)	949	(31.1)	516	(35.1)	46	(1.1)
$0-1,999	66	(1.8)	521	(17.7)	404	(27.5)	99	(2.3)
2,000-3,999	146	(4.0)	331	(10.8)	155	(10.6)	136	(3.2)
4,000-5,999	214	(5.8)	362	(11.9)	121	(8.2)	245	(5.8)
6,000-7,999	285	(7.7)	296	(9.7)	67	(4.6)	282	(6.6)
8,000-9,999	405	(11.0)	212	(6.9)	52	(3.5)	358	(8.4)
10,000-11,999	512	(13.9)	166	(5.4)	47	(3.2)	407	(9.6)
12,000-14,999	699	(19.0)	132	(4.3)	48	(3.3)	742	(17.4)
15,000-19,999	596	(16.2)	56	(1.8)	21	(1.4)	709	(16.7)
20,000-29,999	411	(18.4)	15	(0.5)	21	(1.4)	760	(17.9)
30,000+	270	(7.3)	11	(0.4)	17	(1.2)	471	(11.1)
Total N	3638		3051		1469		4255	

a. Total family income is the sum of midpoints in income categories for
    husband's, wife's, and other income. When the income in a particular
    category was not reported, the case was not figured into the total.

of the wives have incomes over $5,000 annually but less than 1 percent earn over $20,000. Women in Nevada have the highest incomes and Utah and Wyoming women have the lowest incomes.

For husbands in the households sampled, the mean income is between $10,00 and $12,000. Only 2.3 percent record no income while two-thirds of the husbands were earning over $10,000 annually, and over 25 percent have incomes over $20,000 per year. Men in Colorado were earning the most and men in Montana and Utah had the lowest mean incomes.

In addition to the incomes of husbands and wives, 65 percent of the families had other sources of income. For one-fourth of the families, the extra income was less than $12,000, but 10.5 percent received over $10,000. A combination of husband's, wife's, and other income made up the family income for respondents. Only 12.4 percent of the respondents had family incomes less than $4,000, or below the poverty level. Almost half had family incomes over $15,000 and more than one-fourth of all families had at least a $20,000 per year income. Nevada and Colorado families had the highest mean incomes and Utah and Montana families had the lowest.

Bibliography

Ahrons, Constance R. "Divorce: A Crisis of Family Transition and Change," *Family Relations* 29 (October 1980): 533-40.

Bahr, Howard M. "Religious Intermarriage and Divorce in Utah and the Mountain States." *Journal for the Scientific Study of Religion* 20 (September 1981): 251-61.

Bahr, Stephen J. "The Effects of Welfare on Marital Stability and Remarriage." *Journal of Marriage and the Family* 41 (August 1979): 553-60.

Bahr, Stephen J., and Day, Randal D. "Sex Role Attitudes, Female Employment, and Marital Satisfaction." *Journal of Comparative Family Studies* 9 (No. 1, 1978): 53-67.

Becker, Gary. "A Theory of Marriage: Part I." *Journal of Political Economy* 81 (July/August 1973): 813-46.

————. "A Theory of Marriage: Part II." *Journal of Political Economy* 82 (March/April 1974): S11-S26.

————. *The Economic Approach to Human Behavior*. Chicago: University of Chicago Press, 1976.

Becker, Gary; Landes, Elizabeth; and Michael, Robert. "An Economic Analysis of Marital Instability." *Journal of Political Economy* 85 (December 1977): 1141-87.

Bernard, Jessie. *Remarriage: A Study of Marriage*. New York: Russell & Russell, 1956, 1971.

————. "No News, but New Ideas." In Paul Bohannan (ed.), *Divorce and After*. Garden City, N.Y.: Doubleday, 1970, pp. 3-25.

————. "Foreword." In George Levinger and Oliver C. Moles (eds.), *Divorce and Separation: Context, Causes, and Consequences*. New York: Basic Books, 1979.

Blake, Nelson M. *The Road to Reno: A History of Divorce in the United States*. New York: Macmillan, 1962.

Bloom, Bernard L.; White, Stephen W.; and Asher, Shirley J. "Marital Disruption as a Stressful Life Event." In George Levinger and Oliver C. Moles (eds.), *Divorce and Separation: Context, Causes, and Consequences.* New York: Basic Books, 1979, pp. 184-200.

Bohannan, Paul. "Divorce Chains, Households of Remarriage, and Multiple Divorcers." In Paul Bohannan (ed.), *Divorce and After.* Garden City, N.Y.: Doubleday, 1970.

Bohannan, Paul (ed.). *Divorce and After.* Garden City, N.Y.: Doubleday & Co., 1970.

Brandwein, R. A.; Brown, C. A.; and Fox, E. M. "Women and Children Last: The Social Situation of Divorced Mothers and Their Families." *Journal of Marriage and the Family* 36 (August 1974): 498-514.

Brown, Carol A.; Feldberg, R.; Fox, E. M.; and Kohen, J. "Divorce: Change of a New Lifetime." *Journal of Social Issues* (no. 1, 1976): 119-33.

Bumpass, Larry L. "The Trend of Interfaith Marriage in the United States." *Social Biology* 17 (1970): 253-59.

Bumpass, Larry L., and Sweet, James A. "Differentials in Marital Instability: 1970." *American Sociological Review* 37 (December 1972): 754-66.

Bureau of Labor Statistics. *Work Experience and Earnings in 1976 by State and Area,* Report 536. Washington, D.C.: U.S. Government Printing Office, 1978.

―――. *Marital and Family Status of Workers by State and Area,* Report 545. Washington, D.C.: U.S. Government Printing Office, 1978.

Carter, Hugh, and Glick, Paul C. *Marriage and Divorce: A Social and Economic Study.* Cambridge, Mass.: Harvard University Press, 1976.

Cherlin, Andrew. "Remarriage as an Incomplete Institution." *American Journal of Sociology* 84 (November 1978): 634-50.

―――. "Work Life and Marital Dissolution." In George Levinger and Oliver C. Moles (eds.), *Divorce and Separation: Context, Causes, and Consequences.* New York: Basic Books, 1979, pp. 151-66.

―――. "Religion and Remarriage—Reply." *American Journal of Sociology* 86 (no. 3, 1980): 636-40.

―――. *Marriage, Divorce, and Remarriage.* Cambridge, Mass.: Harvard University Press, 1981.

Chester, R. "Is There a Relationship Between Childlessness and Marriage Breakdown?" In E. Peck and J. Senderowitz (eds.), *Pronatalism: The Myth of Mom and Apple Pie.* New York: Cromwell, 1974, pp. 114-26.

Chiriboga, David A., and Cutler, Loraine. "Stress Responses Among Divorcing Men and Women."*Journal of Divorce* 2 (Winter 1978): 95-106.

Condie, Spencer J. "Role Bargains and Role Profits of First Married and Subsequently Married Couples." Unpublished manuscript, Department of Sociology, Brigham Young University, 1978.

Coombs, L. C., and Zumeta, Z. "Correlates of Marital Dissolution in a Prospective Fertility Study: A Research Note." *Social Problems* 18 (Summer 1970): 92-102.

Crosby, John F. "A Critique of Divorce Statistics and Their Interpretation." *Family Relations* 29 (January 1980): 51.

Cull, John C., and Hardy, Richard E. *Deciding on Divorce.* Springfield, Ill.: Charles C. Thomas, 1974.

Curin, Gerald; Veroff, Joseph; and Feld, Sheila. *Americans View Their Mental Health.* New York: Basic Books, 1979.

Cutright, Phillips. "Income and Family Events: Marital Stability." *Journal of Marriage and the Family* 33 (May 1971): 291-306.

Cutright, Phillips, and Scanzoni, John. "Income Supplements and the American Family." In Joint Economic Committee (eds.), *The Family, Poverty, and Welfare Programs: Factors Influencing Family Instability*, Studies in Public Welfare, Paper No. 12, Part I. Washington, D.C.: U.S. Government Printing Office, 1973.

Dailey, R. "Divorce (Moral Aspect)." *New Catholic Encyclopedia*, Vol. IV. New York: McGraw-Hill, 1967, p. 931.

Day, Lincoln. "Those Unsatisfactory Statistics on Divorce." *Australian Quarterly* (December 1979): 26-31.

Duberman, Lucille. *Marriage and Other Alternatives*. New York: Praeger, 1977.

Eckhardt, Kenneth W.; Grady, William R.; and Hendershot, Gerry E. "Expectations and Probabilities of Marriage: Findings from the National Survey of Family Growth, Cycle II." Paper presented at the meetings of the Population Association of America, Denver, Colo., April 10-12, 1980.

Everly, Kathleen. "New Directions in Divorce Research." *Journal of Clinical Child Psychology* 6 (Summer 1977): 7-10.

Falasco, Dee. "A Multivariate Analysis of the Factors Associated with Divorce and Remarriage." Paper presented at the meetings of the Population Association of America, Denver, Colo., April 10-12, 1980.

Farber, Bernard. "Introduction," pp. xviii, xxxiv in Willard Waller, *The Old Love and the New*. Carbondale: Southern Illinois University Press, 1967.

Feldberg, Roslyn, and Kohen, Janet. "Family Life in an Anti-Family Setting: A Critique of Marriage and Divorce." *Family Coordinator* 25 (April 1976): 155-56.

Fenelon, Bill. "State Variations in United States Divorce Rates." *Journal of Marriage and the Family* 33 (no. 2, 1971): 321-27.

Fisher, Esther Oshiver. *Divorce; The New Freedom*. New York: Harper & Row, 1974.

———. "The Journal of Divorce." *Journal of Divorce* 1 (Fall 1977): 5.

Freed, Doris Jonas, and Foster, Henry H. Jr. "Divorce in the Fifty States: An Overview." Unpublished manuscript obtained from Doris Jonas Freed, 60 East 42nd Street, New York, NY 10017, 1978.

Furstenberg, Frank F. "Premarital Pregnancy and Marital Instability." *Journal of Social Issues* 32 (no. 1, 1976): 67-86.

———. "Premarital Pregnancy and Marital Instability." In George Levinger and Oliver C. Moles (eds.), *Divorce and Separation: Context, Causes, and Consequences*. New York: Basic Books, 1979, pp. 83-98.

Gettleman, Susan, and Markowitz, Janet. *The Courage to Divorce*. New York: Simon and Schuster, 1974.

Glaser, Barney G., and Strauss, Anselm. *The Discovery of Grounded Theory*. Chicago: Aldine, 1967.

Glenn, Norval D. "The Contribution of Marriage to Psychological Well-Being of Males and Females." *Journal of Marriage and the Family* 37 (August 1975): 594-600.

———. "The Well-Being of Persons Remarried After Divorce." *Journal of Family Issues* 2 (March 1981): 61-75.

Glenn, Norval D., and Weaver, Charles N. "The Marital Happiness of Remarried Divorced Persons." *Journal of Marriage and the Family* 39 (May 1977): 331-37.

Glick, Paul C. *American Families*. New York: John Wiley, 1957.

———. "Remarriage: Some Recent Changes and Variations." *Journal of Family Issues* 1 (December 1980): 455-78.

Glick, Paul C., and Norton, Arthur J. "Frequency, Duration, and Probability of Marriage and Divorce." *Journal of Marriage and the Family* 33 (May 1971): 307-17.

————. "Marrying, Divorcing, and Living Together in the U.S. Today."*Population Bulletin* 32 (October 1977): 1-41.

Goffman, Erving. *The Presentation of Self in Everyday Life*. Garden City, N.Y.: Doubleday, 1959.

Goode, William J. *After Divorce*. Glencoe, Ill.: Free Press, 1956.

————. *Women in Divorce*. New York: Free Press, 1956.

Grady, William R. *Remarriages of Women 15-44 Years of Age Whose First Marriage Ended in Divorce: United States, 1976*. U.S. Department of Health, Education, and Welfare, Public Health Service, Hyattsville, Md.: U.S. Government Printing Office, 1980.

Gullahorn, Jeanne E. *Psychology and Women: In Transition*. New York: John Wiley & Sons, 1979.

Gurak, Douglas T., and Dean, Gillian. "The Remarriage Market: Factors Influencing the Selection of Second Husbands." *Journal of Divorce* 3 (Winter 1979): 161-73.

Halliday, Terrence C. "Remarriage: The More Complete Institution?" *American Journal of Sociology* 86 (no. 3, 1980): 630-35.

Hammond, Janice M. "Children of Divorce: A Study of Self-Concept, Academic Achievement, and Attitudes." *Elementary School Journal* 80 (no. 2, 1979): 55.

Hannan, M. T.; Tuma, N. B.; and Groeneveld, L. P. "Income and Marital Events: Evidence from an Income Maintenance Experiment." *American Journal of Sociology* 82 (May 1977): 1186-1211.

Hart, Nicky. *When Marriage Ends: A Study in Status Passage*. London: Tavistock, 1976.

Hayes, Maggie P.; Stinnett, Nick; and DeFrain, John. "Learning About Marriage from the Divorced." *Journal of Divorce* 4 (Fall 1980): 23-29.

Haynes, John M. *Divorce Mediation: A Practical Guide for Therapists and Counselors*. New York: Springer, 1981.

Herman, Sonja J. "Women, Divorce, and Suicide." *Journal of Divorce* 1 (Winter 1977): 108.

Hetherington, E. M.; Cox, M.; and Cox, R. "The Aftermath of Divorce." In J. H. Stevens, Jr. and Marilyn Mathews (eds.), *Mother-Child, Father-Child Relations*. Washington, D.C.: National Association for Education of Young Children, 1978, pp. 149-76.

Hetherington, E. M.; Cox, M.; and Cox, R. "Stress and Coping in Divorce: A Focus on Women." In J. E. Gullahorn (ed.), *Psychology and Women: In Transition*. New York: John Wiley and Sons, 1979.

Hicks, Mary W., and Platt, M. "Marital Happiness and Stability: A Review of the Research in the Sixties." *Journal of Marriage and the Family* 32 (1970): 553-74.

Homans, George C. "Social Behavior as Exchange." *American Journal of Sociology* 63 (1958): 597-606.

————. *Social Behavior: Its Elementaary Forms*. New York: Harcourt Brace Jovanovich, 1974.

Huber, Joan, and Spitze, Glenna. "Considering Divorce: An Expansion of Becker's Theory of Marital Instability." *American Journal of Sociology* 86 (1980): 75-89.

Hunt, Morton M. *The World of the Formerly Married*. New York: McGraw-Hill, 1966.

Hunt, Morton M., and Hunt, Bernice. *The Divorce Experience*. New York: McGraw-Hill, 1977.

Idaho Bureau of Business and Economic Research. *Idaho Statistical Abstract*. Boise: Idaho Department of Health and Welfare, 1981.

Irving, Howard H. *Divorce Mediation: A Rational Alternative to the Adversarial System*. Toronto: Personal Library Publishers, 1980.

Johnson, Douglas W.; Picard, Paul R.; and Quinn, Bernard. *Churches and Church Membership in the United States: 1971*. Washington, D.C.: Glenmary Research Center, 1974.

Kessler, Sheila, *The American Way of Divorce: Prescriptions for Change*. Chicago: Nelson-Hall, 1975.

Kimball, Spencer W. *Marriage and Divorce*. Salt Lake City, Utah: Deseret Book, 1976.

Kitson, Gay C., and Raschke, Helen J. "Divorce Research: What We Know; What We Need to Know." *Journal of Divorce* 4 (Spring 1981): 1-37.

Koo, Helen P., and Suchindran, C. M. "Effects of Children on Women's Remarriage Prospects." *Journal of Family Issues* 1 (December 1980): 497-515.

Krantzler Mel. *Creative Divorce: A New Opportunity for Personal Growth*. New York: M. Evans and Co., 1974.

Landis, Judson T. "The Pattern of Divorce in Three Generations." *Social Forces* 34 (March 1956): 201-7.

———. "Social Correlates of Divorce and Nondivorce Among the Unhappy Married." *Marriage and Family Living* 25 (May 1963): 178-80.

Lenthall, Gerald. "Marital Satisfaction and Marital Stability." *Journal of Marriage and Family Counseling* 3 (October 1977): 25-32.

Levinger, George. "Marital Cohesiveness and Dissolution: An Integrative Review." *Journal of Marriage and the Family* 27 (1965): 19-28.

———. "A Social Psychological Perspective on Marital Dissolution." In George Levinger and Oliver C. Moles (eds.), *Divorce and Separation: Context, Causes, and Consequences*. New York: Basic Books, 1979, pp. 37-60.

Levinger, George, and Moles, Oliver C. (eds.). *Divorce and Separation: Context, Causes, and Consequences*. New York: Basic Books, 1979.

Locke, Harvey J. *Predicting Adjustment in Marriage: A Comparison of a Divorced and a Happily Married Group*. New York: Henry Holt, 1951.

Luepnitz, Deborah A. "Which Aspects of Divorce Affect Children?" *Family Coordinator* 28 (January 1979): 79-85.

McKenry, Patrick C.; White, Priscilla N.; and Price-Bonham, Sharon. "The Fracture Conjugal Family: A Comparison of Married and Divorced Dyads," *Journal of Divorce* 1 (Summer 1978): 4.

Mariano, William E. "Marriage Information." In Jane D. Flatt (ed.), *The World Almanac and Book of Facts*. New York: Newspaper Enterprise Association, Inc., 1982.

Messinger, L. "Remarriage Between Divorced People with Children from Previous Marriage: A Proposal for Preparation for Remarriage." *Journal of Marriage and Family Counseling* 2 (no. 2, 1976): 193-99.

Michael, Robert T. "The Rise in Divorce Rates, 1960-1974: Age-Specific Components," *Demography* 15 (May, 1978): 177.

Miller, Arthur A. "Reactions of Friends to Divorce." In Paul Bohannan (ed.), *Divorce and After*. Garden City, N.Y.: Doubleday, 1970, pp. 56-77.

Moller, A. S. "Jewish-Gentile Divorce in California." *Jewish Social Studies* 37 (Summer/Fall 1976): 279-90.

Mott, F. L., and Moore, S. F. "The Causes of Marital Disruption Among Young American Women: An Interdisciplinary Perspective." *Journal of Marriage and the Family* 41 (May 1979): 355-65.

Mueller, Charles W., and Pope, Hallowell. "Marital Instability: A Study of Its Transmission Between Generations." *Journal of Marriage and the Family* 39 (February 1977): 83-92.

National Center for Health Statistics. *100 Years of Marriage and Divorce Statistics: United States, 1867-1967.* Hyattsville, Md., 1973.

————. *Monthly Vital Statistics Report, Advance Report, Final Marriage Statistics, 1975.* Hyattsville, Md., 1977.

————. *Monthly Vital Statistics Report, Births, Marriages, Divorces and Deaths for 1980.* Hyattsville, Md., 1981.

————. *Vital Statistics of the United States, 1977, Vol. III—Marriage and Divorce.* Hyattsville, Md., 1981.

Norton, Arthur J., and Glick, Paul C. "Marital Instability: Past, Present, and Future." In George Levinger and Oliver C. Moles (eds.), *Divorce and Separation: Context, Causes, and Consequences.* New York: Basic Books, 1979, pp. 6-19.

Nye, F. Ivan, and Berardo, Felix M. *The Family: Its Structure and Interaction.* New York: Macmillan, 1973.

Olson, David H. (ed.). *Inventory of Marriage and Family Literature, Vol. VII, 1980.* Beverly Hills: Sage Publications, 1981, p. vii.

Olson, David H. L., and Dahl, Nancy S. *Inventory of Marriage and Family Literature, Vol. II, 1973 and 1974.* St. Paul: University of Minnesota, Family Social Science, 1975.

Pope, Hallowell, and Mueller, Charles W. "The Intergenerational Transmission of Marital Instability: Comparisons by Race and Sex." *Journal of Social Issues* 32 (1976): 49-66.

Price-Bonham, Sharon, and Balswick, Jack O. "The Noninstitutions: Divorce, Desertion, and Remarriage." *Journal of Marriage and the Family* 42 (November 1980): 959-72.

Renne, Karen S. "Health and Marital Experience in an Urban Population." *Journal of Marriage and the Family* 33 (May 1971): 338-50.

Rheinstein, M. *Marriage Stability, Divorce, and the Law.* Chicago: University of Chicago Press, 1972.

Rice, David G. "Pseudo-Divorce: A Factor in Marital Stability and Growth." *Psychotherapy: Theory, Research and Practice* 13 (Spring 1976): 51-53.

Rose, Vicki L., and Price-Bonham, Sharon. "Divorce Adjustment: A Woman's Problem?" *The Family Coordinator* 22 (July 1973): 291-97.

Rosen, Rhona. "Children of Divorce: What They Feel About Access and Other Aspects of the Divorce Experience." *Journal of Clinical Child Psychology* (Summer 1977): 24-27.

Ross, Heather L., and Sawhill, Isabel V. *Time of Transition: The Growth of Families Headed by Women.* Washington, D.C.: The Urban Institute, 1975.

Salts, Connie J. "Divorce Process: Integration of Theory." *Journal of Divorce* 2 (Spring 1979): 233.

Scanzoni, John. "A Historical Perspective on Husband-Wife Bargaining Power and Marital Dissolution." In George Levinger and Oliver C. Moles (eds.), *Divorce and Separation: Context, Causes, and Consequences.* New York: Basic Books, 1979, pp. 20-36.

Scanzoni, Letha, and Scanzoni, John. *Men, Women, and Change: A Sociology of Marriage and the Family.* New York: McGraw-Hill, 1976.

Schlesinger, Benjamin. "Remarriage—An Inventory of Findings." *The Family Coordinator* (October 1968): 248-50.

Schoettle, Ulrich C., and Cantwell, Dennis P. "Children of Divorce." *Journal of the American Academy of Child Psychiatry* 19 (1980): 453.

Simon, Werner, and Lumry, Gayle K. "Suicide of the Spouse as a Divorce Substitute." *Diseases of the Nervous System* 31 (September 1970): 608-12.

Spanier, Graham B., and Lachman, Margie E. "Factors Associated with Adjustment to Marital Separation." *Sociological Focus* 13 (October 1980): 369-81.

Stetson, Dorothy M. and Wright, Gerald C. Jr. "The Effects of Laws of Divorce in American States." *Journal of Marriage and the Family* 37 (August 1975): 537-47.

Sweet, James A. "Differentials in Remarriage Probabilities," working paper 73-29. Madison, Wisc.: Center for Demography and Ecology, 1973.

Sweet, James A., and Bumpass, Larry L. "Differentials in Marital Instability of the Black Population: 1970." *Phylon* 35 (September 1974): 323-31.

Thibaut, J. W., and Kelly, H. H. *The Social Psychology of Groups.* New York: John Wiley, 1956.

Thornes, Barbara, and Collard, Jean. *Who Divorces?* London: Routledge & Kegan Paul, 1979.

Thornton, Arland. "Marital Dissolution, Remarriage, and Childbearing." *Demography* 15 (August 1978): 361-80.

———. "Marital Instability Differentials and Interactions: Insights from Multivariate Contingency Table Analysis." *Sociology and Social Research* 62 (July 1978): 572-95.

Uldry, J. Richard. *The Social Context of Marriage.* Philadelphia: J. B. Lippincott, 1966.

U.S. Bureau of the Census. *Statistical Abstract of the United States, 1957.* Washington, D.C.: U.S. Government Printing Office, 1957.

———. *Census of Population: 1970. Vol. 1—Characteristics of the Population.* Washington, D.C.: U.S. Government Printing Office, 1973.

———. *Statistical Abstract of the United States, 1979* (100th ed.). Washington, D.C.: U.S. Government Printing Office, 1979.

———. *Statistical Abstract of the United States, 1980* (101st ed.). Washington, D.C.: U.S. Government Printing Office, 1980.

———. *1980 Census of Population and Housing, U.S. Summary, Final Population and Housing Counts.* Washington, D.C.: U.S. Government Printing Office, 1982.

U.S. Department of Health and Human Services, Public Health Service, National Center for Health Statistics. *Monthly Vital Statistics Report,* Vol. 31, No. 6, September 9, 1982, p. 3.

Utah Bureau of Health Statistics. *Utah Marriage & Divorce, 1972-1979.* Salt Lake City, Utah: 1981.

Van Dyck, Peter C., and Brockert, John E. *Adolescent Pregnancy in the 1970s: A Study*

Comparing Utah and the United States. Salt Lake City, Utah: Bureau of Health Statistics, 1980.

Walker, Kenneth N., and Messinger, Lillian. "Remarriage After Divorce: Dissolution and Reconstruction of Family Boundaries." *Family Process* 18 (June 1979): 185-92.

Walker, K., and Whitney, O. *The Family and Marriage in a Changing World*. London: Gallancz, 1965.

Waller, Willard. *The Old Love and the New*. Philadelphia: Liveright, 1930. Republished with introduction by Bernard Farber, Carbondale: Southern Illinois University Press, 1967.

Wallerstein, Judith S., and Kelly, Joan B. "Children and Divorce: A Review." *Social Work* 24 (November 1979): 468.

———. *Surviving the Breakup: How Children and Parents Cope with Divorce*. New York: Basic Books, 1980.

Webb, Eugene J.; Campbell, Donald T.; Schwartz, Richard D.; and Sechrest, Lee. *Unobtrusive Measures: Nonreactive Research in the Social Sciences*. Chicago: Rand McNally & Co., 1966.

Weiss, Robert S. "The Emotional Impact of Marital Separation." In George Levinger and Oliver C. Moles (eds.), *Divorce and Separation: Context, Causes, and Consequences*. New York: Basic Books, 1979, pp. 201-10.

———. *Marital Separation*. New York: Basic Books, 1975.

Westoff, Leslie Aldridge. *The Second Time Around: Remarriage in America*. New York: Viking Press, 1977.

White, Lynn K. "Sex Differentials in the Effect of Remarriage on Global Happiness." *Journal of Marriage and the Family* 41 (November 1979): 869-76.

Williams, Kristen M., and Kuhn, Russell P. *Remarriages*. U.S. Department of Health, Education, and Welfare, Public Health Service, Hyattsville, Md.: U.S. Government Printing Office, 1973.

Wise, Myra J. "The Aftermath of Divorce." *American Journal of Psychoanalysis* 42 (no. 2, 1980): 149-58.

Wright, Gerald C. Jr., and Stetson, Dorothy M. "The Impact of No-Fault Divorce Law Reform on Divorce in American States." *Journal of Marriage and the Family* 40 (1978): 575-80.

Yoder, John D., and Nichols, Robert C. "A Life Perspective Comparison of Married and Divorced Persons." *Journal of Marriage and the Family* 42 (May 1980): 413-19.

Zeiss, Antonette M.; Zeiss, Robert A.; and Johnson, Stephen M. "Sex Differences in Initiation of and Adjustment to Divorce." *Journal of Divorce* 4 (Winter 1980): 21-33.

Index

Adjustment to divorce, 119
    financial arrangements, 120, 122
age at marriage
    effect on divorce, 50-51
    effect on marital happiness, 154
    and marital stability, 77-78, 158
age-specific divorce rates, 45-46
Ahrons, C. A., 6
Asher, S. J., 120-21

Bahr, H. M., 79
Bahr, S. J., 55, 63, 71, 73
Balswick, J. O., 8, 49, 61, 143, 148
Baptists, 51
barriers to divorce, 101-4, 115
    children, 102, 115
    divorce laws, 104
    finances, 102, 115, 158
    religious constraints, 103, 115
Becker, G., 62
Bernard, J., 16, 93, 121
binuclear family, 6
Blake, N. M., 49
Bloom, B. L., 120-21
Bohannan, P., 16, 143
Brandwein, R. A., 125
Brown, C. A., 125
Bumpass, L. L., 55, 60
Bureau of Labor Statistics, 73

Carter, H., 17, 51, 53, 54, 61, 121
Catholics, 51, 52, 53, 76, 79, 81, 161,
    187, 190
changes
    lifestyle, 126
    living arrangements, 126-27
characterization of divorce experience,
    121-23
    "nightmare," 121
    relatively painless, 121
    stressful, 121
    traumatic, 121
    upsetting, 121
Cherlin, A., 17, 142
Chester, R., 55
children
    and likelihood of remarriage, 149
    as barrier to divorce, 102, 115
    custody, 3
    effects of divorce on, 6, 9, 102
    from former marriage, 160
    remain with mother, 158
Chiriboga, D. A., 11, 125
Collard, J., 22-23, 24
common possessions, in divorce settle-
    ment, 127-29, 159
comparison level
    divorce, 98, 104
    marital happiness, 94

comparison level for alternatives
 divorce, 104
 marital happiness, 94
Condie, S. J., 142
Coombs, L. C., 51
correlates of marital success and satisfaction, 143, 150-54, 166
 age at marriage, 154
 length of time married, 154
 occcupation, 153-54
 presence of children, 151
 religion, 151-52, 158, 166
cost-reward framework, 95, 114
court records, 11, 157
crude marriage rates, 30
Cull, J. C., 17
Cutler, L., 11, 125
Cutright, P., 54

data collection, 170-71, 173
 confidentiality, 170
 mail surveys, 170
 response rates, 171, 173
decision to divorce, factors affecting, 94-96
 alternatives, 105
 attractions, 96
 barriers, 95
 financial concerns, 105
 personal unhappiness, 105
DeFrain, J., 88, 100, 125
divorce
 correlates of, 48-61
  age at marriage, 50-51
  children, presence of, 55-59
  church membership, 51-53
  economic factors, 54-55
  education, 53-54
  employment of women, 55
  laws about marriage and divorce, 49-50
  migration, 59-60
  premarital pregnancy, 59
  race, 59-60, 165
  religious homogamy, 53, 166
  transmission of instability, 60
  type of marriage ceremony, 53

 number of, 30
 regional differences, 39-46
 and social change, 75
 and stress, 120-21
  divorce morbidity, 120-21
  motor vehicle accidents, 120
  psychopathology, 120
  suicide, homicide, disease mortality, 121
divorce counseling, 18
divorced ministers, 11
divorce mediation, 18
divorce process, 9
"divorce-proneness," 75-76
divorce rates, 75
 crude, 41
 refined, 45
divorce reporting area, 39

Eckhardt, K. W., 62
economic theory of marriage, 96
education, 83-84, 158
 and divorce, 53-54
 and marital stability, 83-84, 158
"empty shell" marriages, 5
Everly, K., 136

Falasco, D., 62
family and friends, importance of, 108-12, 158
Family Research Center, 171
"Family Stability Study," 169
Feldberg, R., 125
Fenelon, B., 51, 59
fertility rates, 55
Fisher, E. O., 18
Foster, H. H., Jr., 50
Fox, E. M., 125
Freed, D. J., 50
Fundamentalists, 51

Gettleman, S., 17, 127
Glenn, N. D., 87, 89, 121, 142, 145
Glick, P. C., 17, 51, 53, 54, 61, 77, 83, 121, 141
Goffman, E., 97
Goode, W. J., 18, 19, 24, 119, 120, 125

Grady, W. R., 62
"grounded theory," 9
Gullahorn, J. E., 17

Halliday, T. C., 142
Hannan, M. T., 55
Hardy, R. E., 17
Hart, N., 21
Hayes, M. P., 88, 100, 125
Hendershot, G. E., 62
Herman, S. J., 3
Hetherington, E. M., 17
Hicks, M. W., 94
high and low cohesive marriages, 97
    sources of alternate attraction, 97
    sources of attraction, 97
    sources of barrier strength, 97
historical context, marriage and divorce
    trends, 29
Homans, G. C., 94
Hunt, B., 21, 24, 164
Hunt, M. M., 20, 21, 24, 141

income and divorce, 134-36
    downward economic mobility, 136,
    160, 162
initiating divorce action, 112
interfaith marriages, 53, 166
intergenerational stability and instability,
    78-79, 158

Jews, 81, 187, 190

Kelly, H. H., 94, 99, 104, 114
Kelly, J. H., 3, 22-23, 25
Kessler, S., 17
Kitson, G. C., 8, 49
Kohen, J., 125
Koo, H. P., 149
Krantzler, M., 18
Kuhn, R. P., 61

Lachman, M. E., 17, 141
Landes, E., 62
Landis, J. T., 78
laws about marriage and divorce, 49-50
    grounds for marital dissolution, 49

leniency of divorce laws, 49
    residency requirements, 49, 50
legal minimum age at marriage, 51
Lenthall, G., 94
Levinger, G., 16, 95-96, 101, 105
life satisfaction, 142
Locke, H. J., 16
Lunry, G. K., 5

marital adjustment, 16
marital counseling, 112-14, 115, 166
marital happiness
    among the remarried, 144-48, 158
        age at marriage, 144
        effect of children, 144
        length of time married, 144
        religious indicators, 144
        social class, 144
    of previously married, 86-89
Markowitz, J., 17, 127
marriage and divorce rates, 29-30
marriage laws, 33-34
    statutory changes, 33
    residency requirement, 33
marriage reporting area, 34
mean number of children per divorce, 56
Messinger, L., 143
methodological innovation, 164-66
Michael, R., 62
"migratory divorce," 49
modernized societies, 7
Moles, O. C., 16, 101
Mormons, 52, 53, 76, 79, 80, 81, 162,
    187, 190
Mueller, C. W., 60, 78

national divorce rates, 3
National Longitudinal Survey of Labor
    Market Experience, 16
national trends, 4-7
networks, 24
Nichols, R. C., 79, 89
no-fault divorce, 50
Norton, A. J., 61, 77, 83, 141

overcoming barriers to divorce, 104-8
    advice from others, 107

comparison level for alternatives, 104
ease of divorce laws, 107
financial concerns, 105, 115
personal unhappiness, 105, 115

periods of greatest stress, 123-25
Platt, M., 94
Pope, H., 60, 78
post-divorce family, 6
Price-Bonham, S., 8, 49, 61, 119, 143, 148
problems in marriage, 99-101
    emotional, 101, 115, 159
    financial, 101, 115, 159
    infidelity, 100, 115, 159
    loss of love, 101, 115, 159
    physical abuse, 101, 115
    sexual, 101
problems in remarriage, 148-58
    conflict over children, 160
    emotional, 160
    financial, 149
    infidelity, 149
    loss of love, 149
    sexual, 149, 160
process of divorce, 10, 16
Protestants, 63, 76, 79, 81, 82, 161, 162, 187, 190

quality of marriage, 4
quantification, 160-63
questionnaire, description of, 169, 171

race and marital status, 84-86
Raschke, H. J., 8, 49
reconstituted family, 143
    step-parents, 143
refined marriage rates, 39
regional specification, 163-64
regional trends, marriage and divorce, 29
religion, and divorce, 79-83
    church v. non-church setting, 80-81
    religious activity, 82-83
    religious identification, 81-82
religious intermarriages, 79, 160, 161, 162, 166

remarriage, 16, 17, 165
    after divorce, 60
    after widowhood, 60
    correlates of, 61-63
        age at divorce, 62
        children, 62
        duration of marriage, 62
        economic factors, 62
        education, 62
    laws about divorce and remarriage, 61
        previous marital status, 61
        race, 61
        religiosity, 160
        sex, 61
    regional difference, 46-48
    structure of, 143
    success of, 142
remarriage rates, 30, 47
Renne, K. S., 87
replication and extension, 157-60
respondents, characteristics of, 76
    age, 185
    education, 188-89
    income, 190-91
    marital status, 186
    occupation, 189-90
    race, 185
    religion, 186-87
    sex, 185
    women's employment, 190
Rose, V. L., 119
Rosen, R., 107
Ross, H. L., 17

sampling procedures, 169, 171
Sawhill, I. V., 17
Scanzoni, J., 51, 107
Schlesinger, B., 142
Simon, W., 5
social context, 29
social exchange, 94
social participation, changes in, 129-34, 165
    family, 130
    former spouse, 133, 159-60, 162
    organizations and clubs, 129
    spouse's relatives, 130

social service agencies, 157
Spanier, G. B., 17, 141
special interest organizations, 11, 157
    Parents Without Partners, 11
Stetson, D. M., 50
stigmatization, 5, 7, 8
Stinnett, N., 88, 100, 125
Suchindran, C. M., 149
Sweet, J. A., 55, 68, 78

teenage brides, 51
Thibaut, J. W., 94, 99, 104, 114
Thornes, B., 22-23, 24
Thornton, A., 51, 55
"triangulation," 157
Tuma, N. B., 55

Walker, K., 55
Walker, K. N., 143
Waller, W., 19, 25
Wallerstein, J. S., 3, 22-23, 25
Weaver, C. N., 87, 142, 145
Weiss, R. S., 16, 20, 120, 125
Westoff, L. A., 106, 141, 143, 155
White, L. K., 87
White, S. W., 120-21
Whitney, O., 55
Williams, K. M., 61
Wise, M. J., 122
Wright, G. C., Jr., 50

Yoder, J. D., 79, 89

Zumeta, Z., 51

About the Authors

STAN L. ALBRECHT is Professor of Sociology at Brigham Young University, Provo, Utah, and the author of *Social Psychology* and *Social Science Research Methods*.

HOWARD M. BAHR is Director of the Family and Demographic Research Institute at Brigham Young University. He is the author of several books on the subject of family relationships and ethnicity including *Middletown Families, The Sunshine Widows, Women Alone*, and *American Ethnicity*.

KRISTEN L. GOODMAN is a Research and Evaluation Specialist for Correlation Evaluation of the Church of Jesus Christ of Latter-Day Saints in Salt Lake City. She is the author (with Howard M. Bahr and Spencer J. Condie) of *Life in Large Families*.